GOD
AND
REASON

A Historical Approach to Philosophical Theology

GOD and REASON

Ed. L. Miller
University of Colorado

The Macmillan Company, New York

Collier-Macmillan Limited, London

For Yvonne

The Macmillan Company
866 Third Avenue, New York, New York 10022

Collier-Macmillan Canada, Ltd., Toronto, Ontario

Library of Congress catalog card number: 70–176059

First Printing

Preface

It has been said that philosophy looks for a black cat in a dark room when no cat is there, but that theology finds the cat anyway.

This is not very complimentary to philosophy and theology, though it does emphasize something important. We may, at times, be repelled by the obscurity of these disciplines and, at other times, bewildered by their dazzling abstruseness; we suspect that they play tricks upon our minds, and their preoccupations often seem irrelevant. Yet it is almost impossible to desist from thinking about such matters as God, evil, and immortality. These are the perennial issues that press themselves upon us and demand from us a response, however feeble and unenlightened. These are the issues of philosophical theology.

This book is written, then, in the belief that most of us are, for better or for worse, and each in his own way, committed to taking philosophical theology seriously. It is also written in the belief—if there is a thesis in these chapters, this is it—that there is only one really adequate approach to these problems, namely, the historical approach. Surely it is presumptuous, if not ludicrous, to attempt a serious consideration of these problems except against the backdrop of the classical discussions that have converged over the centuries into a whole philosophical-theological tradition.

My purpose is to provide an introduction to the central issues of philosophical theology. I have attempted to delineate the classical concepts and perspectives relative to each of these issues, and though it is not possible for any of the discussions to be complete, it will suffice if they indicate the proper direction for further study and provide the necessary points of departure. Though an introductory survey should seek first to present an accurate statement of the relevant positions, the old pedagogical ideal of absolute objectivity has, in my opinion, probably done more harm than good. The reader will therefore be prepared for an occasional intrusion of my own bias. Every book is written from a particular standpoint, and mine, simply stated, is that God has disclosed himself and spoken to man in the Christian Revelation. But it is the standpoint of one who also believes that faith should be no cloak for ignorance, and that the man of faith too must be intellectually responsible about the thing that he believes most strongly. Finally, it is the standpoint of one who believes that philosophy and theology, if they are to count for anything, must speak to real people about real issues. In all of this the reader may discern the influence of St. Augustine and Sören Kierkegaard on the philosophical side, and, on the theological side, of Karl Barth, Emil Brunner, and Oscar Cullmann (though I am more inclined to believe with Brunner than with Barth that *es gibt eine andere Aufgabe der Theologie*).

In some circles the question of God's existence and the traditional theistic arguments have lost their urgency. Whether that is good may be something that the reader might wish to decide as he moves through these pages. At any rate, the extended consideration of these matters can be justified, I think, on the grounds that they continue to be at the very least useful vehicles for the introduction and discussion of fundamental theories, concepts, and distinctions. It appears more and more difficult these days to consider traditional problems apart from the contributions of various contemporary theologians, especially those who theologize in an existential, analytic, or "secular" style. The concluding chapter is thus intended as a brief introduction to a few of the theological thrusts that have taken shape over the last several years and merit, no doubt, the label "new theologies."

In addition to the bibliographical note at the end, the footnotes provide clues for the reader who wishes to pursue the primary sources further. Most of the relevant primary materials (as well as extended bibliographies on each topic) are collected in my book of readings, *Philosophical and Religious Issues: Classical and Contemporary Statements* (Encino, Calif.: Dickenson, 1971).

All Biblical quotations are from the Revised Standard Version, copyright 1946 and 1952 by the Division of Christian Education, the National Council of the Churches of Christ in the U.S.A., and are used by permission.

Ed. L. Miller
University of Colorado
Boulder, Colorado

Contents

1

Philosophy and Religion

It may seem a bit simplistic to attempt a definition of something like philosophy, as indeed it is. One can hardly appreciate what philosophy is without becoming personally involved with philosophical issues and actual philosophizing. Still, a brief consideration of philosophy, religion, and theology will provide a point of departure and a framework in terms of which our discussion may gain some momentum. Furthermore, even in this preliminary discussion some important ideas will begin to emerge that may illuminate the phenomenon of man and his relation to the world.

What Is Philosophy?

Probably everyone has at least some idea of the nature of philosophy and philosophizing. Upon examination, however, our idea may turn out to be a rather obscure one, though we are certain that philosophy has something to do with thinking, and thinking on a grand scale.

The word itself derives from the Greek φιλοσοφία which means "love of wisdom." (According to one tradition, Pythagoras first called himself a philosopher—lover of wisdom—insisting that wisdom itself is the proper possession of God alone.) A more inclusive

1

statement would spell out the several fields of philosophic inquiry: metaphysics (the theory of reality, or, in a more restricted sense, the theory of transcendent reality), epistemology (the theory of knowledge), axiology (the theory of value), ethics (the study of moral or human values), aesthetics (the theory of art and beauty), and logic (the science of right thinking). If the etymological definition suggests too little about philosophy, this one suggests too much, at least for the present purpose. What is required is a more practical definition, one that expresses concisely but as accurately as possible the character of philosophy.

I submit the following as a working definition of philosophy: *Philosophy is the attempt to provide, within limits, a rational interpretation of reality as a whole.* Though many philosophers reject this conception of philosophy (one of the most difficult questions of contemporary philosophy concerns the nature of philosophy itself), it is, as a matter of fact, suggestive of the broad character of traditional Western philosophy. It is also the conception of philosophy that will lie behind most of the discussion in this book. Let us then consider it more carefully.

The word "rational" is important. It emphasizes that philosophy, more obviously than other disciplines, rejects and condemns all forms of superstition, dogmatism, and uncritical opinion, and seeks to replace them with concepts that are born of hard and coherent thinking. Philosophy is, in this broad sense of the word, rationalistic; its principal tool is reason and its business is reflection, both critical and constructive, analytic (it takes ideas apart) and synthetic (it puts them back together). In short, the philosopher believes with Socrates that the unexamined life is not worth living.

But the phrase "within limits" suggests an important qualification. Though the philosopher eschews irrationalism and embraces reason, his thought necessarily gives way, at one point or another, to non-rational (not irrational) contributions such as presupposition, intuition, poetic vision, mystery, and the like. Does not every position or theory or argument begin, for instance, with certain basic assumptions about something or other? In fact, a strong case could be made for the non-rational and non-arguable foundation (or at least features) of the classical philosophical systems like those of Plato, St. Augustine, Descartes, Spinoza, Kant, and Hegel. It is for this reason (the inevitable presence of the non-rational or subjective element) that there can probably never be a definitive philosophy, one that will command unanimous consent.

Finally, the phrase "reality as a whole" suggests the encompassing or synoptic character of philosophic inquiry. Each of the specialized disciplines (for example, biology, psychology, astronomy, and anthropology) focuses on a particular aspect of reality, whereas the philosopher, surveying all facets of experience, seeks to formulate the ultimate principles. As Plato says, the philosopher is one who desires all wisdom, not only some part of it, he is a spectator of all time and existence. Again, the encompassing scope of the philosopher's interest is suggested in Immanuel Kant's three questions reflecting the theoretical, practical, and personal dimensions of philosophical thought:

> What may I know?
> What must I do?
> What may I hope?

In a sense all other inquiries can be construed as subfields of philosophy inasmuch as they all contribute, ultimately, to answering the questions that philosophers ask, questions concerning the nature of knowledge, of value, of meaning, and of reality itself.

On this view, philosophical activity lies somewhere between that of the scientist and the poet. The philosopher attempts to organize and systematize his encounters with existence and value. He attempts to articulate his *Weltanschauung* or "world-view," his general impression and judgment about the whole of things. The philosopher thus speaks in a way that tends to combine the method of the scientist with the concern of the poet. He attempts to speak rationally and systematically, but he desires also to speak of the things that matter most. Alfred North Whitehead suggests much this same understanding:

Speculative philosophy is the endeavour to frame a coherent, logical, necessary system of general ideas in terms of which every element of our experience can be interpreted. . . . Philosophers can never hope finally to formulate these metaphysical first principles. Weakness of insight and deficiencies of language stand in the way inexorably. Words and phrases must be stretched towards a generality foreign to their ordinary usage; and however such elements of language be stabilized as technicalities, they remain metaphors mutely appealing for an imaginative leap. . . .

Rationalism is an adventure in the clarification of thought, progressive and never final. But it is an adventure in which even partial success has importance.[1]

Contemporary Trends

The conception of philosophy that I have suggested may, with some justice, be regarded as a classical or traditionalist view. Clearly it would be rejected both by the "positivist" and "analytic" strains that dominate a large segment of contemporary philosophical thought, as well as by certain "existential" strains that dominate another.

The positivist school favors a scientific approach to philosophy whereby philosophic inquiry is limited to the empirical world, the world of possible experience. These philosophers discard all speculative or metaphysical statements (for example, "God exists") as being literal nonsense because their truth cannot be verified in terms of sense-experience, the only criterion the positivists admit. It follows, for such thinkers, that traditional (speculative) philosophy has been antiquated by the new scientific approach. We will have more to say about positivism later.

Current analytic (or linguistic) philosophers also find themselves at times far removed from the concerns of traditional philosophy. According to the analytic movement, or at least one version of it, virtually all of the muddledness of traditional philosophy can be laid at the door of linguistic confusion. Philosophers, it is said, too often plunged into questions about reality, God, morals, and the like, without first giving sufficient attention to the nature and ambiguities of the questions themselves, or, more accurately, the language in which the questions were posed. In the following passage, G. E. Moore, a pioneer of the contemporary language approach, expresses succinctly the motivation and interest of the analytic philosopher:

It appears to me that in Ethics, as in all other philosophical studies, the difficulties and disagreements, of which its history is full, are mainly due to a very simple cause: namely to the attempt to answer questions, without first discovering precisely *what* question it is which you desire to

[1] Alfred North Whitehead, *Process and Reality* (New York: Macmillan, 1929), pp. 4, 6, 14.

answer. I do not know how far this source of error would be done away, if philosophers would *try* to discover what question they were asking, before they set about to answer it; for the work of analysis and distinction is often very difficult: we may often fail to make the necessary discovery, even though we make a definite attempt to do so. But I am inclined to think that in many cases a resolute attempt would be sufficient to ensure success; so that, if only this attempt were made, many of the most glaring difficulties and disagreements in philosophy would disappear.[2]

Believing, then, that many (maybe most) of the urgent problems in the history of philosophy are not real problems at all but actually pseudo-problems, problems of language, the analysts undertake to unravel the subtle complexities of philosophical discourse through what is called "linguistic analysis."

Some analysts, such as Moore, believe that the language to be analyzed is the ordinary language in which people communicate daily, and thus these philosophers are often called "ordinary language analysts." Others, like Bertrand Russell, believe that it is necessary to construct and study artificial, symbolic languages (in many ways resembling mathematical languages) which would be free from the incompleteness and imprecision of everyday language. But all linguistic analysts, beginning at the beginning as they see it, have as their common goal the clarification of the meaning of words and concepts, their interrelationships, and the status of various types of languages and propositions. This clarification, for the analytic thinker, is the substance of philosophical activity. It is, as someone has expressed it, "talk about talk." No student of philosophy would deny that this kind of analysis plays a legitimate and even necessary role in philosophic inquiry. On the other hand, it would be a serious error to mistake what is but a part of philosophy for the whole of it.

Very different from either positivistic or analytic philosophy is existentialism, a philosophy that, as we shall see later, repudiates as ultimately unimportant precisely the kind of questions that preoccupy those other thinkers, and shifts the *locus* of philosophical concern to the concretely existing individual. Albert Camus, the late French writer and philosopher, has aptly summarized the existentialist interest in the more crucial issues in this way:

2 George Edward Moore, *Principia Ethica* (Cambridge, England: University Press, 1903), p. vii.

Judging whether life is or is not worth living amounts to answering the
fundamental question of philosophy. All the rest—whether or not the
world has three dimensions, whether the mind has nine or twelve categories—comes afterwards. These are games . . . . I have never seen anyone die for the ontological argument. . . . the meaning of life is the
most urgent of questions.[3]

Insofar as existentialism, at least in certain of its forms, suggests
to some an abandonment of reason, it represents a philosophic sin
quite different from that of the positivist-analyst. The fact remains,
however, that the overarching concern of the existentialists (often
theologians and writers as much as philosophers) is with personal
meaning and decision. This concern was heightened for Camus
and others by the horrors of World War II and the emergence of
technological society with its devaluation of the person, its relativization and loss of moral and spiritual values. Whatever its
shortcomings, existentialism can hardly be accused of irrelevance,
and one might risk the opinion that, for better or worse, it is this
kind of philosophical reflection that bears most obviously on the
situation of contemporary man.

The truth is, of course, that such an either/or bifurcation of
contemporary philosophy into these two essentially different movements is itself misleading. It will become apparent in the course
of the following discussions that a plethora of further alternatives
may be found on either side of both positivistic-analytic and existential philosophy. It may further be hoped that (to say the inevitable thing) the conception of philosophy suggested earlier will
be found to accommodate the best of both of these approaches,
namely, a willingness to think hard and critically without forgetting
why.

Religion and Theology

Our definition of philosophy was offered with the concession
that some philosophers would find it unacceptable. It is even more
difficult to agree on the nature of religion. On this matter the
theologian, anthropologist, psychologist, Hindu, Jew, and Christian

[3] Albert Camus, *The Myth of Sisyphus and Other Essays*, tr. Justin O'Brien
(New York: Vintage Books, 1955), p. 3 f.

may each proffer radically different views. Rather than venturing into such a quagmire of opinions, we may do well to focus upon one element that seems to be present in nearly every conception of religion and to ask whether it is not indeed the central and distinctive one.

The word "religion" is almost always associated with God and the supernatural. It might be argued, however, that religion in itself has nothing necessarily to do with God at all. Certainly if anything is the science or study of the divine, it is theology, not religion, and belief in God makes one a theist, not a religious person. Of course, if one thinks that "religion," "theology," and "theism" are simply different words with the same meaning, then for him that is the end of the matter. But it appears that we can identify "theology" with the study of the divine (which is exactly what the word means) and "theism" with belief in the divine, and still find something important to which we can assign the word "religion."

Theology and theism, like cosmology and Platonism, are intellectual and cognitive affairs; they concern the *theory* about and *belief* in something. It is evident, though, that there is more to a man's position than the theory behind it. If someone claims to be a Christian or a Marxist or a Buddhist, I immediately understand something of his beliefs, how he thinks, what judgments he has made on certain theoretical questions. But he is also telling me about his response or *commitment* to something. And it would appear that it is this latter aspect of a man's position, the more experiential, volitional, or existential aspect, that we have foremost in mind when we speak of someone's "religion"; it is primarily a matter of personal appropriation and devotion. (In fact, the word "religion" derives from the Latin verb *religare*, which meant "to tie" or "to bind," and eventually to be tied or bound in reverence and devotion to something.) Of course we would not be inclined to call every commitment a religious one, but only that commitment to and appropriation of something acknowledged as *ultimate* or in some sense *holy*.

It must be noted that it is possible to be thus responsive and devoted to something ultimate and to be in this sense religious without entertaining even a belief in God, much less passionate commitment. An individual's religion may or may not be theological or theistic in character, that is, it may or may not involve a belief in God; for the Christian it will, for the Marxist it won't, and for the Buddhist it will depend on his brand of Buddhism (Therevada Buddhism, for example, is a wholly non-theistic religion). It has already been hinted that there can be no religious commitment in an intellectual vacuum and that it necessarily rests upon or involves some intellectual judgments or other; religious commitment presupposes reason, and reason is fulfilled in religious commitment. But to identify religion with any *particular* belief, such as belief in the Judeo-Christian God, would be to exclude a vast block of human experience which most of us simply cannot resist calling "religious." According to a fragment of Aeschylus,

Zeus is all, and more than all!

This is a religious response, whatever Zeus may symbolize; there are many gods with a small "g," including wealth, political causes, humanitarian ideals, and pleasure.

The English philosopher F. H. Bradley adopts this very conception of religion when he identifies it as a "fixed feeling of fear, resignation, admiration or approval, no matter what may be the object, provided only that this feeling reaches a certain strength, and is qualified by a certain degree of reflection."[4] This definition is a good one (at least for my purpose) inasmuch as it emphasizes (1) that the essence of religion lies in the existential appropriation or affirmation of an object, though (2) in order to qualify as religious, this affirmation must attain a distinctive power for the individual, (3) that the particular object of the commitment is purely secondary, and (4) that there is no religious commitment apart from reflection and intellectual judgment. I myself would hazard that *religion is the experience of the Highest Good that we grasp and are grasped by, the recognition of an ultimate Power and Purpose standing over against us and eliciting our devotion.*

If our above characterization of philosophy and religion is at all correct, we may ask further whether the distinction between the two is not a reflection of two very different (though in practice inseparable) aspects of an individual's position, be it that of

[4] F. H. Bradley, *Appearance and Reality* (London: Sonnenschein, 1893), p. 439, n.

the Christian, Marxist, Buddhist, or whatever. We may even ask whether the distinction between philosophy and religion is not a reflection of the very *nature* of man as being at once a rational and volitional creature, a creature both of cognition and decision.

The opening sentence of Aristotle's *Metaphysics* is a classic statement of the rational or philosophical nature of man: "All men by nature desire to know." There is no man who is not caught up to some degree in the world of ideas and reflection, no man who does not seek rational grounds for his commitment. Some are, of course, better philosophers than others, and some are more dominated by the intellectual impulse than others. Still, every man reflects upon the things that concern him most; he raises, in his own way, the ultimate questions of his existence.

On the other hand, man is more than a creature of intellect. He is also a being who wills, approves, and sanctions; he is a creature of commitment. Just as no man is altogether devoid of philosophical activity, so also it would appear that there is no man whose life does not revolve around something, an ultimate Good that stirs his deepest feelings, an object of worship, an integrating center of meaning, a highest cause. Paul Tillich called it "ultimate concern." Naturally, one man's commitment may be more clearly defined, more consciously directed, more intense, or more elevated than another's, but every man is committed, in one way or another, to something that he (at least for the moment) recognizes as holding supreme worth and significance—one can usually tell what it is for a given individual by the way he lives. For every man there is a pearl of great price for which he would gladly sell all; and where his treasure is, there will his heart be also.

Not everyone will agree that man's twofold nature is suggestive of the distinction between philosophy and religion, and some will surely balk at the reduction of religion to something like ultimate concern pure and simple. That a passionate stamp collector is for that reason as much a religious man as St. Francis of Assisi may strike us as ludicrous, and we feel thus compelled to distinguish (as Tillich will urge us later) between religious commitment that directs itself to an unworthy object and is, consequently, demonic and idolatrous, and commitment that realizes itself in that which is truly ultimate and worthy of our highest devotion. Be that as it may, I do insist that, as Pascal says, "the knowledge of God is very far from the love of Him,"[5] and that religion clearly has more to do with the latter than it does with the former.

We are by our very nature creatures of both reflection and commitment. About this we have no choice. We do, however, have a choice about what we believe and how we go about demonstrating its truth. That is why philosophical theology is important.

[5] Blaise Pascal, *Pensées*, no. 280, in *Pensées and The Provincial Letters*, tr. W. F. Trotter and Thomas M'Crie (New York: Modern Library, 1941).

2

What Is Philosophical Theology?

The purpose of this book is to provide a survey of the central problems and concepts of philosophical theology. First, let us draw some further distinctions in order that we may grasp more fully the concept of philosophical theology itself.

Two Kinds of Theology

As stated previously, theology concerns the knowledge of God. There are, however, two different kinds of theology: revealed and philosophical. The distinction between revealed and philosophical theology is sometimes a blurry one inasmuch as they are interrelated and interdependent in ways that often make it difficult, if not impossible, to consider one apart from the other. Nevertheless they do represent, in general, very different approaches to the knowledge of God.

One of the distinctive features of the Judeo-Christian tradition is its belief in a divine self-disclosure: God has intervened in human history and spoken to man; he has unveiled himself in a "special revelation." And the knowledge of God drawn from this revelation is an example of revealed theology. Such theology is sometimes called "dogmatic" (in the best sense of the word) or "confessional" theology because it seeks to elucidate the divinely bestowed articles of faith (dogmas) which it takes as its fundamental and non-negotiable datum. Not unlike the mathematician, the dogmatic theologian begins with certain givens; his system is self-contained and is offered, so to speak, as a package deal. Philosophical theology, on the other hand, is the attempt to attain knowledge of God through the *lumen naturale,* man's "natural light," independently of special revelation. It assumes a "general revelation" whereby at least some rudimentary knowledge of God is accessible to all men. Further, in the confrontation with special revelation one is more or less passive, whereas a knowledge of God through general revelation is contingent upon the active employment of our natural faculties, including observation, inference, reflection, and interpretation. It is the difference between God's movement toward man and man's movement toward God.

Many theologians insist that the Bible itself witnesses to a general revelation, a theology or knowledge of God attainable in a purely rational or philosophical manner. No doubt the best example of this is to be found in Romans 1:19–20 where St. Paul indicts the ungodly who suppress the manifest truth of God: "For what can be known about God is evident to them, because God has shown it to them. Ever since the creation of the world his invisible nature, namely, his eternal power and deity, has been clearly perceived being understood through the things that have been made. So they are without excuse."[1] Philosophical theology is otherwise known as "natural" theology. The latter may suggest to some a knowledge of God through nature, though the term is usually intended to emphasize that knowledge of God may be acquired through the intellect in its natural state, unaided by supernatural illumination or grace. We shall soon see that some of the arguments for the existence of God have nothing whatever to do with the world of nature or sense-experience.[2]

---

[1] My translation.

[2] For a discussion of the Greek and Roman origins of the concept of natural theology, see Werner Jaeger, *The Theology of the Early Greek Philosophers,* tr. Edward S. Robinson (Oxford, England: Clarendon Press, 1947), pp. 1 ff. and notes.

The Idea of Revelation

We will return to philosophical theology presently. For the moment, we might dwell a bit on the concept of special revelation. If it is accepted that God has indeed revealed himself to man through a supernatural self-disclosure, then there are open to us at least two different interpretations of that special revelation. The more traditional of the two is often called the "propositional" view of revelation. As the word suggests, this view holds that the divine revelation is contained in the language, statements, or propositions of a text, such as the Bible; it involves a certain conception of the way in which God has revealed himself (God spoke to men who in turn wrote down what he said).

Often associated with the propositional view of revelation is the traditional doctrine of the inspiration of the Scriptures, for it is the supernatural inspiration that is thought to guarantee the validity and truth of the statements contained in the Bible. Adherents of this doctrine usually defend it with St. Paul's statement, "All scripture is inspired by God . . ." (II Tim. 3:16), and St. Peter's comment that "no prophecy ever came by the impulse of man, but men moved by the Holy Spirit spoke from God" (II Peter 1:21). They then proceed to explain inspiration in any one of several ways. One view, sometimes called the "dictation theory," holds that the writers of the Bible were, like typewriters, completely passive or even oblivious to the promptings of the Spirit who articulated through them the divine and infallible message. This interpretation, or at least one version of it, was emphatically embraced by Pope Leo XIII in his 1893 encyclical *Providentissimus Deus*:

All of the books, and the whole of each, which the Church receives as sacred and canonical were written down at the dictation of the Holy Spirit; and, in fact, so far from there possibly being *any error present in divine inspiration,* this latter of itself not only excludes but rejects it with the same necessity that God himself, who is the supreme Truth, cannot be the author of any error whatever. . . . For the Holy Spirit himself with supernatural power so stirred and moved them to write, and so assisted as they wrote, that they both conceived correctly in mind, and wished to write down faithfully, and expressed aptly with infallible truth, all and each of those things which he bade; otherwise he himself would not be author of the entire Holy Scripture.[3]

Another theory, that of verbal inspiration, allows for the obvious differences in the style and vocabulary of the various writers, while holding that every word is, nonetheless, divinely insured against error. According to the conceptualist interpretation, what is inspired is not each and every word but rather general ideas and concepts that the writers then expressed in their own way, drawing upon their individual experiences, recollections, and reflections.

In some theological circles many battles have been waged, sometimes bitterly, over questions concerning the inspiration and infallibility of the Biblical text. This preoccupation is, however, understandable, for if the propositional view of revelation is correct, then the proposition is everything.

In contemporary theology this conception of revelation has largely given way to a non-propositional view. What could it mean to say that God has revealed himself otherwise than in the statements contained, for example, in the Bible? The non-propositional understanding of revelation, too, takes several forms, though the dominating one conceives it to be (as the German theologians have expressed it) *Heilsgeschichte,* "redemptive-history." This view directs our attention from what God has said to what he has done and is doing, to his "mighty acts" in the unfolding of history. God is revealed, for example, throughout the history of Israel, in his repeated and continuing interventions on behalf of his Covenant people. And of course divine revelation would according to this theory be epitomized in the cluster of redeeming events surrounding Jesus Christ: his incarnation, ministry, death, and resurrection. Revelation is thus not so much a collection of canonical books, or a system of theological assertions concerning God, man, and salvation, as it is revelatory acts, God himself acting even yet in history and bringing to completion his redemptive purpose.

Both the propositional and *heilsgeschichtlich* views of revelation result in unfortunate distortions when pushed to extremes. If the former tends to degenerate into a literalistic "bibliolatry" or Bible-

[3] Pope Leo XIII, *Providentissimus Deus,* in *Enchiridion Symbolorum,* secs. 1951 f., ed. Heinrich Denzinger, et al., thirty-first ed. (Freiburg im Breisgau: Herder, 1957) (my translation).

worship, the latter may slip into an overly subjective interpretation of the divine will. The truth is, of course, that these are not mutually exclusive views of revelation, and many theologians have managed to steer between the two, allowing each to make its contribution.

The neo-orthodox theologian Emil Brunner (1889–1966) represents such a mediating position. After attacking the "fatal equation" of revelation with propositions, a misunderstanding which, as he says, dates from the Apostolic Fathers and hangs like a dark shadow over the whole history of the Christian Church, Brunner interprets revelation primarily as the unrepeatable, unique, absolute, and personal *event* of Jesus Christ:

In the time of the Apostles, as in that of the Old Testament Prophets, "divine revelation" always meant the whole of the divine activity for the salvation of the world, the whole story of God's saving acts [*Heilsgeschichte*], of the "acts of God" which reveal God's nature and His will, above all, Him in whom the preceding revelation gains its meaning, and who therefore is its fulfillment: Jesus Christ. He Himself is the Revelation. Divine revelation is not a book or a doctrine; the Revelation is God Himself in His self-manifestation within history. Revelation is something that *happens*, the living history of God in His dealings with the human race . . . .

But the Bible, for Brunner, is nonetheless indispensable as a witness and *interpretation* of God's dealing with men: "The Bible is the word of God because in it, so far as He chooses, God makes known the mystery of His will, of His saving purpose in Jesus Christ."[4] On this understanding, then, the Bible is not a body of theological information but rather the response of those to whom it was vouchsafed to be witnesses to the acts of God among men; it is not itself the revelation of God, but rather the record of the revelation, necessary for an understanding of God's redemptive plan.

Still another important concept is that of "progressive revelation," a position that is compatible with both propositional and non-propositional views though usually associated more closely with the latter. Progressive revelation denies that revelation is something that drops out of heaven, complete and intact. Rather,

---

[4] Emil Brunner, *Revelation and Reason*, tr. Olive Wyon (Philadelphia: Westminster Press, 1946), pp. 8, 135.

it understands God's self-manifestation to man as something that happens over the ages of human history, always appropriate to the developing stages of man's evolving intellectual, moral, and spiritual consciousness. We should not therefore be surprised that God dealt crudely with the primitive people of Israel's early history, though later dealing with them on more exalted planes, commensurate with their developing response. The ethical monotheism of the later prophets is far removed from the henotheism (belief in a supreme god) of the First Commandment: "Thou shalt have no other gods before me." Ezekiel's promise that the sins of the father will not be visited on the sons reflects, ethically, a considerable advance on the Exodus promise that they will. And does not the Sermon on the Mount, with its recurring distinction "You have heard that it was said to the men of old. . . . But I say to you . . . ." exemplify a radical reinterpretation and elevation of earlier revealed principles?

It does not follow from this that all revelation must be relativized in terms of a certain people, a particular place, a particular time, and a given level of intellectual, moral, and spiritual attainment. "Thou shalt not murder" is as universally binding now as ever, and even "Thou shalt not have any other gods before me" can be easily translated into a timeless religious principle. And, as suggested above, the Christian will insist that revelation has achieved some kind of finality in Jesus Christ:

In many and various ways God spoke of old to our fathers by the prophets; but in these last days he has spoken to us by a Son, whom he appointed the heir of all things through whom also he created the world. He reflects the glory of God and bears the very stamp of his nature, upholding the universe by his word of power. (Heb. 1:1–3).

The Spirit of Xenophanes

Though our main concern is not with revealed theology but with philosophical theology, historically these two approaches to the knowledge of God have been closely though sometimes unhappily allied.

Xenophanes of Colophon, an early Greek philosopher of the fifth century B.C., is an excellent example of the spirit and concern of philosophical or natural theology. There is even some justification for calling Xenophanes the father of philosophical theology in the West. He, more emphatically and articulately than any other early philosopher, repudiated the old mythological and superstitious theology propagated by Homer and Hesiod. Consider his attack upon their naïve, anthropomorphic concept of the gods: "If oxen or horses or lions had hands, or could draw with hands or create works like men, the horses would draw the forms of their gods like horses, and the oxen like oxen; and they would make their bodies in accordance with the body that they themselves each possess." Or consider his distress over the way the poets impiously attributed immoral acts to the gods: "Both Homer and Hesiod have ascribed to the gods all the things which are among men reproachful and a disgrace: stealing, committing adultery, and deceiving one another." But Xenophanes' theologizing was not wholly negative and critical. He does appear also to have propounded a positive and philosophically more adequate theory of the divine than his Greek predecessors. "There is one God, greatest among both gods and men, who resembles mortals not at all in body or in mind." Again, "He always remains in the same place, not moving at all. Nor does it befit him to move about at different times to different places."[5]

Xenophanes reflects the theological and philosophical revolution from which the Western intellectual tradition was born, and he himself anticipated many of the ideas of subsequent theology. But the main reason for mentioning Xenophanes is that he represents so well the rationalist (both critical and constructive) bent of all philosophical theology.

It would be a mistake, however, to conclude that all philosophical theologians have, like Xenophanes, opposed and rejected traditional authority. Actually, natural and dogmatic theology have often been amiable partners in the theological enterprise. St. Thomas Aquinas, one of the most influential of philosophical theologians, repeatedly emphasized the necessity of special revelation:

Even as regards those truths about God which human reason can investigate, it was necessary that man be taught by a divine revelation. For the truth about God, such as reason can know it, would only be known

[5] Xenophanes, Fragments 15, 11, 23, and 26, tr. Ed. L. Miller, in "Xenophanes: Fragments 1 and 2," *The Personalist*, LI (Spring, 1970), pp. 143 f.

by a few, and that after a long time, and with the admixture of many errors; whereas man's whole salvation, which is in God, depends upon the knowledge of this truth. Therefore, in order that the salvation of men might be brought about more fitly and more surely, it was necessary that they be taught divine truths by divine revelation.[6]

The problem, when it has arisen, has usually arisen from the other side. For even though all Christian theologians may acknowledge the authority of divine revelation, not all of them acknowledge the authority of natural reason, at least not in the sphere of spiritual or theological truth. Thus there have been some trying moments, with the rationalists usually under attack. Martin Luther, for example, declares that a man cannot be saved unless he is willing to tear out the eyes of his reason, kill it, and bury it. Further,

If all the smart alecks on earth were to pool their wits, they could not devise a ladder on which to ascend to heaven. . . . he who would deal with the doctrines of the Christian faith [should] not pry, speculate, and ask how it may agree with reason, but, instead, merely determine whether Christ said it. If Christ did say it, then he should cling to it, whether it harmonizes with reason or not, and no matter how it may sound.[7]

This does not mean that Luther had no respect for reason when it is relegated to its proper realm or illuminated by divine grace: "I don't say that men may not teach and learn philosophy; I approve thereof, so that it be within reason and moderation. Let philosophy remain within her bounds, as God has appointed, and let us make use of her as of a character in a comedy; but to mix her up with divinity may not be endured."[8]

Even with his concession to philosophy Luther clearly represents a very different attitude toward the natural reason than does Thomas. There has been, in fact, such an undercurrent throughout

---

[6] St. Thomas Aquinas, *Summa Theologica*, Part One, Qu. I, Art. 1, in *Basic Writings of Saint Thomas Aquinas*, ed. Anton C. Pegis (New York: Random House, 1945), Vol. I.

[7] Martin Luther, "Tenth Sermon on John 6," tr. Martin H. Bertram, in *Luther's Works*, ed. Jaroslav Pelikan (St. Louis, Mo.: Concordia, 1959), Vol. XXIII.

[8] Martin Luther, *Table Talk*, tr. and ed. William Hazlitt (London: George Bell, 1884), p. 23.

the history of Christian thought. At the present time we witness the rejection of all forms of philosophical theology by a lingering (usually fundamentalist) anti-intellectualism and, more important, by a dominant strain within the neo-orthodox movement. The most obvious example of the latter is to be found in the Swiss theologian Karl Barth who answers a dogmatic "No!" (the title of one of his early essays) to natural theology, denying (against Brunner) that there is any "point of contact" between God's Word and the human consciousness in its natural, fallen state, and denying that there is any "other task" of theology either before or beyond the proclamation of God's special revelation. He held, in fact, that even man's "Yes!" to the revelation in Christ is wholly the work of God, concurring with the Lutheran formula, "I believe that not of my own reason and power do I believe in my Lord or am able to come to him. . . ." As for Romans 1:20 (quoted earlier), Barth explains that far from a proof-text for natural theology this passage is actually a proof-text against it, as a careful reading reveals: Nature itself testifies to the invisibility, hiddenness, and inaccessibility of God and directs us instead to the divine self-disclosure in Jesus Christ.

This tension, and even conflict, between natural and revealed theology raises, obviously, the crucial problem of the relation between faith and reason, a problem to be considered later.

Philosophy of Religion

The labels "philosophy of religion"[9] and "philosophical theology" are often used interchangeably, though they do not necessarily mean the same thing. Philosophical theology is a certain subject matter, namely, God or the divine, approached in a certain way, namely, philosophically. But philosophy of religion is, strictly speaking, what is called a "second-order" study. It is important to know what this means since second-order inquiry is thought by some these days to be the main task of philosophy.

To ask a second-order question is to ask a question about a ques-

---

[9] Here, and in many places throughout our discussions, it will be most convenient to use the word "religion" in its more usual sense rather than the special and refined sense suggested in Chapter 1.

tion. Thus the analytic movement in contemporary philosophy, concerned as it is with the analysis of language, is essentially a second-order study. Now, philosophy *of* religion is philosophizing in a more or less analytic manner *about* religion. It should be apparent that this is something quite different, and considerably more restricted, from the broader concerns of actual theologizing. Similarly, philosophy of science is not science itself but the critical analysis of scientific language, concepts, and methods. It engages in no scientific research and requires no laboratory. In the same way, one can entertain all sorts of discussion *about* religion and theology without being a religious person or without actually theologizing.

On the other hand, philosophical theology (as I am using the term) by no means excludes the analytic concern of philosophy of religion. In fact, at certain points the two are inseparable. All important philosophers have been to some degree analytic in their methodology inasmuch as they have been forced, at one point or another, to grapple with problems of meaning and language. St. Thomas Aquinas, for example, contributed much to the understanding of the nature of religious language and concepts. Still, Thomas knew—or thought he knew—what was meant by a question such as "Does God exist?," whereas many contemporary philosophers have declared a moratorium on all God-talk or theological discourse until the meaning and status of such language can be clarified. In fact, some thinkers find more interest in the question "What does it mean to ask 'Does God exist?' " than in the primary question itself.

It is not a simple matter to suggest all that is involved in philosophical theology, but clearly it is a more comprehensive concept than philosophy of religion taken in its strict sense. As we shall see, the interests and methods of philosophical theology extend much further than second-order and linguistic analyses.

Philosophical Theology Proper

Philosophical theology encompasses a great number of issues such as immortality, faith and reason, the problem of evil, and so forth. For the most part, however, discussion revolves around one central issue: God. This should not be surprising since God is, after all, the proper object of theological inquiry; if there is no God, then there is nothing for theology to study. Further, and perhaps more important, it should be seen that the question of God is at least in some sense presupposed by many of the others. What is the problem of faith and reason if there can be no divine authority to have faith *in?* What is the problem of evil to the person who rejects the existence of a loving and just God anyway? Accordingly, St. Thomas Aquinas announced as he began to unfold his theological system, ". . . we must first establish, as the necessary foundation of the entire work, the investigation by which it is demonstrated that God exists. For if we do not demonstrate that God exists, all investigation of divine matters is impossible."[10]

Our discussion too will be directed first to this fundamental problem. However, before beginning our survey of the traditional approaches to God, it might be helpful to offer a brief outline and summary of the whole domain of philosophical theology proper, even though such a summary must at many points be overly simplified and inadequate.

To begin, let us recall that theology is strictly, the science or study of God. There are two different kinds of theology, revealed theology which provides a supernatural knowledge of God, and philosophical or natural theology which ascends to a natural knowledge of God by way of the unaided intellect. Within the sphere of purely philosophical or natural knowledge of God, we can further distinguish two approaches, the rational and the non-rational. Under the non-rational approach would fall, for example, the various sorts of religious experiences. The mystic, for instance, claims to have a knowledge of God that transcends reason and possesses an experiential and self-authenticating certainty. On the other hand, the rational approach is argumentative and attempts to establish a knowledge of God in a logical, rational, discursive manner.

(In defense of the division of philosophical theology into the rational and non-rational categories one might appeal to Plato, Kierkegaard, the mystics, and others as belonging to the philosophical tradition even though there is in their positions a strong strain of the non-rational, perhaps even the distinctive strain. Philosophical activity need not be wholly discursive as I attempted to suggest in the first section of the first chapter. Further, we have a natural inclination to import under the non-rational certain kinds of re-

---

[10] St. Thomas Aquinas, *Summa Contra Gentiles,* I, 9 (my translation).

ligious experience which, properly, should be considered in relation
to revealed theology. This only emphasizes that such distinctions
and classifications are, after all, rather artificial.)

Under the rational approach to the knowledge of God fall the
traditional theistic arguments, that is, arguments for God's existence.
Because these arguments occupy an important place in the history
of philosophy, and therefore also in the following chapters, we
should grasp at the very beginning something of their nature, and
this means still another important distinction. There are two kinds
of theistic arguments, the *a priori* and the *a posteriori*. A *priori*
knowledge is knowledge acquired prior to or independently of
sense-experience. A person who believes in *a priori* knowledge is
known as a rationalist (using the word now in a more technical or
restricted sense than before), as opposed to an empiricist who believes that all knowledge is acquired *a posteriori,* that is, through
sense-experience. Accordingly, the *a priori* arguments seek to demonstrate God's existence without any reference to the sense-world.
These arguments are completely rationalistic, in the narrower meaning of the word. By contrast, the *a posteriori* arguments attempt to
infer the existence of God from sense-experience. These arguments
are empirical.

Of the many theistic arguments, we will consider four that are
truly classical and representative. Both the Ontological Argument
and the Moral Argument claim to prove the existence of God *a
priori,* apart from sense-experience: the Ontological Argument,
through an analysis of the concept of God or the idea of the most
perfect being; the Moral Argument on the basis of moral experience
or the universal sense of duty. Both the Cosmological and Teleological Arguments, on the other hand, try to demonstrate the existence of God *a posteriori,* from the evidence of sense-experience. The
Cosmological Argument begins with the sheer existence of the universe and concludes that God must exist as its ultimate cause.
According to the Teleological Argument, God must exist in order
for us to account for a certain feature of the universe, namely, its
apparent design and intelligibility.

One last point and our preliminaries are over. We can hardly
talk about God unless we have some idea of what we are talking
about. But it is not easy to say what God is. He has been called
the Supreme Being, the One, the Absolute, the All, the Nothing, the
Infinite, the Void, and so on. In the following discussions "God"

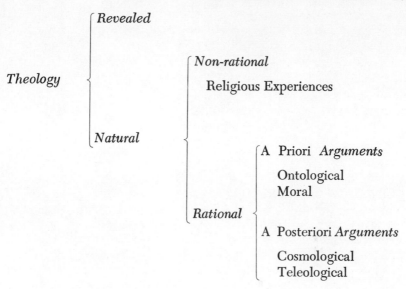

Theology
- Revealed
- *Natural*
  - *Non-rational*
    - Religious Experiences
  - *Rational*
    - A Priori *Arguments*
      - Ontological
      - Moral
    - A Posteriori *Arguments*
      - Cosmological
      - Teleological

refers to the God of traditional theism. Theism (from the Greek θεός, "god") is the belief in one transcendent, absolute, and necessary being, the condition and ultimate cause of everything. (In its loosest sense, theism is simply the belief in God or gods and thus includes monotheism or the belief in one God, pantheism or the belief that God is everything, polytheism or the belief in many gods, and deism, the belief in a God who after creating the world ceased to be interested in it.) Let us, then, begin our survey of the classical approaches to God, *pro et contra*.

3

The Ontological Argument

Of all traditional proofs for the existence of God, none is more enigmatic than the Ontological Argument. Originally formulated over eight-hundred years ago, it has always been the subject of much perplexity, and in recent years has once again gravitated to the forefront of philosophical discussion. In every age, including our own, some have regarded the Ontological Argument as an example of philosophical sleight-of-hand, others as the most profound and certain demonstration of God's existence. Whatever else may be decided about the Ontological Argument, it is no doubt the best example of a purely *a priori* proof, unfolding as it does without any reference whatsoever to the world of sense-experience. The argument begins with the concept or idea of God as the most perfect being ("ontological" derives from the Greek participle ὄν, ὄντος, "being") and through an analysis of this mere concept deduces God's objective reality.

St. Anselm and Descartes

St. Anselm (1033–1109), Archbishop of Canterbury, first conceived this demonstration of God's existence. It is important to notice that Anselm's Ontological Argument was part of an extended prayer that included a contrite confession of sin along with a plea for illumination. Far from a piece of detached academicia, Anselm's argument is imbued with a deep piety and motivated by a desire to enrich the spiritual life by demonstrating through reason what one already believes and is committed to as an article of faith:

I do not endeavor, O Lord to penetrate thy sublimity, for in no wise do I compare my understanding with that; but I long to understand in some degree thy truth which my heart believes and loves. For I do not seek to understand that I may believe, but I believe in order to understand.[1]

Anselm thus disarms at the very beginning those, usually skeptics, who delight in pointing out that the people who seek to demonstrate the existence of God are usually believers already. Not only is this true (nobody ever pretended otherwise), but most religious thinkers themselves would insist that the real nature of their proofs concerning God, his attributes, and so forth can be appreciated only against the background of faith, that is, as a rational unfolding of revealed truths.

Anselm begins his argument with a reference to Psalms 14:1: "The fool says in his heart, 'there is no God.'" But what does "God" mean? Anselm answers that even the atheist understands "God" to mean—in Anselm's famous formula—*aliquid quo nihil maius cogitari possit,* "that than which nothing greater can be conceived." (It is important to appreciate that by this Anselm does not mean the greatest being that happens to exist, but the greatest *possible* being.) Now the atheistic fool agrees that the idea of God exists, otherwise he could not employ that idea as he does even when he says, "God does not exist." The atheist does not therefore deny God's existence as an idea in the mind; what he denies is that God exists objectively, outside the mind, in reality. But Anselm counters that it is greater for a thing to exist in reality than for it to exist only as an idea in the mind. God (a being than which nothing greater can be conceived) must then exist in reality, not merely as an idea in the mind, for if he existed in the mind only he would not be God, because then something greater could be conceived. In Anselm's own words,

[1] St. Anselm, *Proslogium,* Ch. 1, in *St. Anselm: Basic Writings,* tr. Sidney Norton Deane, second ed. (La Salle, Ill.: Open Court, 1962).

if that, than which nothing greater can be conceived, exists in the understanding alone, the very being than which nothing greater can be conceived, is one than which a greater can be conceived. But obviously this is impossible. Hence, there is no doubt that there exists a being, than which nothing greater can be conceived, and it exists both in the understanding and in reality.[2]

By this reasoning, anyone who denies the existence of God is denying the existence of a being who must exist in order to be the very thing he is talking about. It is like saying: God—a being who must exist in order to be "God"—does not exist. According to Anselm, when the atheist denies the existence of God he obviously does not realize what he is saying, and that is why he is called a fool.

Some readers, seeing that the argument revolves on the notion of God as the greatest possible being, will invariably object that this is not in fact how they use the linguistic symbol "God." But obviously it is not the symbol "God" that is crucial to the argument but the *idea* that is usually associated with it, namely, the idea of the greatest possible being. If someone were to persist in an unorthodox use of "God," Anselm might simply ask him, "Well, by what symbol do you denote the greatest possible being? X, you say? Now, if X is the greatest possible being does it not follow that X must exist, since . . . ." Even if one were to have *no* name for the greatest possible being, he nonetheless has at least the idea of it otherwise all of the present discussion would be utterly unintelligible to him, and that idea (even if it must be spelled-out as "the greatest possible being" or "that than which nothing greater can be conceived") is all that Anselm requires.

René Descartes (1596–1650), a French philosopher and mathematician who is often called the father of modern philosophy, also argued the existence of God with a version of the Ontological Proof. Whereas St. Anselm begins with the formula "that than which no greater can be conceived," Descartes begins with "the most perfect being." It should be noted that Descartes is thinking of metaphysical perfection, that is, the full actualization of possible being, rather than moral perfection, though clearly the former implies the latter. There is a second and perhaps more important difference. Anselm, exemplifying the Augustinian principle of faith in search of understanding, derived his concept of God from Scripture. Des-

[2] *Ibid.*, Ch. 2.

cartes, on the other hand, proceeding in a purely philosophical manner, seizes the idea of God as a necessary deduction from the data of pure reason. Briefly, he moves by means of "clear and distinct ideas" from the indubitable reality of his own mind to a reflection on the fact that he doubts, to an awareness of his own limited or finite perfection, to the idea of infinite perfection. This is not to say that Descartes was, at the start, an unbeliever; he did in fact accept the authority of the Scriptures and of the Church, though in a manner unlike Anselm he distinguished philosophy from theology and sought to provide a philosophical demonstration of God's existence independently of revelation, one that proceeds solely in terms of intellectual intuition and deduction and that delivers a conclusion as certain as the conclusion of any mathematical demonstration.

Descartes begins with the philosophical concept of the most perfect being and then asks what this concept involves, or, in other words, what is included in the attributes of the most perfect being. We must say, of course, that God possesses all perfections: omniscience, omnipotence, justice, benevolence, and so on. Now since it is more perfect to exist than not to exist, existence too is a perfection. (Clearly, an actually existing thing possesses more metaphysical power than an imaginary one; if someone doubts this he should try sweeping the house with a non-existent broom.) If, then, we neglect to ascribe existence to God, he cannot be the most perfect being or the sum of all perfections. God must therefore exist because actual existence is a necessary attribute or perfection of the most perfect being, one of his defining properties, "that crown of perfections without which we cannot comprehend God," and (as Anselm had argued) a property that can be found in the concept of no other thing.[3] The very concept of God entails his real existence, says Descartes, just as the idea of a triangle entails the equality of its angles to two right angles, or the idea of a sphere or circle entails the equidistance of all its parts from its center. But whereas it does not follow from the nature of triangles or circles that they must exist, ". . . I cannot conceive of a God without existence, anymore than of a mountain without a valley. . . . from the fact

---

[3] René Descartes, "Notes Against a Programme," in *The Philosophical Works of Descartes*, tr. Elizabeth S. Haldane and G. R. T. Ross, revised ed. (Cambridge, England: University Press, 1934), I, 445.

alone that I cannot conceive God except as existing, it follows that existence is inseparable from him, and consequently that he does, in truth, exist."[4]

Two Early Rebuttals

Anselm had no sooner propounded his proof than it was challenged by Gaunilon, a monk of the monastery of Marmoutier near Tours. Though Gaunilon was, of course, a believer, he was persuaded that Anselm's argument was unsound and he felt constrained to answer Anselm in the interest of intellectual honesty. Gaunilon's criticisms, which reduce essentially to two, are contained in his reply entitled *In Behalf of the Fool.*

First, Gaunilon denies that the idea of God does in fact exist in his understanding on the grounds that we understand only what is familiar to us. Naturally, Gaunilon employs the word "God" and even the locution "that than which nothing greater can be conceived," though he insists that the meaning or *signification* of these entirely transcend him. Second, Gaunilon argues that even if we did have in our minds the idea of God, or the concept of that than which nothing greater can be conceived, we could not conclude that such a being exists in reality. We might as well argue that because we have in our minds the idea of a lost island, most wonderful, glorious, and perfect, it must actually exist, otherwise it would not be most perfect inasmuch as we could then conceive of a better one. Gaunilon wonders who would be the bigger fool— the one who submits such an argument or the one who accepts it. Our minds are in fact replete with ideas of wonderful things that have, nonetheless, no counterparts in the real world.[5]

To Gaunilon's first objection Anselm replied (recalling an idea suggested above) that if Gaunilon did not have God at least in his mind, that is, if he did not understand the meaning of "God" or "that than which nothing greater can be conceived," then he would not have been able even to follow the argument. Further, is it not

[4] René Descartes, *Meditations,* V, in *Discourse on Method and Meditations,* tr. Laurence J. Lafleur (Indianapolis, Ind.: Library of Liberal Arts, 1960), pp. 121 f.

[5] Gaunilon, *In Behalf of the Fool,* in *St. Anselm: Basic Writings, op. cit.*

a simple matter to formulate an idea of that than which nothing greater can be conceived by ascending from the lesser to the greater? from that which has a beginning to that which has no beginning? from that which has no beginning but an end to that which has neither beginning nor end? from that which changes to that which is immutable? and so on? And is not this procedure quite in accord with the teaching of the Scriptures that God's invisible nature may be grasped through his creation (Rom. 1:20)? Finally, says Anselm, even if it is not possible to entertain an idea of what God is, there is a difference between saying that God is inconceivable and that his inconceivability is inconceivable. An experience may be ineffable, but I can say that it was ineffable; I may not be able to grasp the infinite itself, but I can surely grasp the concept of infinity; and though God may be inconceivable, I can at least know what that means.

With respect to Gaunilon's second (and more familiar) objection Anselm responded as follows. Concerning the most perfect island, or the most perfect unicorn, or the most perfect man, Gaunilon was right. It is impossible to deduce the real existence of any of these from only an idea, for the idea of none of these involves existence as a defining property. If one were to look up "island" in the dictionary he would not find it defined as "an area of land completely surrounded by water *and which exists,*" nor does the perfection of a unicorn lie in the addition of still another attribute (existence) but in the excellence of its proper attributes, namely, the straightness of its ivory horn, the whiteness of its coat, and the like. It is clear, then, that one can just as easily conceive of the non-existence of such things as their existence. But there is one thing, Anselm argues, the non-existence of which is inconceivable. God, unlike an island or a unicorn or a man, is by his conception the sum of *all* perfections, which must therefore include existence. A lost desert island, however resplendent and glorious, and a unicorn, however elegant, hardly qualify as that than which nothing greater can be conceived; or as Descartes might have said, it is one thing to be the most perfect island imaginable but quite another to be the most perfect of all beings, it is one thing to possess certain perfections but quite another to possess all of them. As was observed above, it does not matter what name we give to the greatest possible being, and if Gaunilon's "lost island" turns out to be, in fact, the greatest possible being, then (Anselm dryly remarks) it does exist, it will be found, and it will never again be lost![6]

The Dominican monk St. Thomas Aquinas (1225–1274) also attacked Anselm's argument but on very different grounds. Obviously, Anselm was a rationalist (in the technical sense) who believed, as his argument shows, that we can acquire knowledge of God independently of sense-experience. St. Thomas Aquinas, on the other hand, was a classical empiricist whose whole philosophy is built on the epistemological principle *Nihil est in intellectu quod non fuerit prius in sensu,* "Nothing is in the intellect which was not first in the senses." This includes the knowledge of God which, as will be shown in the next chapter, Thomas reduces ultimately to our knowledge of the world.

For Thomas, the essence of every created thing (*what* it is) is distinct from its existence (*that* it is) just by virtue of the fact that its being is derived; it is easy enough to distinguish the whatness of a table from its whatness plus actual existence or thatness. In God, however, essence and existence are identical as required by his self-subsistent and indivisible being. God's existence as seen from the standpoint of God himself is therefore self-evident, because his existence is immediately seen to be inseparable from his essence. But from *our* standpoint—the crucial difference—God's existence is not self-evident, because we can know God only indirectly and imperfectly by means of his effects in the created world of nature; bound as we are to our five senses, we can never ascend to a knowledge of God as he is in himself, we can only know him as he is reflected to us in the empirical world (a fuller explanation of this doctrine is provided in the first section of Chapter 11). Thomas' own analogy may help. It is absolutely self-evident that a whole is greater than any of its parts, though this would not be self-evident to someone who was for some reason incapable of conceiving of wholes or parts. We are in a similar position *vis-à-vis* God. God's existence is self-evident in itself *though not to us* who are incapable of grasping the divine being as it is in itself. And if we cannot know what God's essence is, how can we show that his existence follows from it? We might as well try to show that a conclusion follows from its premises without knowing what the premises are.[7]

[6] St. Anselm, *Reply to Gaunilon,* in *St. Anselm: Basic Writings, op. cit.*

[7] St. Thomas Aquinas, *Summa Contra Gentiles,* I, 10 f., tr. Anton C. Pegis (Garden City, N.Y.: Image Books, 1955).

For our present purpose it is enough to emphasize that Anselm and Thomas bring to the discussion very different conceptions of knowledge. Anselm (operating in the Platonic tradition) begins with knowledge that is *a priori* and immediately present to the soul. Thomas (in the Aristotelian tradition) believes that we can have knowledge only of what can be imperfectly discerned in sense-experience. It is further important to realize that this fundamental difference is necessarily reflected at every point in their philosophies, including their judgments concerning our knowledge of God.

The Logic of "Exists"

Of all the criticism of the Ontological Argument, one in particular stands out as especially significant. The German philosopher Immanuel Kant (1724–1804) was the first to emphasize what many regard as the real fallacy of this proof. Kant correctly observed that the Ontological Argument, which he knew primarily in its Cartesian and later formulations, treated existence as though it were a predicate; that is, it attributes existence to God in the same manner that it attributes omnipotence, justice, and benevolence to him. Though there is some question whether this is technically true of Anselm's formulation, there can be no question but that it is true of Descartes': "Here I do not see . . . why [existence] may not be said to be a property as well as omnipotence, taking the word property as equivalent to any attribute or anything which can be predicated of a thing. . . . necessary existence in the case of God is also a true property in the strictest sense of the word . . . ."[8] But is existence, in fact, an attribute or predicate? Can existence be attributed to a thing in the same way as blue or rectangularity? Kant answered, No.

According to Kant, existence adds absolutely nothing to a concept. Take, for example, the concept "unicorn." The idea of a unicorn is not the least bit augmented or otherwise changed by the addition of existence, nor is it in any way diminished by the subtraction of existence. Whether one says, "The unicorn exists" or "The unicorn does not exist," the concept "unicorn" remains

[8] Descartes, *Reply to Objections*, in *The Philosophical Works of Descartes, op. cit.*, II, 228.

unaltered: "white, shaped like a horse, and having an ivory horn." Or, to use Kant's own example, a hundred actual dollars do not contain the least coin more than a hundred possible dollars. Of course, there is a difference between a hundred actual dollars and a hundred possible dollars, as will become apparent if you try to spend the possible ones. Still, what is involved in the *concept* of a hundred dollars is not different. What is different is the relation of the concept to the actual world, but that has nothing to do with the predicates or attributes of the thing for these have already been exhausted in the concept. Kant summarizes his objection as follows:

By whatever and by however many predicates we may think a thing— even if we completely determine it—we do not make the least addition to the thing when we further declare that this thing *is*. Otherwise, it would not be exactly the same thing that exists, but something more than we had thought in the concept; and we could not, therefore, say that the exact object of my concept exists.[9]

The question of a thing's existence, then, has nothing to do with the content of a concept but with the application of the concept to the real world.

Furthermore, according to the usual interpretation of the Onto- logical Argument, the existence of God cannot be denied without self-contradiction. The existence of God is thought to be, as we learned from Descartes, an integral part of the very concept of God in the same way that the idea of a triangle necessarily involves the equality of its angles to two right angles. That is, "God exists" is what is called an "analytic" statement (a tautology or redun- dancy), the predicate simply restating what is contained already in the subject as in "A triangle is a plane figure having three angles," "All bachelors are unmarried males," and "All barking dogs bark." Now, says Kant,

to posit a triangle, and yet to reject its three angles, is self-contradictory; but there is no self-contradiction in rejecting the triangle together with

[9] Immanuel Kant, *Critique of Pure Reason,* tr. Norman Kemp Smith (London: Macmillan, 1929), p. 505. Actually, Kant's objection was anticipated by David Hume: "To reflect on anything simply, and to reflect on it as existent, are nothing different from each other. That idea, when conjoin'd with the idea of any object, makes no addition to it" (*A Treatise of Human Nature,* ed. L. A. Selby-Bigge [Oxford, England: Clarendon Press, 1888], pp. 66 f.).

its three angles. The same holds true of the concept of an absolutely necessary being. If its existence is rejected, we reject the thing itself with all its predicates; and no question of contradiction can then arise.[10]

In other words, the truth of any analytic or tautologous statement is purely conditional or hypothetical. It is analytically certain, for example, that *if* there are any barking dogs, *then* they bark, but from this absolutely nothing can be inferred concerning the actual existence of barking dogs, or, for that matter, the existence of anything. Similarly, if we understand "God exists" as an analytic statement, then it is translatable into "If God exists, then he exists" —a true statement, but not very informative.

A more recent variation on this Kantian theme may be found in Bertrand Russell's "theory of descriptions" that has provided a whole new analysis of the word "exists." According to Russell, the paradox of how such things as unicorns can "be" non-existent results from the failure to distinguish (echoes of Kant) between the grammatical and the logical function of "exists." In the statement "Sirius exists," the word "exists" is, of course, grammatically a predicate. But its logical function is not to ascribe a certain property (existence) to a subject, but rather to assert that there is an actual something that can be described by the name "Sirius." The real significance of the statement "Sirius exists," becomes more apparent in Russell's translation "There is an x such that 'x is Sirius' is true." And "Unicorns do not exist" may be better expressed as "There are no x's such that 'x is a unicorn' is true." In this way, the statement "Unicorns do not exist" is not a statement about the nature of unicorns but about the *application* of the concept "unicorn."[11] We saw that for Anselm (maybe) and Descartes (certainly) existence was conceived as a defining property of God, something that could be predicated of him in the same way as goodness

---

[10] Kant, *op. cit.*, p. 502.

[11] Bertrand Russell, *A History of Western Philosophy* (New York: Simon & Schuster, 1945), p. 831. For a more extended discussion of Russell's theory of descriptions, see his *Introduction to Mathematical Philosophy* (London: George Allen & Unwin, 1919), Ch. 16. My statement above follows John Hick (*Philosophy of Religion*, [Englewood Cliffs, N.J.: Prentice-Hall, 1963], p. 19), whose brief summary is difficult to improve. One should also note (and in relation to Russell's discussion) G. E. Moore's highly praised 1936 article, "Is Existence a Predicate?," reprinted in *The Ontological Argument*, ed. Alvin Plantinga (Garden City, N.Y.: Anchor Books, 1965).

and omnipotence. But if "God exists" means "There is an x such that 'x is God' is true," then in the first statement "exists" says nothing about the nature of God, though it does say something about the universe, namely, that there is an instance of what is described by the word "God." Existence is not a predicate, so the Ontological Argument, as it is usually understood, must be invalid.

But even Russell at one time believed in the Ontological Argument as he himself relates:

I remember the precise moment, one day in 1894, as I was walking along Trinity Lane, when I saw in a flash (or thought I saw) that the ontological argument is valid. I had gone out to buy a tin of tobacco; on my way back, I suddenly threw it up in the air, and exclaimed as I caught it: "Great Scott, the ontological argument is sound."[12]

Closely related to all of this is the suggestion, often made these days, that only propositions are necessary, not things. Clearly, the statement "A triangle has three angles" is necessarily true because, as we have seen, by "triangle" we *mean* a plane figure having three angles; the statement must be true in view of the rules that govern the symbols of our language; its truth is analytically or *logically* necessary. On the other hand, the statement "Sirius is 8.7 light years away" is contingent—contingent upon whether or not Sirius is, in fact, 8.7 light years away. It is argued further that an existential statement (a statement that either affirms or denies the existence of something) cannot be logically necessary, because its truth depends not upon the conventions of language but, like the statement about Sirius, upon reality or the way things actually are. If so, the Ontological Argument cannot possibly work; it cannot tell us that God is necessary if only propositions are necessary. If, on the other hand, the Ontological Argument transposes itself into the proposition "The statement 'God exists' is necessarily true," then the necessity it involves is merely a matter of verbal stipulation and the truth of its conclusion is, as we saw above, purely hypothetical. In short, the Ontological Argument cannot affirm the real existence of God and at the same time claim the logical certainty thereof.

On this understanding, it has been argued that any theistic argument that leads to or otherwise involves the idea of God as a

---

[12] Bertrand Russell, "My Mental Development," in *The Philosophy of Bertrand Russell,* ed. Paul Arthur Schilpp (New York: Tudor, 1951), p. 10.

logically necessary being involves an absurdity, for that idea is self-contradictory. This position, nowadays espoused by many, receives probably its best-known expression in two very influential articles by the British philosophers J. J. C. Smart and J. N. Findlay.

Smart, in his article "The Existence of God," announces that

in asking for a logically necessary first cause we are doing something worse than asking for the moon. It is only *physically* impossible for us to get the moon; if I were a few million times bigger I could reach out for it and give it to you. That is, I know what it would be *like* to give you the moon, though I cannot *in fact* do it. A logically necessary first cause, however, is not impossible in the way that giving you the moon is impossible; no, it is *logically* impossible. 'Logically necessary being' is a self-contradictory expression like 'round square.'[13]

Findlay, in "Can God's Existence be Disproved?," shrewdly fashions an ontological *disproof* of God's existence on the basis of the same distinction. On the one hand, he says, our conception of God as an adequate object of religious devotion demands that he be conceived as a being who "towers infinitely" above and beyond all other objects, and this conception includes not only the unthinkableness of other things existing without him but also the unthinkableness of his own non-existence. On the other hand, we modern philosophers know that only propositions—not things—can be necessary, and that the idea of a being whose non-existence is unthinkable or inconceivable (that is, whose existence is necessary) is therefore unintelligible. Findlay concludes, quite the contrary to St. Anselm, that what follows from an adequate conception of God is that he cannot possibly exist: "It was indeed an ill day for Anselm when he hit upon his famous proof. For on that day he not only laid bare something that is of the essence of an adequate religious object, but also something that entails its necessary non-existence."[14]

It should be apparent that whether an existential statement can be certain or necessary without being *logically* certain or necessary is still another important possibility, one that we will encounter in the next section and again in the next chapter.

[13] J. J. C. Smart, "The Existence of God," in *New Essays in Philosophical Theology*, ed. Antony Flew and Alasdair MacIntyre (London: Student Christian Movement Press, 1955), p. 39.

[14] J. N. Findlay, "Can God's Existence Be Disproved?," in *ibid*.

A Recent Reformulation

In 1960 Norman Malcolm, Professor of Philosophy at Cornell University, published an important article entitled "Anselm's Ontological Arguments" in which he argued that Anselm actually (though perhaps unintentionally) presented two different proofs, an invalid one and a valid one. The first (and invalid) of Anselm's proofs is found in *Proslogium*, Chapter 2, and the second (and valid) is found in Chapter 3 and also in Anselm's reply to Gaunilon.

With respect to Anselm's first proof, which was summarized in the first section of this chapter, Malcolm judges that it does indeed presuppose that existence is a predicate, though he agrees with Kant in the rejection of this assumption: "It makes sense and is true to say that my future house will be a better one if it is insulated than if it is not insulated; but what could it mean to say that it will be a better house if it exists than if it does not?"[15] But Malcolm finds a second proof in Anselm that is significantly different from the first. The substance of the second argument is contained in the following passage from *Proslogium*, Chapter 3:

it is possible to conceive of a being which cannot be conceived not to exist; and this is greater than one which can be conceived not to exist. Hence, if that, than which nothing greater can be conceived, can be conceived not to exist, it is not that, than which nothing greater can be conceived. But this is an irreconcilable contradiction. There is, then, so truly a being than which nothing greater can be conceived to exist, that it cannot even be conceived not to exist; and this being thou art, O Lord, our God.[16]

The difference between the two proofs is the following. The first takes existence as a predicate inasmuch as it reasons that something is greater if it exists than if it does not exist. The second, on the other hand, takes *necessary existence* as a predicate when it reasons that something the non-existence of which is logically impossible is greater than something the non-existence of which is logically possible.

[15] Norman Malcolm, "Anselm's Ontological Arguments," *Philosophical Review*, LXIX (January, 1960), reprinted with minor changes in *Knowledge and Certainty* (Englewood Cliffs, N.J.: Prentice-Hall, 1963), pp. 143 f.

[16] St. Anselm, *Proslogium*, Ch. 3, *op. cit.*

There are some recognized advantages to this second formulation. Though it may be somewhat strange to predicate existence of something that is already something, it would appear to be perfectly possible and meaningful to ask of something existing whether its existence is necessary or not, and if so, to adjudge it more perfect. In this way the second formulation bypasses completely the whole problem of whether existence is a predicate. It also bypasses the problem (if it is a problem) of whether existence is better than non-existence. At any rate, Malcolm agrees that Anselm's first argument is fallacious because existence is not a predicate, but he thinks that the second argument is sound because necessary existence is a predicate (he speculates that Descartes' argument too was of this second sort), and he sets out to develop his own version of this argument.

How is it, then, that necessary existence can be legitimately construed as a predicate or defining property of God? Malcolm's argument may be outlined as follows. If God is that than which nothing greater can be conceived, or an unlimited being, then obviously by his very conception he is not the sort of being whose existence or non-existence can be caused, or simply happen. In either case he would be dependent or contingent upon something outside himself and therefore a limited being. It follows that if he does not exist, his existence is logically impossible; if he does exist, his non-existence is logically impossible. Now such a being either exists or does not exist. We are, then, driven to a twofold conclusion: God—the unlimited being—either necessarily does not exist, or he necessarily does exist. But the only reason one could possibly have for saying that he necessarily does not exist would be if the concept of such a being were self-contradictory or in some way logically absurd. The concept of that than which no greater can be conceived or of an unlimited being would appear, however, to be a perfectly consistent and meaningful one. We cannot, therefore, say that his existence is impossible, and thus we must say that his existence is necessary.[17]

(It is important to see—because Malcolm's argument will not

---

[17] Malcolm, *op. cit.*, pp. 149 f. Even before Malcolm, Charles Hartshorne had done extensive work along the same lines, formulating versions of the Ontological Argument on the basis of Anselm's second statement. See his *Man's Vision of God* (New York: Harper & Row, 1941) and his more recent *Anselm's Discovery* (La Salle, Ill.: Open Court, 1965).

work without this—that nothing prevents the possible truth of an idea so long as the idea is logically consistent, that is, so long as it is free from self-contradiction. Thus, however empirically implausible, it is at least *logically* possible that there are green men inhabiting the far side of the moon. But it is not even logically possible that there might exist a square circle for that concept is from the start self-contradictory.)

It will be recalled that Kant reduced "God necessarily exists" to an analytic, tautologous statement, and this Malcolm finds problematic. Kant and others had reasoned that as any analytic statement is translatable into a conditional or hypothetical "If . . . then" statement, "God necessarily exists" is equivalent to "If God exists, then he necessarily exists." But according to Kant this statement (with its *"if"*) positively implies that far from a being who cannot not-exist, God perhaps may not exist. Malcolm countered this conclusion with the observation that far from asserting anything, the statement "God necessarily exists" as understood by Kant to be an analytic statement involves, when translated into its hypothetical equivalent, a downright contradiction. *"If* God exists . . ." suggests that maybe he does not exist, and that is clearly incompatible with the original assertion that he necessarily does! It follows that there is an important difference (Malcolm calls it a lack of symmetry) between "A triangle has three angles" and "God necessarily exists": The former may be translated in a meaningful conditional ("If a triangle exists, then it has three angles"), whereas the latter cannot. The upshot of this is that whatever else might be said about the statement "God necessarily exists" (or "God is a necessary being"), it is not equivalent to the hypothetical "If God exists, then he necessarily exists," and here, at least, is an important exception to what Malcolm calls the "contemporary dogma" that no existential propositions can be necessary.[18]

Malcolm has hardly had the last word on the subject. As might be expected, his article produced an avalanche of replies and was attacked from several directions.[19] One of these objections, some-

---

[18] *Ibid.,* pp. 151 ff.

[19] Malcolm himself provides an index to many of these critical responses in a footnote added in the reprinted version of his article, *ibid.,* p. 162. Special note should be made of *Philosophical Review,* LXX (January, 1961) containing six different discussions of Malcolm's article.

thing of a historical one, charges that Malcolm's "necessary being" is probably a far different sort of being from Anselm's original "that than which nothing greater can be conceived." Malcolm's argument delivers a being whose existence is logically necessary or whose non-existence is logically impossible, whereas Anselm (so the objection goes) no doubt conceived the greatness of his God not in terms of logical necessity or impossibility, but in terms of his unity, immutability, omnipotence, eternity, sovereignty, and the like. But this is too harsh on Malcolm who did, in fact, emphasize that there are many different conceptions of what a necessary being might be, depending on the different "language games" (as Wittgenstein expressed it) in which they perform their duties. As a matter of fact, in defense of one of these legitimate conceptions (and "games") Malcolm appeals to Psalms 90:2,

> Before the mountains were brought forth,
> > or ever thou hadst formed the earth and the world,
> > from everlasting to everlasting thou art God.

which may be, after all, more akin to how Anselm had conceived God's greatness long before the necessary/existential distinction was drawn by the modern mind, a distinction that fails to do justice to the full breadth of philosophical and linguistic experience.

A different kind of challenge to Malcolm is levelled by those who claim to find fatal infelicities in the logic of his position. One example may be mentioned. Malcolm had concluded that (1) if God does not exist, his existence is logically impossible, and (2) if God does exist, his existence is logically necessary. With respect to (1), it has been charged that Malcolm is mistaken in deducing from the observation that God can neither begin to exist or cease to exist that if he does not now exist then his existence (or "God exists") is logically impossible; what follows, rather, is that it is logically necessary that if God does not exist, then he simply never will, and that is quite a different idea. Similarly, with respect to (2), from the truth that God can neither come into or pass out of existence it does not follow that if God exists then his existence (or "God exists") is logically necessary; what is logically necessary is that if he exists, then he always exists. In this way, what may be legitimately deduced from the impossibility of God's coming into or passing out of existence is nothing that bears on the contingency or necessity of God's existence or non-existence, but only on the necessity of his remaining in existence (if he exists) or out of it (if he doesn't).[20]

What to Make of It?

Neither have Malcolm's critics had the last word. Some philosophers believe that it is possible to construct a version of the argument that dispenses entirely with all existence-as-a-predicate talk, some have now claimed to find three and even four arguments in Anselm's statement, others have urged a return to the original one-argument hypothesis, and someone else has turned the proof into an Ontological Argument for the Devil! It is no wonder that the reader by now may be tempted to side with the German philosopher Arthur Schopenhauer who regarded the Ontological Argument as a "charming joke," and a "piece of scholastic jugglery." To be sure, many important philosophers have dismissed the Ontological Argument as an optical illusion of the philosophical imagination, but those who have embraced it as a sound and forceful witness to the reality of God form an impressive list also, including Spinoza, Leibniz, Hegel, and (in their own ways) Barth and Tillich.

This last observation may be taken, I think, as sufficient evidence that the significance of the Ontological Argument (and this applies equally to many of the positions considered in this book) cannot be decided on logical grounds alone. If it were guilty of some simple (or even complicated) logical fallacy, the argument would have been discarded long ago. It has, instead, remained a center of controversy to the present day. The real issue lies much deeper. We have already seen that there are fundamentally different conceptions of knowledge, reality and language, and it is probably at this level that the success or failure of the Ontological Argument must be decided.

---

[20] See Alvin Plantinga, "A Valid Ontological Argument?," *Philosophical Review, ibid.,* reprinted with minor changes in his *God and Other Minds* (Ithaca, N.Y.: Cornell University Press, 1967), pp. 82 ff.

4

The Cosmological Argument

If, in the midst of a street corner conversation, you were to ask your companion why he believes in God, he might answer something like this: "Well, here is the world, and it had to come from *something*." For all its lack of sophistication, this response represents a rudimentary expression of the Cosmological Argument (from the Greek κόσμος: "world" or "universe"), which purports to demonstrate the existence of God from the existence of the world, or some part of it. More specifically, this argument reasons from contingent or dependent being to the necessary or independent being of God. The argument states, in effect, that neither the universe, nor any part of it, contains within itself its own *raison d'être*, and that God must be posited as the ultimate cause of things. In fact, this argument is often called the First-Cause Argument.

The Five Ways of St. Thomas Aquinas

Of all the philosophical arguments ever propounded for the existence of God, none are more famous than the *Quinque Viae*, or "Five Ways," that St. Thomas Aquinas presents in a few brief paragraphs near the beginning of his *Summa Theologica*. Before considering the substance of Thomas' position, a few preliminary comments may be in order.

Briefly, Thomas' first argument begins with the evidence of motion and concludes that God must exist in order for there to be, as is rationally required, an unmoved first mover of all things. The second argument attempts to prove that God must exist as the ultimate efficient cause of things, otherwise the series of causes and effects would have no beginning. The third argues that there must exist a self-subsistent necessary being, otherwise all things and the universe itself would be merely possible and therefore ultimately non-existent. The fourth reasons that the gradation in things, such as more and less being, more and less good, more and less true, more and less noble, implies the existence of an absolute being as the ground of all other, relative being. The fifth is usually regarded as a version of the Teleological Argument according to which God must exist as the intelligent architect of the orderly cosmos.[1] It will be noted that, wholly unlike the Ontological Argument of St. Anselm or Descartes, Thomas' arguments each begin with some aspect or other of the sensible world, claiming to prove the existence of God in a completely *a posteriori* manner. He sees this procedure as sanctioned by St. Paul's exhortation (Rom. 1:19–20) that the invisible God may be known, even apart from revelation, through his visible creation. Further, each argument is a causal argument, proceeding by means of the principle *ex nihilo nihil fit*, "from nothing, nothing comes," or, to put it in more modern terms, the principle that for everything that happens there is a necessary and sufficient cause.[2]

Some further observations may be helpful. First, the precise nature of Thomas' Cosmological Argument and its relation to the Teleological Argument (to be considered at length in Chapter 5) is

---

[1] St. Thomas Aquinas, *Summa Theologica,* Part One, Qu. II, Art. 3, in *Basic Writings of Saint Thomas Aquinas,* ed. Anton C. Pegis (New York: Random House, 1945), Vol. I.

[2] The continuing influence of Thomistic natural theology is reflected in the decrees of the Vatican Council of 1870: "The same holy mother Church holds and teaches that God, the beginning and end of all things, can certainly be known by the natural light of human reason from created things. . . ." (in *Enchiridion Symbolorum,* sec. 1785, ed. Heinrich Denzinger, et al., thirty-first ed. [Freiburg im Breisgrau: Herder, 1957]). Thomism was commended by Pope Leo XIII in the 1879 encyclical *Aeterni Patris* as the unofficial philosophy of the Roman Catholic Church.

not always agreed upon. Some would object, for example, that the imposition of this later distinction on Thomas (a distinction popularized by Kant) distorts the essential unity of his fivefold argument which, after all, he does not call five demonstrations but five "ways." Nevertheless, if we distinguish between reasoning toward God from the existence of some empirical reality or other (usually the world or universe itself) and reasoning toward God from something *about* reality or the world, then only the first three of Thomas' Ways are versions of the Cosmological Argument. Of course, that motion, efficient causality, and contingency are (in Thomas) not facts about the world in the same way that design is would require more explanation, if indeed such could be provided. It is also sometimes thought (the influence of Kant again) that the Fourth Way stands in a somewhat different relation to the first three, being perhaps more of a Moral Argument (Chapter 6). But this distinction too is regarded with suspicion by Thomist scholars. The Five Ways, it would be argued, converge on one ultimate cause of one reality, though arrived at *via* different aspects of that reality: its moved, caused, contingent, graduated, and ordered character.

Second, it is sometimes objected that even though Thomas concludes each of his proofs with some such locution as ". . . and this everyone understands to be God," the God that Thomas proves is actually not much more than an abstract philosophical principle, hardly the object of faith and prayer. Obviously, Thomas is aware of the difference between knowing that God exists and knowing what he is. Over the chapters of his main works Thomas believes that he is able to establish (though imperfectly) a knowledge of God's attributes, and in the *Summa Contra Gentiles* it takes him hundreds of pages to move from the First Cause to the God and Father of our Lord Jesus Christ. Nonetheless, in the present passages he is content to establish the foundation of theology, namely, the existence of the First Cause or Necessary Being, though the demonstration of this "philosophical" God is no small task, nor, as Thomas sees it, is it an unimportant one. A philosophical knowledge of God, for Thomas, is a "preamble to faith"; it provides a rational foundation both for the unbeliever in his approach to Christianity and, as for St. Anselm, for the individual who already believes what he does not yet understand.

Finally, it might be noted that none of the Five Ways are entirely original with Thomas. The first two reflect the influence of

Aristotle's *Physics* and *Metaphysics;* the third suggests Thomas' indebtedness to the *Guide for the Perplexed* by the Jewish philosopher Maimonides; the fourth echoes the Platonic *Dialogues;* and the fifth should be considered in light of St. John Damascene's *On the Orthodox Faith.* This is not to say that Thomas' arguments are not his own. Certainly they bear the distinctive imprint of his own reinterpretation and are filled with new significance. Still, this serves to remind us that none of the philosophical and/or theological contributions considered in this book were born in an intellectual vacuum, not even the celebrated proofs of St. Thomas Aquinas.

Of the Five Ways it will suffice for our purposes to consider the Second and the Third. Thomas' full statement of the Second Way is as follows:

In the world of sensible things we find there is an order of efficient causes. There is no case known (neither is it, indeed, possible) in which a thing is found to be the efficient cause of itself; for so it would be prior to itself, which is impossible. Now in efficient causes it is not possible to go on to infinity, because in all efficient causes following in order, the first is the cause of the intermediate cause, and the intermediate is the cause of the ultimate cause, whether the intermediate cause be several, or one only. Now to take away the cause is to take away the effect. Therefore, if there be no first cause among efficient causes, there will be no ultimate, nor any intermediate, cause. But if in efficient causes it is possible to go on to infinity, there will be no first efficient cause, neither will there be an ultimate effect, nor any intermediate efficient causes; all of which is plainly false. Therefore it is necessary to admit a first efficient cause, to which everyone gives the name of God.[3]

Stated as simply as possible, the argument is that (1) the universe could not be the cause of itself; (2) it could not come from nothing; (3) the chain of causes and effects cannot be extended to infinity; (4) therefore, there must be a first, uncaused cause of all things. Any form of the Cosmological Argument will look roughly like this.

In a deductive argument such as this one, any uncertainty or ambiguity in the premises is necessarily passed along to the conclusion. We must, then, look carefully at the three premises of the above argument. The first presents the least difficulty. As Thomas

---

[3] St. Thomas, *op. cit., loc. cit.*

observes, if the effect is truly dependent upon the cause (and that is the essence of the cause–effect relationship), then the cause must in some sense precede the effect. For something to be the cause of itself it would have to exist before it exists, and that is absurd. Thomas, like Aristotle, thought that the truth of the Law of Non-Contradiction is self-evident: A thing cannot both be and not-be at the same time in the same respect. Thus, we may pass over the first premise of the argument. The other two premises, however, may not prove so agreeable, and the major criticisms of the Cosmological Argument have, in fact, revolved largely around these.

First in the Order of Time

One of the most obvious criticisms of the First-Cause argument is that a first cause is simply not necessary at all. Why could the universe not have existed from eternity? Why can we not say that the present universe is just one of an infinite number of states extending backward in time without end? Actually, there are two forms of the First-Cause Argument, and it is extremely important to grasp this distinction at this point in our discussion. According to one version, the argument leads to a first cause in time, a being who stands at the beginning of the *temporal* series. The other form of the argument interprets God as first not in time but in the order of *being*. This last, which is the position of Thomas, is not always easy to comprehend, and we will return to it in a moment. For the present, we will suspend our discussion of Thomas and direct ourselves to the more popular form of the Cosmological Argument according to which God must exist as the first cause in time or first cause of the temporal series.

Almost everyone feels an urge to posit a temporal origin of the universe on the rather instinctive—but not very philosophical— grounds, "There just had to be a beginning of things!" Others believe that it is possible to provide persuasive arguments for this hypothesis. The scholastic theologian-philosopher St. Bonaventure (a contemporary of Thomas) argued, perhaps more emphatically than anyone else, the impossibility of a *creatio aeterna,* a world that has always existed. Through a series of *reductio ad absurdum* arguments Bonaventure tried to show that the thesis that the world or universe has always existed leads to absurd and impossible conclu-

sions. If, for example, the universe has existed from eternity, then
an infinite number of days has already passed by, and every new
day is added to the already infinite number of days; yet it is impossible to add to the infinite. Further, there are twelve lunar
revolutions for every one solar revolution; but if the world has always existed, then the moon has gone round the earth an infinite
number of times and likewise the sun; but two infinite numbers,
one of which is twelve times the other, is absurd.[4]

Bonaventure's position may more easily be represented by trans-
lating it into the following argument: If the world has existed from
eternity, then prior to the present moment an infinite number of
years has elapsed; but an infinite series can never elapse or be
consummated or concluded—that is precisely why it is an *infinite*
series. In this way, the suggestion that the universe has always
existed is self-contradictory. Or, simplifying the argument still further: If the world has always existed, we would spend forever
arriving at the present point in time, in which case we would never
have finally arrived at this point. To avoid this absurd conclusion,
we must concede that a *finite* number of years, days, or hours has
elapsed and that time therefore must have had a beginning. And
because something cannot come from nothing or be its own cause,
we must posit a transcendent being, God, the first cause of the
whole spatio-temporal, cause-and-effect series.

This kind of reasoning may possess a *prima facie* plausibility, but
a warning should be issued against all arguments having anything
to do with infinity. The concept of infinity is a most perplexing one.
In fact, 2,500 years ago the Greek philosopher Zeno of Elea posed
a series of paradoxes concerning the infinite, some of which continue to baffle philosophers and mathematicians to this day.

We can, however, settle at least two things. First, when Bonaventure speaks of an infinite span of time having gone by, he does
not mean an infinity of infinite divisibility. Any finite segment of
time contains, of course, an infinite number of moments, just as a
segment of a line contains an infinite number of geometrical points.
But here we are referring to an infinity of actual and determinate
units such as years or minutes, not merely theoretical or ideal points

[4] St. Bonaventure, *Commentaria in II Sententiarum*, Dist. One, Part One,
Art. I, Qu. 2, in *St. Thomas Aquinas, Siger of Brabant, St. Bonaventure: On
the Eternity of the World*, tr. Cyril Vollert, et al. (Milwaukee, Wis.: Marquette
University Press, 1964).

on a geometric line. Second, it is inevitably countered that we should have no more difficulty conceiving of an infinite number of years stretching into the past than we have of an infinite series of negative numbers (0, −1, −2, −3, *ad infinitum*). But there is an important difference between this hypothetical or purely conceptual infinity and an infinity of actually existing spatio-temporal states. It is one thing to entertain the concept of infinite series and quite another to pass through one. I can easily conceive of an infinite number of numbers, but I cannot succeed in counting them, not even if I lived forever. Similarly, I can conceive of an infinite number of years stretching into the past, but it is impossible that they have actually elapsed.

God and Cosmology

Not all of the arguments that the universe had a beginning in time are of a purely logical, philosophical nature. More recently, cosmologists have emerged with scientific empirical evidence for the temporality of the universe. One of the most important of these is the Second Law of Thermodynamics or, as it is also called, the Law of Entropy. According to this principle, the energy in the universe is being progressively and uniformly distributed throughout. Some regions of the universe are hotter than others, and heat is constantly flowing from the hotter to the cooler. The end of this process would be a state of thermal equilibrium, that is, a completely random distribution of energy and the stagnation of all physical activity. It should be apparent how all of this may be construed as evidence for a beginning of the universe. If the universe has always existed, then by now such a uniform distribution of energy would have come about, which is obviously not the case. Some rather astute scientists have been willing to affirm a beginning of the cosmos on the evidence of entropy, including the physicist and astronomer Sir Arthur Eddington who claimed that since the universe is running down it must have once been "wound up."[5] Even Bertrand Russell, writing in 1931, concluded, ". . . as arguments of this nature go, it is a good one, and I think we ought provisionally to accept the

[5] A. S. Eddington, *The Nature of the Physical World* (New York: Macmillan, 1928), p. 83.

hypothesis that the world had a beginning at some definite, though unknown, date."[6]

Other, and closely related, cosmological evidence for a temporal beginning of the universe is the Lemaître-Gamow concept of the evolutionary cosmos. According to this theory (often called the Big Bang Theory), all of the matter of the universe was originally compressed into something resembling a huge, super-dense atom. At a definite point in time, calculated at 10 or 15 billion years ago, the primeval atom exploded, flinging matter into the expanses of space. Our expanding universe, in which galaxies are receding from one another at enormous velocities, is the effect of this colossal nuclear reaction and cosmic explosion.[7] That this piece of cosmology has been seized as pointing to an original creation is understandable.

The Second Law of Thermodynamics has been called the best established of natural laws, and the Big Bang Theory appears now to have won out over its nearest competitor, the Steady State Theory, as the most adequate explanation of the expanding universe.[8] But how these theories bear on the question of the world's beginning is less certain. It is not impossible, for example, that the present world-order, with its entropic scattering is but one stage in a cyclic expansion and contraction. More generally, it might be objected that such speculation tends to obscure the honored boundaries between physics and metaphysics: Is it really possible to move so easily from considerations about the origin and nature of this particular configuration of matter to conclusions about the absolute beginning of all matter? It would seem, though, that the theist

[6] Bertrand Russell, *The Scientific Outlook* (London: George Allen & Unwin, 1931), p. 122.

[7] George Gamow, *The Creation of the Universe,* revised ed. (New York: Viking Press, 1961).

[8] According to the Steady State model, hydrogen atoms are continually being created; they then coalesce into clouds that further condense into stellar systems or galaxies which recede from one another leaving new emptiness to be filled up by coalescing hydrogen atoms. The result is that from any position in space (the Cosmological Principle) and at any point in time (the Perfect Cosmological Principle) the universe would appear the same, at least in terms of the distribution of galaxies. The evidence of quasars (quasi-stellar objects) detected by radio astronomy now suggests, however, that this is not the case. Furthermore, according to the Big Bang Theory, a remnant of the original thermal radiation should even yet be detectable, and something at least like it (an isotropic radiation of a wave length of 7.2 cm) has been.

might appropriately claim that the evidence of physics tends at least to converge, along with his philosophical and perhaps revealed evidence, that the universe was indeed created *ex nihilo* by an omnipotent being at some definite point in the past.

First in the Order of Being

"First cause" is usually understood, as above, to mean "temporal beginning," and for most people the Cosmological Argument proves, if anything, that there must be a God who created the world once upon a time, at an original moment in the past. But to return now to our earlier discussion, we have seen that there is another form of the argument, a more classical version, and that this latter is the version of St. Thomas.

If we asked someone, "What is the cause of the universe?," and he were to answer, "The universe has always existed," we might legitimately respond, "We did not ask for the *age* of the universe but for its *cause*." That is, even if something has always existed it would still appear quite meaningful to ask why there is something rather than nothing. Accordingly, Thomas formulated a version of the Cosmological Argument on the supposition of the world's eternity, proving not a first cause in a temporal series at all, but rather a being who is first on the ontological scale, in other words, first in the order of being. As he says in another context, ". . . God is the cause of an everlasting world in the same way as a foot would have been the cause of an imprint if it had been pressed on sand from all eternity."[9] Similarly, Aristotle (whom Thomas reverently called "The Philosopher") did not regard his Unmoved Mover as a first cause in time. He believed that the world has always existed, but that the evident activity and change in the world at every moment derives from the motion of the heavenly spheres (which carry the sun, moon, planets, and the fixed stars in their orbits), which in turn derive their motion from the Unmoved Mover, God.[10] Of course, Thomas believed as an article of faith that the world did have a beginning in time (Gen. 1:1), but he also believed that on

[9] St. Thomas Aquinas, *Summa Contra Gentiles*, I, 43, tr. Anton C. Pegis (Garden City, N.Y.: Image Books, 1955).

[10] Aristotle, *Metaphysics*, XII, 6 (1071b ff.).

purely philosophical grounds the eternity of the world could be neither affirmed nor denied, and he freely grants it for the sake of the argument.[11]

The first cause to which this form of the argument leads is, in this way, "first" in the sense of *ultimate*: God is the ultimate being. One might represent the temporal cause-and-effect series by a horizontal line, and the ontological cause-and-effect series by a vertical line. If the horizontal series were to extend infinitely in both directions, it would, nevertheless, represent a collection (though an infinite collection) of contingent things. And because an infinite number of contingent things can no more be the cause of itself than a single contingent thing, the infinite series is itself wholly contingent. The horizontal or temporal series, even if infinite, is therefore subject to, conditioned by, and contingent upon a higher and different order of causality. But if there were no first term or ultimate

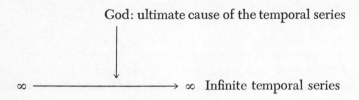

God: ultimate cause of the temporal series

∞ ⟶ ∞ Infinite temporal series

cause in the vertical or ontological series, then the universe as a whole would have no ground, no condition, no cause, no reason for being. There would be, in the final analysis, no final analysis.

This form of the argument, according to which there must be at any moment in the life of the universe an ultimate, necessary being upon which the contingent universe depends, is more clearly seen in Thomas' Third Way:

The third way is taken from possibility and necessity, and runs thus. We find in nature things that are possible to be and not to be, since they are found to be generated, and to be corrupted, and consequently, it is possible for them to be and not to be. But it is impossible for all things which are, to be of this sort, for that which can not-be at some time is not. Therefore, if everything can not-be, then at one time there was nothing

11 St. Thomas (the Angelic Doctor) and St. Bonaventure (the Seraphic Doctor) carried on a running debate on this very question, and their relevant statements have been translated and included in the work mentioned in note 3 above.

in existence. Now if this were true, even now there would be nothing in existence, because that which does not exist begins to exist only through something already existing. Therefore, if at one time nothing was in existence, it would have been impossible for anything to have begun to exist; and thus even now nothing would be in existence—which is absurd. Therefore, not all beings are merely possible, but there must exist something the existence of which is necessary. But every necessary thing either has its necessity caused by another, or not. Now it is impossible to go on to infinity in necessary things which have their necessity caused by another, as has been already proved in regard to efficient causes. Therefore we cannot but admit the existence of some being having of itself its own necessity, and not receiving it from another, but rather causing in others their necessity. This all men speak of as God.[12]

Here it should be clear that Thomas argues for a self-subsisting necessary being, not a first cause in time, and in fact assumes, as he does in all of the Ways, that the universe has always existed. The argument may be restated as follows. If all things are merely possible or are the sorts of things that come into being and pass away, and if the universe has always been here, then nothing would now exist. For at some time in the infinite past all things would not-be at once (given enough time everything possible will happen, and it is possible that everything that can not-be will not-be all at the same time). Now out of nothingness, nothing can possibly come. But we exist. It is therefore not the case that all things are merely possible, and there must exist something that is necessary. But this is not the end. By "necessary being" Thomas does not necessarily mean (as Malcolm did in the last chapter) a being who cannot not-exist for all eternity. For Thomas there are, as a matter of fact, *created* necessary beings, beings who might not have existed though once created they cannot cease to exist (for example, angels and the souls of men). But a series of such necessary beings as these (necessary *ab alio*) cannot extend *ad infinitum,* so there must exist an ultimate and self-existent necessary being (necessary *a se*) upon

12 St. Thomas, *Summa Theologica, op. cit., loc. cit.* The translation of the third sentence is emended in accordance with the correct textual reading: *Impossibile est autem omnia quae sunt, talia esse.* It is often remarked that Thomas' Third Way best displays the kernel of his theistic proof. In some ways that may be so, but it should be qualified with the observation that in the *Summa Contra Gentiles* (I, 13) he unfolds not summarily but completely a proof for God and it is not the Third Way but the First Way.

which all other beings (both necessary and possible) depend for their existence. There you have it.

We raised in the previous chapter the problem of the concept "necessary existence," and cannot here raise it all over again in relation to Thomas. But for those who cannot bear the suspense it may at least be noted that "God exists" is for Thomas (and this *is* similar to Malcolm) a necessary proposition though one that bears, obviously, on the existence of something. Whether it is a *logically* necessary proposition is another question; it will be recalled that Thomas has already informed us that God's existence is identical with his essence, which would suggest that one cannot deny "God exists" without self-contradiction. Be that as it may, many interpreters view Thomas' proofs as involving not a logical but a sort of factual or metaphysical necessity dictated by the self-subsistent nature of God which in turn is arrived at through a reflection on the nature of things. We have seen that a whole strain of contemporary philosophers would reject such a proposition as "God necessarily exists" on the grounds that only propositions, not things, can be necessary, but of course St. Thomas did not know that.[13]

It should be apparent by now that it misses the point entirely to represent the most classical theistic argument (Thomas') as reducing the world to antecedent states which originate in a being who stands at the beginning of the spatio-temporal process. The inevitable pictures of falling dominoes or bumping billiard balls is wholly out of place here. What the argument leads to is an ultimate being who at this moment (as at every moment) underlies the whole

[13] John Hick, citing J. J. C. Smart and J. N. Findlay (see above, Chapter 3, pp. 35 f.), explains: "It is said that only propositions, not things, can be logically necessary, and that it is a misuse of language to speak of a logically necessary *being*. This particular objection to the cosmological argument is based upon a misapprehension, for the argument does not make use of the notion of a logically necessary being" (*Philosophy of Religion* [Englewood Cliffs, N.J.: Prentice-Hall, 1963], pp. 22 f.). But it is probably not so much a matter of any misapprehension as it is a matter of a fundamental difference as to the nature of philosophical language. People like Smart and Findlay simply deny that philosophical language can function in the way that people like Thomas make it function; they simply deny that there can be any kind of necessity other than logical or propositional necessity. For a defense of the notion of factual as opposed to logical necessity, see Hick's article, "God as Necessary Being," *Journal of Philosophy*, LVII (October 27 and November 10, 1960).

structure of the cosmic process. As someone has expressed it, God is arrived at not by noting what has gone before something, but by looking *into* it. The First Way, then, teaches that if there is now no ultimate mover, then there is now no motion either; the Second Way teaches that if there is no ultimate efficient cause, then there are no cause-and-effect relations; the Third teaches that if there is no ultimate necessary being, then there are no other beings either; the Fourth teaches that if there is no maximal being, truth, and goodness, then neither is there any relative being, truth, and goodness; the Fifth teaches that if there is no intelligible end of things, then there is even now no purposeful activity. It is all a matter of what must exist right now in order to account for the way the world exists right now.

The Cosmological Argument attempts in various ways to demonstrate the existence of God by beginning with the sensible world and then trying to penetrate to its ultimate cause. But of course the argument in none of its forms can prove anything to someone who insists that the world is simply "gratuitous" (Jean-Paul Sartre) or "just there" (Bertrand Russell), and who is unwilling to subject that opinion to rational scrutiny.

Common Objections

Surely the most popular complaint against the Cosmological Argument (in any of its forms) is that if everything must have a cause, then so must God. But this will not do. When the theist claims that God caused the world and everything else, he is affirming that all things are dependent upon a being who himself necessarily *transcends* space and time as well as all coming and going. The question "Where did God come from?" can thus be discarded as ill conceived, because it construes God to be, like other things, the sort of being that can come and go. If God himself can come into being, then he cannot possibly be the *cause* of things that come into being and would not therefore be what the theist means by "God." Similarly, St. Augustine (354–430) observes that the question "What was God doing before he created the world?" is nonsensical. What possible meaning can there be in asking what God was doing "then" before the creation, since before the creation there was no time and therefore no "before"? And he castigates those who, enmeshed in the temporal flux of before and after, are incapable of transcending time and grasping the all-is-present and the all-at-once character of eternity in which God exists impassible and unmoved. (Augustine suggests that his answer is more respectable than the clever but trivial one provided by others: "What was God doing before he created the world? Why, he was preparing Hell for people who pry into mysteries!")[14]

More serious is the charge that the Cosmological Argument (especially in its Thomistic form) is guilty of the fallacy of composition, the mistake of thinking that what is true of the part is necessarily true of the whole. Bertrand Russell, for example, once complained that it no more follows from the fact that everything in the universe has a cause that the universe itself has a cause, than it follows from the fact that every man has a mother that mankind has a mother. But it must be observed that the fallacy of composition is not a formal but a material fallacy; that is, the fallacy cannot be identified by taking note of the form of a statement but rather by considering the nature of the ideas involved. It does follow from the fact that every thread in the carpet is green that the carpet itself is green, though it does not follow from the fact that all the books comprising a library have 500 pages that the library has 500 pages, even though both inferences are identical in form: If x is true of each of the members of y, then x is true of y. Similarly, the charge that the Cosmological Argument commits the fallacy of composition fails, perhaps, to pay sufficient attention to the kind of causality or contingency involved in the reasoning. If the argument were reasoning from the fact that everything in the universe has a cause in space and time, then it would indeed have to conclude that the universe too has a cause in space and time—which is exactly what the argument denies. In reality, however, the Cosmological Argument reasons from the contingency (or possible non-being) of every sensible thing to the contingency (or possible non-being) of all sensible things (a quite valid inference), and further reasons that the necessary cause of all sensible things cannot itself be one of those things (another valid inference).

Another common objection charges that the Cosmological Argu-

[14] St. Augustine, *The Confessions*, XI, 10 ff., tr. R. S. Pine-Coffin (Baltimore, Md.: Penguin Books, 1961).

ment is rendered sterile by the modern physical concept of the conservation of energy, which encompasses also the older principle of the indestructibility of matter. The reasoning (often directed against Thomas' Third Way) is that whereas particular configurations of matter do indeed come into being and pass away, energy itself abides. But a confusion lurks here. No one who affirms the principle of the conservation of energy has ever denied, at least not on those grounds, that energy is created. If the conservation of energy were incompatible with creation, then no man who is both a scientist and a Christian could believe in the conservation of energy! What the principle actually claims is not that energy can be neither created nor destroyed, but that once it exists it cannot be destroyed of itself, or that if left to itself in a closed system the total amount of energy remains constant. Moreover, it should be stressed that Thomas himself believed in something similar to the principle when he affirms that the physical world is, along with angels and souls, a necessary (though created) reality, the same kind of necessary being that he explicitly mentions in his Third Way as being dependent for its existence upon some uncreated necessary being.

This still leaves unraised, however, what is for many the greatest difficulty.

Hume on Causality

Obviously, the principle "From nothing, nothing comes," or the idea that for everything that happens there must be a necessary and sufficient cause, lies at the heart of the Cosmological Argument and has been assumed throughout our discussion thus far. Indeed, the concept of causality is one of the most fundamental in philosophy; it is also one of the most problematic.

The question before us is this: Is the statement "Every event must have a cause," or "From nothing, nothing comes," necessarily and universally binding? It is difficult for many to resist an *a priori* feeling of certainty with respect to causality, though as a metaphysical and rational principle it has been attacked by a good many philosophers. One of these was the British empiricist David Hume (1711–1776) who probably did more than anyone else in the history of philosophy to undermine this traditional concept. His treatment of causality is the product of his phenomenalism, the epistemological doctrine that all knowledge reduces to the phenomena or appearances given in sense-perception.

According to Hume's analysis, when we observe a causal relation between A and B, all we actually observe is that A is next to B and that A comes before B. These two factors, "contiguity" and "succession," are all that is disclosed to us through sense-experience. But clearly, though A may be contiguous with B and precede B, it is not therefore necessarily the cause of B. Hume concludes that a genuine causal relation must involve something more than mere contiguity and succession:

Shall we then rest contented with these two relations of contiguity and succession, as affording a complete idea of causation? By no means. An object may be contiguous and prior to another, without being consider'd as its cause. There is a NECESSARY CONNEXION to be taken into consideration; and that relation is of much greater importance, than any of the other two above-mention'd.[15]

It is over the nature of this necessary connection that Hume abandons the road followed by most of his predecessors. As traditionally conceived, causality was viewed as a metaphysical principle, that is, one of the fundamental laws of reality, a kind of power out there in the world binding things together with universal and necessary connections. Such an understanding of causal necessity could, of course, never be admitted by Hume the empiricist who took causality to be not a "relation of ideas" (that is, an analytic statement) but a "matter of fact" derived ultimately from sense-experience, and for whom causality therefore could never amount to anything more than the observed "constant conjunction" of one thing with another. As far as observation and experience goes, there is no more certainty, universality, or necessity in the statement "Every event must have a cause" than in "All swans are white."

It must be noted, however, that Hume is not denying causal necessity as such; what he is denying is that causality can be

---

[15] David Hume, *A Treatise of Human Nature,* ed. L. A. Selby-Bigge (Oxford, England: Clarendon Press, 1896), p. 77 (slightly edited).

rationally grounded, that it is cognitively or theoretically certain, that it is knowable: ". . . I never asserted so absurd a Proposition as *that any thing might arise without a Cause:* I only maintain'd, that our Certainty of the Falsehood of that Proposition proceeded neither from Intuition nor Demonstration; but from another Source."[16] What is this source? Hume answers: a propensity of human nature, a feeling or sentiment, a habit or custom, a rationally unjustified *belief.* In light of Hume's doctrine of "natural belief," the necessity or power which unites experiences together in a causal relation is now understood to lie in the mind's habit of passing from one experience to another, and causal necessity turns out to be a psychological rather than a metaphysical principle, though not for that reason any less important for our thinking about the world, and living:

> though the powers and forces by which the course of nature is governed, be wholly unknown to us; yet our thoughts and conceptions have still, we find, gone on in the same train with the other works of nature. Custom is that principle, by which this correspondence has been effected; so necessary to the subsistence of our species, and the regulation of our conduct, in every circumstance and occurrence of human life.[17]

The full significance of Hume's translation of metaphysical necessity into natural belief has sometimes been slighted by his interpreters in favor of his more negative and critical contribution. In this way the Humeian analysis has contributed more than Hume might have wished to the radical empiricist understanding of causality which, in its extreme form, dissolves it into an empirical generalization, a mere expression of statistical probabilities, or a methodological postulate. Be that as it may, Hume himself did, in fact, challenge the traditional metaphysical necessities (restricting all necessary truths to the logically necessary relations of ideas) including the metaphysical necessity of causality. And if we cannot be certain that every event must have such a cause, then we

---

[16] David Hume, "Letter to John Stewart," in Norman Kemp Smith, *The Philosophy of David Hume* (London: Macmillan, 1941), p. 413 (slightly edited).

[17] David Hume, *An Enquiry Concerning Human Understanding*, ed. L. A. Selby-Bigge, second ed. (Oxford, England: Clarendon Press, 1902), pp. 54 f.

cannot be certain that the world did either. Whether the world is an event to start with brings us to Kant.

Kant on Causality

We saw in Chapter 3 that all of us are certain of such truths as, "All barking dogs bark" or "All bodies occupy space," because these are analytic statements or tautologies; the predicate repeats what is already given in the subject such that they cannot be denied with self-contradiction; their truth is analytic and *a priori*. But Kant insisted that there is also a universality and necessity about many "synthetic" statements, statements in which the predicate adds something to what is given in the subject. That is, he believed (unlike Hume and a whole string of contemporary philosophers) that there are synthetic *a priori* truths, truths that are both *a priori* certain *and* existentially informative, and he believed that "Every event must have a cause" was one of them. Consider Kant's rejection of Hume's analysis of causality:

the very concept of a cause so manifestly contains the concept of a necessity of connection with an effect and of the strict universality of the rule, that the concept would be altogether lost if we attempted to derive it, as Hume has done, from a repeated association of that which happens with that which precedes, and from a custom of connecting representations, a custom originating in this repeated association, and constituting therefore a merely subjective necessity.[18]

But how, then, does Kant account for causality as a necessary and universal principle?

According to Kant, the reason every event must have a cause is that the concept of causality is built into the mind itself as one of the ways in which the mind (of its very nature) is disposed to represent reality. Causality is one of the *a priori* "categories" of the understanding through which space and time, also contributed by the intellect, is organized into intelligible experience; it is constitutive of experience, a necessary element of experience, part of what we *mean* by experience. Kant thus salvaged the concept of causality as a philosophical principle from Hume's skepticism, as

[18] Immanuel Kant, *Critique of Pure Reason,* tr. Norman Kemp Smith (London: Macmillan, 1929), p. 44.

well as explained how synthetic *a priori* knowledge in general is possible.[19]

But, alas, a high price must be paid for this reinstatement of causality. The *a priori* concepts, such as causality and substance, can now have no application whatever beyond the world of possible experience, inasmuch as they themselves constitute experience —and there goes the Cosmological Argument. In fact, says Kant, when the "theoretical reason" (which operates by means of the spatio-temporal and categorical structure of the understanding) ventures into the metaphysical and transcendent realm, the inevitable result is confusion and contradiction. If causality is a spatio-temporal relation constituting an aspect of experience, and if God transcends space and time, then what possible application can the concept of causality have to God? We saw above that if God is not the sort of being that can come and go, then surely he cannot be the effect of something. Kant shows that for the same reason God cannot be the cause of anything. In a word, the Cosmological Argument is unsound because it tries to apply the concept of causality, which has appropriate application to the sensible world only (what Kant calls the "phenomenal world" or the world of appearance) to the transcendent world (the "noumenal" or real world) where it has no application at all. The gulf between the supreme being and the chain of natural causes is rationally unbridgeable.[20]

Kant provides a series of "antinomies" (two incompatible propositions both of which can be proved true) as examples of the difficulties that plague the theoretical reason when it trespasses beyond its empirical limits. It so happens that his First Antinomy concerns the beginning of the world in time, a question that is not irrelevant (as we have seen) for one version of the Cosmological Argument. According to Kant, the thesis "The world had a beginning in time" can be demonstrated by a sound argument: If the world did not have a beginning in time, then an infinite number of years has elapsed, but this conclusion is self-contradictory. Unfortunately, the antithesis "The world did not have a beginning in time" can also be demonstrated: If the world did have a beginning in time, then in that empty period preceding time

[19] Immanuel Kant, *Prolegomena to any Future Metaphysics,* tr. Lewis W. Beck (New York: Library of Liberal Arts, 1951), pp. 42 ff.

[20] Kant, *Critique of Pure Reason, op. cit.,* pp. 511 f.

there could have been no distinguishing condition favoring existence over non-existence, and thus nothing at all would have been
initiated into existence.[21] What does this mean? It means that this
piece of speculative reasoning is illegitimate. Because the beginning of the world is not an object of possible experience, we cannot discuss it by means of concepts that have to do only with
experience. And so it is, for Kant, with all speculative issues;
concerning these issues we can expect no help from the theoretical
reason—only antinomies.

It should be noted that both Hume and Kant viewed causality
as a way of relating objects of experience, Hume psychologizing
it and Kant idealizing it. Kant, for example, thinks that the Cosmological Argument has something to do with "the impossibility
of an infinite series of causes, given one after the other, in the
sensible world"[22]—like falling dominoes. We have seen, however,
that the notion of causality employed by, say, St. Thomas was
conceived more richly as an ontological or metaphysical relation,
a condition of being itself. The Cosmological Argument defended
by the great scholastics was, in fact, unknown to Hume and Kant
—not that it would have mattered.

One further observation. Even aside from his delimitation of the
theoretical reason to objects of possible experience, Kant judges
that the Cosmological Argument would lead us, at best, to the
mere idea of an *ens realissimum* ("most real being"). But here
we are once again confronted with the difficulty encountered in
the Ontological Argument, namely, how to get from the concept
of such a being to its objective reality. For Kant, then, the Cosmological Argument rests ultimately upon the Ontological Argument, and the Ontological Argument is fallacious.[23]

We see, then, that an empiricist like Hume presents us with a
concept of causality that is taken to be descriptive of the real
world but that can never possess any rationally grounded universality or certainty. Kant, on the other hand, presents us with a
concept of causality that is universal, necessary, and certain, but
applicable only to an idea-istically constituted world of appearances. Many will be unable to suppress the suspicion that neither
of these approaches is correct, and, rejecting both of them, they

[21] *Ibid.*, pp. 396 ff.
[22] *Ibid.*, p. 511.
[23] *Ibid.*, pp. 509 ff.

will insist that the principle "Every event must have a cause" is somehow both certain *and* descriptive of the way things really are. How to explain the derivation of such a concept would be another problem and to pursue it here would be to open an epistemological Pandora's Box that would involve us in issues that range far beyond the scope of these chapters. But they are important issues and sooner or later must be confronted by the serious reader. We have already seen that much can rise or fall with the concept of causality, including the Cosmological Argument.

5

The Teleological Argument

Man has always been impressed by the apparent order of the cosmos, and, not surprisingly, has seized upon it as awesome evidence for an intelligent creator. This almost universal response no doubt inspired the Psalmist's exclamation,

> The heavens are telling the glory of God;
> and the firmament proclaims his handiwork (Ps. 19:1).

and the ancient judgment that Widsom

> . . . reaches mightily from one end of earth to
> the other,
> and she orders all things well (Wis. 8:1).

It is too much to believe, some have reasoned, that this vast array of orderly and purposive activity is but the product of mere chance, an accidental and fortuitous concurrence of atoms. The universe is rational, and rationality is the product of mind. This argument for the existence of God is called the Teleological Argument (from the Greek τέλος "end," "purpose," "completeness") or the Design Argument, since it reasons from the apparent design in the universe to the existence of a Designer.

Paley and the Watch-Analogy

The Teleological Argument has its roots in Plato and Aristotle for whom order and purpose were central facts about reality. In a well-known passage from the *Phaedo,* Plato represents Socrates as reflecting upon his earlier despair over the prevailing mechanistic explanations of nature and his subsequent joy upon discovering the philosophy of Anaxagoras with its doctrine of an all-governing Mind, for therein he found, or at least thought he found, a truly adequate cause of nature's unfolding. This interest in teleology was passed along to later thinkers, most notably to Aristotle and his Christian disciple St. Thomas Aquinas who employed it most obviously in his Fifth Way:

We see that things which lack knowledge, such as natural bodies, act for an end, and this is evident from their acting always, or nearly always, in the same way, so as to obtain the best result. Hence it is plain that they achieve their end, not fortuitously, but designedly. Now whatever lacks knowledge cannot move towards an end, unless it be directed by some being endowed with knowledge and intelligence; as the arrow is directed by the archer. Therefore some intelligent being exists by whom all natural things are directed to their end; and this being we call God.[1]

But we have seen already that it probably does violence to the unity of Thomas' theistic proof to separate the Fifth Way as being a different argument from his others. For a statement of the Teleological Argument, in distinction to the Cosmological Argument, we would do well to look elsewhere.

The most famous statement of the Teleological Argument is (for better or for worse) that of the Anglican divine William Paley (1743–1805) who in 1802 published a book entitled *Natural Theology, or Evidences of the Existence and Attributes of the Deity Collected from the Appearances of Nature.* From the opening pages of this book comes Paley's famous analogy of the watch. Let us imagine ourselves, he says, stumbling across a shiny object lying on the ground. A closer examination reveals an intricate mechanism of wheels, springs, and levers, precisely constructed and

[1] St. Thomas Aquinas, *Summa Theologica,* Part One, Qu. II, Art. 3, in *Basic Writings of Saint Thomas Aquinas,* ed. Anton C. Pegis (New York: Random House, 1945), Vol. I.

adjusted so as to set it ticking and telling the time of day. We would judge as incredible any suggestion that this watch is the product of mere chance, as if falling snow, rustling leaves, blowing sands, and flaking of minerals, just happened to shape the required pieces, bring them together, and combine them in just this manner! Rather, our irresistible tendency would be to attribute the watch to an intelligent designer:

There cannot be design without a designer; contrivance without a contriver; order without choice; arrangement without anything capable of arranging; subserviency and relation to a purpose without that which could intend a purpose; means suitable to an end, and executing their office in accomplishing that end, without the end ever having been contemplated or the means accommodated to it. Arrangement, disposition of parts, subserviency of means to an end, relation of instruments to a use imply the presence of intelligence and mind.[2]

The universe displays at every point an infinitely greater order, purpose, and design than that of the watch: ". . . every indication of contrivance, every manifestation of design which existed in the watch, exists in the works of nature, with the difference on the side of nature of being greater and more, and that in a degree which exceeds all computation."[3] Actually, says Paley, the physiological features of man himself present the most compelling evidence of all; he writes at great length documenting the complexities of the human eye and praising its design, claiming that if there were no other instance of design in the whole of experience, the human eye alone would suffice as evidence for the existence of a supreme designer. The fact is, however, that *everything* in the universe and the universe itself manifests "special design." And since, as everyone knows, a cause must be adequate to the effect, any rational person will hold the universe to be ultimately unintelligible apart from the concept of a cause that is commensurate with the overwhelming order and plan of the cosmos. Thus we are compelled by the display of order in the universe, analogous to that of the watch, to draw the inevitable inference to creative intelligence. Such a cause, Paley concludes, is supplied by natural

[2] William Paley, *Natural Theology*, ed. Frederick Ferré (Indianapolis, Ind.: Library of Liberal Arts, 1963), pp. 8 f.
[3] *Ibid.*, p. 13.

theology which assures us that "there must be something in the
world more than what we see," and that "among the invisible
things of nature there must be an intelligent mind concerned in
its production, order, and support."[4]

Hume: the Limits of Experience

David Hume's criticism is rightly considered the classic critique
of the Design Argument. In *Dialogues Concerning Natural Religion*
(published posthumously in 1779, several years before Paley's *Natural Theology*), Hume attacks the argument from many angles,
but these reduce essentially to four, and they all reinforce the
Humeian principle that belief must be proportioned to the evidence.

First, Hume argues that if we grant (which we might or might
not) that matter and motion have existed from eternity, and that
given enough time every possible situation will be actualized, then
due to "the eternal revolutions of unguided matter" every possible
arrangement and configuration of the elements—even watches—will
of necessity come about sooner or later. Further, once a world
such as ours is actualized, its displays of contrivance and design
should not be surprising. Would not each part stand necessarily in
some relation to every other part, and the world itself in some
relation to other worlds? Would not the form of something always
be adapted to its function? Would not all phenomena take on the
appearance of some organization or other and of a disposition by
natural laws and regular processes? The observation that the universe bears the marks of "special design" would now appear to be
empty.[5] Indeed, one might carry this point even further than Hume
did and suggest that a completely chaotic universe is inconceivable: If the constellations of stars were fixed according to some
other arrangements, or the planets were shifted from their present
orbits, or the parts of animals were adapted differently, what would
we have? Not chaos, but simply a different order.

We just saw that the Teleological Argument (at least in its

---

[4] *Ibid.*, p. 86.
[5] David Hume, *Dialogues Concerning Natural Religion*, ed. Henry D. Aiken
(New York: Hafner, 1948), pp. 52 ff.

Paleyan form) rests on an analogy when it concludes that there must be something (God) that is to the universe what the watchmaker is to the watch ("like effects prove like causes"). Hume's second and most telling criticism is that this is a dubious analogy, for it assumes that the universe as a whole is the effect of some cause in the same way that a house or watch is the effect of a carpenter or watchmaker. The only reason for judging that a house must be caused by a carpenter, or a watch by a watchmaker, is (as was explained in our discussion of Hume in Chapter 4) that the constant conjunction between house and carpenter, watch and watchmaker is given over and over again in experience. That is, on the basis of past and repeated experiences we are led to believe that this house too must have been constructed by a carpenter: "When two *species* of objects have always been observed to be conjoined together, I can *infer*, by custom, the existence of one wherever I *see* the existence of the other; and this I call an argument from experience."[6] The universe as a whole, however, is unique and without parallel, and its creation is certainly not something that is given over and over again in experience. There is, therefore, nothing within our experience that can possibly serve as an analogue to the creation of the world, and there is nothing within our experience analogous to a creator. "An intelligent being of such vast powers and capacity as is necessary to produce the universe . . . exceeds all analogy and even comprehension."[7]

Third, even if the world as a whole were analogous to something in our experience, Hume observes that it would not be most strikingly analogous to human contrivances or machines. For example, the world resembles more an organism than an artifact; it is more like an animal or vegetable than a watch or a loom. And because like effects have like causes, it would appear most reasonable to seek the cause or origin of the world in something analogous to generation and vegetation. On the most likely analogy, then, we should rather say that the world came from something like a seed or an egg than from a watchmaker. It may be answered, of course, that the mechanism of generation itself points to an original and creative reason. But Hume, who admits only experience and observation as our guides, responds in turn that the presence of rea-

[6] *Ibid.*, p. 23.
[7] *Ibid.*, p. 40.

son in the world points rather to the primacy of generation, for "reason, in innummerable instances, is observed to arise from the principle of generation, and never to arise from any other principle."[8]

Finally, Hume argues that such reasoning can at best lead only to a disappointing and unsatisfying concept of the divine. If, *per impossibile,* the Teleological Argument were to convince us that nature is the product of an intelligent being, there is little in nature that reflects the infinity, unity, and perfection of God. If significant at all, the analogy requires only a cause that is *adequate* to the effect. God, or the intelligent creator of the cosmos, may be many rather than one, imperfect rather than perfect, limited in power rather than omnipotent, and still be an adequate or sufficient cause of the world. Perhaps a committee of dim-witted gods, without even a chairman, performing experiments in cosmology to amuse themselves, botched who knows how many worlds before settling on this one—which, come to think of it, they may have botched also. Is there anything in this alternate analogy that is incompatible with our experience?[9] And, if a further note may be added, how much less able are we through such reasoning to ascend to a knowledge of the holy and benevolent God of Christianity, the Father of Jesus Christ, the author of our salvation?

Kant: The Limits of Reason

Neither does the Teleological Argument escape the devastating critique of Immanuel Kant. It is almost paradoxical, though, that before destroying the argument (which he calls the "physico-theological" argument), he eulogizes it:

[8] *Ibid.,* p. 51.

[9] *Ibid.,* Part V. In fairness to Hume, it should be added that though the above criticisms are, in the *Dialogues,* put into the mouth of Philo, to what extent Philo represents Hume is not always clear. Further, Philo, though a skeptic with respect to the traditional arguments, is not an atheist. At the beginning of Part II he announces that his quarrel is not with the being of God but with the anthropomorphic character of God to which the Teleological Argument leads: "He is infinitely superior to our limited view and comprehension, and is more the object of worship in the temple than of disputations in the schools."

This world presents to us so immeasurable a stage of variety, order, purposiveness, and beauty, as displayed alike in its infinite extent and in the unlimited divisibility of its parts, that even with such knowledge as our weak understanding can acquire of it, we are brought face to face with so many marvels immeasurably great, that all speech loses its force, all numbers their power to measure, our thoughts themselves all definiteness, and that our judgment of the whole resolves itself into an amazement which is speechless, and only the more eloquent on that account. . . . This knowledge . . . so strengthens the belief in a supreme Author [of nature] that the belief acquires the force of an irresistible conviction.[10]

Thus, Kant praises the argument to which he is about to lay waste.

For Kant, two main difficulties are involved in the Teleological Argument. First, and this exactly parallels one of Kant's critiques of the Cosmological Argument, the theoretical concepts and categories with which the mind confronts the world are entirely inappropriate and inadequate to establish a supreme being, a supreme architect, or a supreme anything. Kant believed that the concept of causality is an *a priori* category of the mind, a way in which reality is experienced (recalling our earlier discussion of Kant, one has only to speculate on what his experience would be without the relating and unifying contribution of cause-and-effect relations to see that it would not be what is called "experience" at all), and that the concept of causality has therefore no application beyond the domain of possible experience. Now God is obviously not an object of possible experience, he is not a spatio-temporal reality, and thus by his very conception he absolutely transcends the causal relation as Kant conceives it. What efficacy can there possibly be, then, in talking about God (or God's relation to the world) in terms of causality? But the Teleological Argument, no less than the Cosmological Argument, is a *causal* argument, it moves from the observation of the world's order to the *cause* of that order. It follows that the Teleological Argument (at least for Kant) requires an illegitimate extension of the mind's theoretical concepts.[11]

Second, and apart from the above criticism, the Teleological Ar-

---

[10] Immanuel Kant, *Critique of Pure Reason*, tr. Norman Kemp Smith (London: Macmillan, 1929), pp. 519 f. (translator's bracketing). Kant further honored the Teleological Argument as "the oldest, the clearest, and the most accordant with the common reason of mankind" (p. 520).

[11] *Ibid.*, pp. 518 f.

gument in itself would still be powerless to demonstrate the reality of a supreme being. At best, the argument demonstrates the necessity of an architect of the cosmos, a being who, for all we know, merely imposes order on an already existing material. But this is something quite different from an all-sufficient primordial being. It is logically conceivable that though the universe depends for its order upon a higher and more powerful being, this being in turn depends for its existence upon a still higher and more powerful being. As Hume has already said, there is clearly a difference between a being who is capable of creating the world and a being who is *omnipotent*. For its full force the Teleological Argument rests, therefore, upon the Cosmological Argument which does lead to the concept of the necessary and supreme being. But we have already seen that, according to Kant, the Cosmological Argument in turn presupposes the truth of the Ontological Argument, and that the Ontological Argument is unsound.[12]

By now it should be apparent that David Hume and Immanuel Kant have played central roles in the history of philosophical theology, and, as it would seem up to this point, decidedly critical and unsympathetic roles. We have seen that in his *Dialogues Concerning Natural Religion* Hume attacks the traditional theistic arguments, and in his famous essay "On Miracles," in the *Enquiry Concerning Human Understanding*, he dealt a blow against belief in the miraculous from which it has never quite recovered. Even so, it can be detected that Hume speaks cautiously at a time when the Calvinistic Church of Scotland levied heavy penalties even for an abuse of the Sabbath. His bitterest polemic was the posthumously published *Natural History of Religion* in which he attacks, among other things, the opinion that the "higher religions" such as Judaism, Christianity, and Mohammedanism have produced great benefits for society. On this point Hume judges, to the contrary, that the narrowness, bloodiness, and intolerance of these religions lead rather to the conclusion that they are "sick men's dreams."[13]

[12] *Ibid.*, pp. 520 ff.

[13] David Hume, *The Natural History of Religion*, ed. H. E. Root (Stanford, Calif.: Stanford University Press, 1956), p. 75. This reminds one of Bertrand Russell's quip: "I regard [religion] as a disease born of fear and as a source of untold misery to the human race. I cannot, however, deny that it has made some contributions to civilization. It helped in early days to fix the calendar, and it caused Egyptian priests to chronicle eclipses with such care that in

With Kant it is very different. Born of pietist parents, Kant was throughout his life sympathetic to religion, though he sought to translate the Biblical faith of his upbringing into rational and philosophically respectable terms. As Kant saw it, his own demarcation of reason made possible a more religiously adequate approach to God: "I have . . . found it necessary to deny *knowledge* [*Erkenntnis*], in order to make room for *faith* [*Glaube*]."[14] This more positive side of his philosophical theology is reflected most notably in his *Religion Within the Bounds of Reason Alone* and the *Critique of Practical Reason*. In the latter work Kant himself presents a new argument for the existence of God (which we will consider in the next chapter) replacing the ones he destroyed, providing a practical knowledge of God (*Glaube*) in place of theoretical knowledge (*Erkenntnis*).

A Scientific Restatement

The traditional Teleological Argument began with the evidence of special design, and from the beauty and adaptability of nature it postulated a special creation. This argument possessed some force as long as one believed that organisms originated in their present forms. In 1859, however, Charles Darwin published *The Origin of Species* which resulted in the abandonment of this common sense conviction and, along with it, the whole idea of supernatural creation. It was now possible to account for organic structures in a purely natural way. In place of a special creation by an almighty watchmaker, Darwin, with his principles of "natural selection" and the "survival of the fittest," substituted long sequences of mechanical and proximate causes. What was once thought to be the most obvious example of God's handiwork turns out to be the product of nature alone. And the most forceful evidence for the Teleological Argument turns out to be none.

At least so it appeared to many. For others, evolution was not

---

time they became able to predict them. These two services I am prepared to acknowledge, but I do not know of any others" (*Why I Am Not a Chrisian, and Other Essays,* ed. Paul Edwards [New York: Simon & Schuster, 1957], p. 24).

[14] Kant, *op. cit.,* p. 29.

at all incompatible with theism, and Darwin himself concluded *The Origin of Species* with a doxology:

There is grandeur in this view of life, with its several powers, having been originally breathed by the Creator into a few forms or into one; and that, whilst this planet has gone cycling on according to the fixed law of gravity, from so simple a beginning endless forms most beautiful and most wonderful have been, and are being evolved.[15]

Of the many expressions of theistic evolution, one of the most influential was that of F. R. Tennant (1866–1957), a trained chemist, biologist, and physicist. Tennant, who developed his position in full consciousness of the critical contributions of Hume, Kant, and others, believed that though complete proof of God's existence is unattainable, it is possible, proceeding inductively, to amass facts and generalizations that taken collectively may provide a basis for "reasonable belief." God is, for Tennant, a kind of scientific hypothesis, the most rational explanation for a network of empirical facts. (This reminds us of John Stuart Mill who referred to the Design Argument as "an argument of a really scientific character, which does not shrink from scientific test, but claims to be judged by the established canons of Induction."[16])

In his important work *Philosophical Theology,* Tennant suggested a wider conception of teleology—teleology "on a grander scale"—that is not only compatible with organic evolution but is in fact prompted by it: "The discovery of organic evolution has caused the teleologist to shift his ground from special design in the products to directivity in the process, and plan in the primary collocations."[17] Though evolution may force us to abandon the Paleyan brand of teleology, a broader, richer teleology replaces it, a teleology in which the progressive and purposive evolution of organisms is itself a powerful evidence.

---

[15] Charles Darwin, *The Origin of Species,* sixth ed. (New York: Appleton-Century-Crofts, reprint 1923), II, 305 f. The explicit reference to "the Creator" was added subsequently to the first edition in an attempt, no doubt, to placate hostility.

[16] John Stuart Mill, "Theism," in *Three Essays on Religion,* third ed. (New York: Longmans, Green & Co., reprint 1923), p. 167.

[17] F. R. Tennant, *Philosophical Theology* (Cambridge, England: University Press, 1928, 30), II, 85.

Tennant's more comprehensive teleology focuses not upon particular evidences of design (such as the purposive adaptation of the parts of animals to one another and of the animals to their environments), but rather upon the apparent intelligibility and meaningfulness of nature as a whole:

The forcibleness of Nature's suggestion that she is the outcome of intelligent design lies not in particular cases of adaptedness in the world, nor even in the multiplicity of them. . . . The forcibleness of the world's appeal consists rather in the conspiration of innumerable causes to produce, by their united and reciprocal action, and to maintain, a general order of Nature.[18]

This universal conspiration manifests itself in six main "fields of fact." In Tennant's words these are (1) the knowability or intelligibility of the world (or the adaptation of thought to things); (2) the internal adaptedness of organic beings; (3) the fitness of the inorganic to minister to life; (4) the aesthetic value of Nature; (5) the world's instrumentality in the realization of moral ends; (6) the progressiveness in the evolutionary process culminating in the emergence of man with his rational and moral status.[19] Though Tennant considers each of these at length, our comments must necessarily be limited.

Consider, for example, the aesthetic value of nature. The beauty and sublimity of nature may certainly fail in themselves as conclusive evidence that the universe is teleological. Strictly speaking, the beauty of nature need not be attributed to artistic production; much that is capable of evoking aesthetic sentiment is not always the result of conscious design. Still, the aesthetic response that nature elicits at every turn is such as to suggest what Tennant called an "alogical probability" that the aesthetic display of nature is grounded in mind. (The concept of alogical probability is a recurring and important one in Tennant's work. The phrase suggests the way in which the mind is often overwhelmed by the weight of evidence, but of a kind that cannot be calculated in terms of statistical or logical probabilities. According to Tennant, many of the fundamental principles upon which we think and act, includ-

[18] *Ibid.*, p. 79.
[19] *Ibid.*, p. 81.

ing the principle of scientific induction itself, are grasped and affirmed in just this alogical way.) Thus, the undeniable aesthetic aspect of nature becomes at least a "link in the chain of evidence" presented by the wider teleology.[20]

But nature is more than aesthetic, it is "a theatre for moral life." The whole of the natural process has come to fruition in man, the moral being: "In the fullness of time Nature found self-utterance in a son possessed of the intelligent and moral status. . . . The world-process is a *praeparatio anthropologica*, whether designedly or not, and man is the culmination, up to the present stage of the knowable history of Nature, of a gradual ascent."[21] Surely, any account of nature, if it is to be scientifically impartial and philosophically significant, will have to be written in light of the spiritual and moral character of man, her ultimate product. Tennant is careful, however, not to commit himself to a naturalistic interpretation of moral value. He emphasizes, in Kantian fashion, that there is an aspect of man that belongs properly to the "noumenal" realm and that can never be given a purely naturalistic explanation. This aspect of man includes his soul and moral constitution. Having observed this important "proviso," as he calls it, we may go on to speak of man as he is represented in the "phenomenal" realm of nature: ". . . we can affirm that man's body, with all its conditioning of his mentality, his sociality, knowledge and morality, is 'of a piece' with Nature; and that, *in so far as he is a phenomenal being*, man is organic to Nature, or a product of the world."[22]

The aesthetic and the moral are but two aspects of nature. There are many others, and they all conspire for the production of unity and intelligibility. Though no one of them, nor all of them together, constitute incontrovertible evidence for a Divine Mind, considered collectively they do support, says Tennant, a reasonable belief.

In this way, the evolutionary hypothesis undermined the old special teleology, while at the same time providing the foundation for a new one. This wider and more compelling teleological interpretation of nature turns our attention from products to processes; it asks us not to look here or there for a particular evidence of

[20] *Ibid.*, p. 88 ff.
[21] *Ibid.*, p. 101.
[22] *Ibid.*, p. 101 (my italics).

design in nature, but rather to consider the coherence and consummate effect of her well-nigh infinite and diverse strands. As Tennant puts it,

Theism no longer plants its God in the gaps between the explanatory achievements of natural science, which are apt to get scientifically closed up. . . . It is rather when these several fields of fact are no longer considered one by one, but as parts of a whole or terms of a continuous series, and when for their dovetailing and interconnectedness a sufficient ground is sought, such as mechanical and proximate causation no longer seems to supply, that divine design is forcibly suggested.[23]

Tennant believes that we are forced, finally, to explain nature either in terms of wisdom or undesigned coincidence. If we opt for the latter, we are yet confronted with nature's overwhelming complexity and wondrous coherence, and we have provided "not explanation but statement of what calls for explanation."[24]

It remains for Tennant to distinguish his position from the position of those who claim to explain the same unfolding of nature in terms of some "unconscious" will or purpose. Here he has in mind primarily the French thinker Henri Bergson who taught, in his *Creative Evolution*, that all nature is charged with an *élan vital*, or "life-force," carrying her forward into ever higher states of organization. Tennant holds, aside from the fact that the notion of "unconscious purpose" is a contradiction in terms, it is irreconcilable with the self-corrective course of nature: The simple fact is, as he expresses it in a lively metaphor, that nature seems to keep her head though the unconscious-purpose theorists claim she is brainless. Furthermore, nature does not appear to be equally propelled in all of her several kingdoms by blind purpose, contrary to what one would expect on the basis of such a theory. In fact, natural selection moves the species forward only by means of misadaptations and dead ends. In order to explain the facts, what is required is not a force but a Mind. As Tennant puts it rather aphoristically, "If Nature evinces wisdom, the wisdom is Another's."[25]

23 *Ibid.*, p. 104.
24 *Ibid.*, p. 109.
25 *Ibid.*

If any theistic argument could prove persuasive in our empirically minded age it would undoubtedly be Tennant's or one like it.

The Central Problem

Clearly the Cosmological and Teleological Arguments are closely related. They begin with the same reality, they employ many of the same concepts, and they proceed in much the same manner. For this reason many of the critical issues have already been considered in the previous chapter. With respect to the most obvious objections to the Teleological Argument alone, these too have now been aptly represented in our discussion of Hume and Kant.

It may be appropriate, however, to single out for emphasis the problem that may in fact lie at the bottom of every version of the Teleological Argument, including that of Thomas, Paley, and Tennant: the subjective interpretation of order. We have already observed that both Hume and Kant interpreted (though in very different ways) the teleologist's idea of order or purpose as being a product of the mind itself. Hume and Kant aside, it takes no great imagination to appreciate that the mind does often impose order where there is none, at least none in the sense of deliberate design, and this happens in two ways. Sometimes an otherwise haphazard arrangement assumes an orderly shape, at least in our minds, befitting what our present need or desire calls for. At other times we uncritically assume that certain features of nature exist for the purpose of producing certain ends, failing to observe that those ends follow rather from the particular character of nature. Thus, someone crossing a stream may optimistically regard the stones so conveniently placed as having been deliberately placed, or view a Rorschach ink blot as fraught with significant configurations, or regard it as a mark of divine prudence that God appropriately situated the nose and ears so as to enable us to hang eyeglasses on them!

Understandably, the question is often raised whether teleologists have been, on a large scale, guilty of maybe not so flagrant but equally misplaced judgments. It is against this general tendency that Hume poses the following question and warning: "What peculiar privilege has this little agitation of the brain which we call *thought*, that we must thus make it the model of the whole universe? Our partiality in our own favour does indeed present it on all occasions, but sound philosophy ought carefully to guard against so natural an illusion."[26] To this may be added the charge (anticipated earlier) that the teleologist who waxes rhapsodic over nature's abundant order may be simply uttering a truism or tautology. If order involves (as it appears it must) pattern, relation, sequence, and the like, what in the natural world *isn't* possessed of order? This applies especially to the kind of teleologist who is fond of talking about the just-right distance of the earth from the sun or about the aesthetics of the heavenly system.

For these reasons the teleologist may suitably feel called upon to show that the purpose implied in his teleological view is inexplicable except as involving (1) consideration of a goal and (2) intention of actualizing it. Presumably this would be shown either in Paleyan fashion by piling up as many specific instances as the skeptic requires (it will be recalled that even though Paley called his a "cumulative argument," he himself required only the eye), or, *à la* Tennant, by conducting broad surveys of whole spheres of continuities in nature. Even so, such evidence is in the end wholly empirical and finite, and whether a teleologist such as Tennant is able to succeed depends inevitably on a subjective interpretation of the evidence he points to.

Argument or Point of View?

It must not be taken lightly that reflective men of all ages have found in teleology cogent grounds for belief in God. To the list of thinkers already mentioned many others might be added. The "beautiful system" revealed by astronomy led Newton, in his *Principles of Nature* (1687), to reject blind necessity in favor of divine will. More recently, the English physicist Sir James Jeans, in *The Mysterious Universe* (1930), concluded from the new influx of scientific knowledge that the universe must have been constructed by a mathematician. Lecomte du Nuöy reasons in his well-known

---

[26] Hume, *Dialogues Concerning Natural Religion, op. cit.,* p. 22.

Human Destiny (1947) to the presence of divine intelligence from the staggering improbability of chance organization of the atoms of even a single protein molecule. The contemporary Catholic theologian-biologist Teilhard de Chardin, *The Phenomenon of Man* (1955), found it necessary to posit a divine "Omega point" as the end and explanation of nature's unfolding. The catalogue of those who argue in these ways for the existence of God could be extended seemingly without end.

But a similar catalogue could be constructed on the other side. Hume, for example, expresses a quite different sentiment: "The whole presents nothing but the idea of a blind nature, impregnated by a great vivifying principle, and pouring forth from her lap, without discernment or parental care, her maimed and abortive children!"[27] And a contemporary writes, "If we are to be intellectually honest, we must frankly admit that we can detect no purpose or meaning in the vast distances and wild eruptions of the universe—and certainly no purpose centered on the welfare of man."[28]

So, the question becomes this: If the universe thus abounds with an overwhelming display of order, why do so many fail to see it or interpret it aright? The answer is probably very simple and has little to do with the nature of scientific hypotheses, or analyses of "purpose," or issues in probability theory. At the beginning of this chapter St. Thomas told us: "We see that things which lack knowledge, such as natural bodies act for an end, and this is evident from their acting always, or nearly always, in the same way, so as to obtain the best result." It has been said that anyone who sees that much is no doubt prepared to see God also. That is, the Teleological Argument, like many important arguments, begins with a feeling about things rather than ending with one.

---

[27] *Ibid.*, p. 79.
[28] H. J. Paton, *The Modern Predicament* (London: George Allen & Unwin, 1955), p. 218.

6

The Moral Argument

Many remain unswayed by the icy logic of the Ontological Argument as well as by the more tangible evidence adduced by the Cosmological and Teleological Arguments. There is, however, yet another argument for God's existence. This argument, turning our attention from the world of sense-experience to the world of moral experience, seizes moral consciousness as its evidence for God, and hence it has come to be called the Moral Argument.

Kant and the Moral Law

As was mentioned earlier, even though Immanuel Kant rejected the Ontological, Cosmological, and Teleological Arguments, thereby undermining traditional philosophical knowledge of God, he himself proposed a new and very different one. And now there begins to emerge the positive side of Kant's contribution.

Kant's argument for the existence of God begins with a kind of fundamental sense or apprehension of moral meaningfulness. If one does not share the conviction that there is moral rhyme or reason to the world and human experience, then this argument is, for him, doomed to failure from the very start. Kant, however, believed that most of us find ourselves inescapably confronted with moral experience. There is no better expression of this confrontation than Kant's own lines which occur near the conclusion of his *Critique of Practical Reason:* "Two things fill the mind with ever new and increasing admiration and awe, the oftener and the more steadily we reflect on them: the starry heavens above me and the moral law within me."[1] At the very least, this important statement suggests that for Kant the reality of moral experience can no more be doubted than the reality of sensible experience. In the same way that I find myself in a sensible world, conditioned by objects outside me and to which I can only respond passively, so do I find myself in a moral world, conditioned by an objective moral law existing independently of my own opinions or inclinations. If we ask someone to survey the starry heavens above and he responds, "What starry heavens?", we judge the man to be blind, irrational, or otherwise lacking in a certain faculty present to normal people. Similarly, we would certainly entertain serious doubts about someone who appears utterly oblivious to moral duty and responsibility. Like the starry heavens above, moral law is just there, it is given.

It is extremely important to realize that when we speak here of the givenness of moral law we are not talking about any *particular* moral law such as "Thou shalt *x*" or "Thou shalt not *y*." There is an important difference between moral consciousness and conscience.

Some people do think that a more or less specific moral code can be detected in virtually all societies and in every period of human history. The cultural relativists and anthropologists have, in fact, probably exaggerated the moral diversity among societies, and C. S. Lewis, the late Oxford scholar and Christian writer, invites us to consider rather the essential unity of the moral doctrines of different civilizations and cultures:

If anyone will take the trouble to compare the moral teaching of, say, the ancient Egyptians, Babylonians, Hindus, Chinese, Greeks and Romans, what will really strike him will be how very like they are to each other and to our own. . . . Men have differed as regards what people you ought to be unselfish to—whether it was only your own family, or your fellow countrymen, or everyone. But they have always agreed that you

[1] Immanuel Kant, *Critique of Practical Reason,* tr. Lewis White Beck (Indianapolis, Ind.: Library of Liberal Arts, 1956), p. 166.

ought not to put yourself first. Selfishness has never been admired. Men have differed as to whether you should have one wife or four. But they have always agreed that you must not simply have any woman you liked.[2]

Furthermore, some believe that the Bible, too, supports the belief in a universally apprehended moral order, as in St. Paul's statement (a counterpart to his earlier statement about the invisible God who is evidenced in nature) that "When Gentiles who have not the [Mosaic] law do by nature what the law requires, they are a law to themselves, even though they do not have the law. They show that what the law requires is written on their hearts, while their conscience also bears witness . . . ." (Rom. 2:14–15). Not surprisingly, there is a version of the Moral Argument based on just the sort of empirical observations that Lewis indicates above, and he himself speaks of "a Somebody or Something behind the Moral Law."[3]

Though the question of universal moral laws (in the plural) may be an interesting one, and it certainly is a debated one, it has nothing whatever to do with Kant's *a priori* concept of moral law (in the singular), and it has nothing to do with his formulation of the Moral Argument. It is essential to note that Kant does not claim that there is a universal sense as to *what* is right, though he does claim that there is a universal sense that *something* is right. Duties may vary but duty itself does not. And it is this feeling of "ought," this feeling of being morally conditioned, this sense of duty, that points to an objective moral order and moral law. If there were no objective basis for morality, then all moral experience and moral judgments would be ultimately unfounded and unintelligible.

What has all this to do with God? Kant answers that the basis for moral law and the source of the moral consciousness can be nothing other than a supreme being or intelligence. His reasoning is this. Moral law or duty requires for its fulfillment nothing less

[2] C. S. Lewis, *Mere Christianity*, revised ed. (New York: Macmillan, 1952), p. 5.

[3] *Ibid.*, p. 23. Concerning the relation of the moral law to Christianity, Lewis says, "It is after you have realized that there is a real Moral Law, and a Power behind the law, and that you have broken that law and put yourself wrong with that Power—it is after all this, and not a moment sooner, that Christianity begins to talk" (p. 24).

than the *summum bonum,* the highest good, which is perfect happiness. The attainment of the highest good must therefore be possible if the idea of moral duty is not to be completely vacuous. That is, there must be some proportion or agreement between our acting in accordance with moral duty and our achievement of the Highest Good. And this requires God as a kind of guarantor that the moral agent will receive the just consequence of his act. Kant concludes that

it [is] our duty to promote the highest good; and it is not merely our privilege but a necessity connected with duty as a requisite to presuppose the possibility of this highest good. This presupposition is made only under the condition of the existence of God, and this condition inseparably connects this supposition with duty. Therefore, it is morally necessary to assume the existence of God.[4]

Kant thus builds his argument for the existence of God on the very evidence that is so often used to disprove God's existence, namely, the observed disparity between moral worthiness and the possession of happiness. If the universe is, so to speak, a truly moral place, then God must exist as an omnipotent being capable of insuring a just relation (if not in this world then in the next) between moral worthiness and the attainment of its reward.

For Kant, then, we can have absolutely no knowledge of God through the theoretical reason, though we can ascend to a knowledge of God (and, as we shall see in Chapter 10, to a knowledge of immortality and freedom as well) through the "practical reason." The theoretical reason begins and ends with sense-experience, whereas the practical reason begins with the moral law within, or moral consciousness, through which it is enabled to penetrate the reality (the noumenal world) that lies behind appearance (the phenomenal world). Kant's Moral Argument is not, in fact, a proof in the sense that the other traditional arguments are. In the Moral Argument, the existence of God is not, strictly, deduced from premises or in any way inferred from empirical evidence. He is seen, rather, to be *practically* required in the sense that he must exist as a "postulate" or necessary condition of an objectively valid morality. Kant makes clear what such knowledge isn't and what it is: "By a postulate of pure practical reason, I understand a theo-

---

[4] Kant, *op. cit.*, p. 130.

retical proposition which is not as such demonstrable, but which is an inseparable corollary of an *a priori* unconditionally valid practical law."[5]

Many thinkers after Kant formulated their own versions of the Moral Argument. One of the most influential was Hastings Rashdall (1858–1924), an English theologian and idealist philosopher. In the second volume of his *The Theory of Good and Evil* Rashdall conceded that if God does not exist it does not follow necessarily that there can be no morality at all. The materialist, for example, can devise for himself a purely naturalistic and relative morality by which to order his practical life. But if God does not exist it *does* follow that there can be no such thing as objective morality:

The belief in God, though not . . . a postulate of there being any such thing as Morality at all, is the logical presupposition of an "objective" or absolute Morality. A moral ideal can exist nowhere and nohow but in a mind; an absolute moral ideal can exist only in a Mind from which all Reality is derived. Our moral ideal can only claim objective validity in so far as it can rationally be regarded as the revelation of a moral ideal eternally existing in the mind of God.[6]

If one chooses to acknowledge the reality of moral ideals, he might be asked, not unfairly, where they exist. Obviously they do not exist in tables or in chairs or other such brute things. It is of the nature of an ideal to subsist in a mind. But whose mind? Surely not in any human, finite mind for these are constantly changing. We must therefore believe in an eternal and unchanging Mind as the only adequate *locus* of eternal and unchanging ideals.

It will be observed that Rashdall uses the words "objective" and "absolute" interchangeably. But inasmuch as these words are often the source of much confusion a distinction may be in order. Whereas an *objective* moral principle derives its validity and authority outside of and independently of the individual (for example, from God), an *absolute* moral principle is often regarded as claiming in addition to be universally binding on all men in all circumstances. In the matter of going to war, for example, an objectivist would insist that there is involved here a genuine moral truth and

<hr>

[5] *Ibid.*, p. 127.

[6] Hastings Rashdall, *The Theory of Good and Evil* (Oxford, England: Clarendon Press, 1907), II, 212.

an objective good to be realized through going or not going, and presumably he would attempt to consider all facets of the situation in order to arrive as best he can at his moral decision. The absolutist, on the other hand, may insist that war is wrong in any way, shape, or form, and that no possible circumstances can ever justify participation in it. Clearly, moral absolutism implies moral objectivism, though the converse does not hold; and both are incompatible with subjectivism or relativism, the doctrine that there is no moral value outside of individual or collective opinion. What is important for our present discussion is that it would appear that a Moral Argument such as Kant's or Rashdall's (in spite of Rashdall's terminology) requires only belief in moral objectivism.

In any event, all Moral Arguments teach that ideals and duties are unintelligible until viewed in light of their divine origin, understood in some sense or other. Like the Teleological Argument, the Moral Argument begins with a confrontation with order, though now understood of course as an order or teleology of moral experience rather than sense-experience, which it judges as inexplicable apart from God. As yet another proponent expresses it, "Either our moral values tell us something about the nature and purpose of reality . . . or they are subjective and therefore meaningless."[7] That they are meaningless is, for many of us, too much to accept.

(Before moving on it might be useful to point out that there are, by a happy coincidence, two different forms of each of the theistic arguments that we have considered. In the case of the Ontological Argument it will be recalled that Malcolm and others found two different arguments in St. Anselm. In our discussion of the Cosmological Argument we distinguished between the popular version that leads to a first cause in time and the more classical version that involves a first cause in the order of being. The Teleological Argument has been developed both on the grounds of special teleology as well as a broader, evolutionary teleology. And now we have seen that there are also two different Moral Arguments, one taking its evidence from the empirical fact of universal moral convictions and the other beginning with the *a priori* givenness of the general moral consciousness.)

---

[7] D. M. Baillie, *Faith in God and its Christian Consummation* (Edinburgh: T. & T. Clark, 1927), p. 173.

The Rejection of Objective Value

Many do, nevertheless, reject the idea of a universal moral consciousness and the belief in an objective moral order. And inasmuch as the Moral Argument rises or falls with just this question we must consider it a bit further.

One of the most popular objections to the belief in objective values is that we come by moral consciousness through learning or conditioning, and far from its being universally and objectively binding it is therefore purely subjective and relative. At least two responses may be made to this charge. First, that something is learned is hardly evidence against its objective truth and validity. We learn that two plus two equals four, and that war is bad, and we learn all kinds of things which we believe to be nonetheless true. Is there, in fact, anything that we claim to know that we have not learned in one way or another? And though people may disagree upon their interpretation of "good," it does not follow from this that there *is* no objective good. We may just as easily conclude from the fact that people often disagree in their interpretation of the world that the world does not exist, or from the fact that some people cannot see that two plus two equals four that perhaps it doesn't.

Second, this objection is usually directed toward specific moral codes like "Thou shalt not commit adultery." Admittedly, these codes or laws are usually learned or acquired through conditioning and are therefore in many instances relative to a given culture—no one cares to deny that. But, as we have already emphasized, this is not what Kant and others mean by our consciousness of moral law. They are referring, rather, to our fundamental feeling of "ought" or duty. The knowledge of what I ought to do may be something that I learn through culture and upbringing, but the awareness that I ought to do something is part of my very humanity. If someone is found to be completely devoid of any such moral consciousness, we may simply judge that he lacks the faculty of moral sensitivity in the same way that we would judge that a man who denies the reality of red is obviously lacking in a certain sense faculty. We may, in fact, judge that a completely amoral man is not a man at all.

More important is the rejection of objective value on philosophical grounds. Of these we will briefly consider two examples: the reductionistic naturalist and the atheistic existentialist. Naturalism is the doctrine that nature is the ultimate reality, but there are many different naturalisms just as there are many interpretations of "nature." When it is said, then, that the naturalist believes that the criterion of what is good, along with everything else, is nature, it matters very much just what brand of nature is being entertained. Clearly some form of ethical naturalism is exemplified by the ancient Greek philosopher Epicurus who reasoned from the fact that men seek pleasure above all else to the conclusion that pleasure must be the highest good. Similarly, John Stuart Mill (in his *Utilitarianism*) provides a naturalistic justification for the utilitarian principle that one ought to seek the greatest happiness for the greatest number: There is only one proof that a sound is audible, namely, that people hear it; likewise, the only evidence that something is desirable is that people do desire it; it follows, for Mill, that only one proof that happiness is desirable can be given, namely, that each person does in fact desire happiness.

One extreme version of naturalism takes "nature" to mean physics and chemistry and reduces statements of value to statements about the empirical world and psychology. This crude reductionism holds that the ultimate basis of value commitments is an individual's own desires or feelings about things. The judgment "Stealing is wrong" simply expresses one's subjective feelings or emotions concerning something in the same way as "Cherry pie is good." This interpretation of moral judgments finds support in Bertrand Russell who (at least in one place) suggests that our varying opinions on moral questions, just as our varying perceptions of colors, can no doubt be explained by the physicist.[8] The criterion for condemning immoral conduct is, by this view, no more objective than for condemning color blindness, with the result that morality is simply the way a majority of people feel. Morality is just a reflection of subjective empirical or psychological states.

Whereas the reductionistic naturalist bases his morality somehow or other in empirical or psychological states, some other

---

[8] Bertrand Russell (with Frederick Copleston), "The Existence of God: A Debate," reprinted in *Philosophical and Religious Issues,* ed. Ed. L. Miller (Encino, Calif.: Dickenson, 1971), Ch. 13. For a statement of the similar and influential position known as "emotivism," see Alfred Jules Ayer, *Language, Truth and Logic,* second ed. (London: Gollancz, 1946), Ch. 6.

thinkers give the appearance of denying any justification whatsoever for moral ideals and choices. The best contemporary example
of this position is probably the French existentialist Jean-Paul
Sartre. Sartre's point of departure is God's demise, especially as
eternal law giver and justifier of morality. For Sartre, God is un-
believable, dead, and gone, and gone with him is all possibility of
any objective and binding moral principles:

> The existentialist . . . thinks it very distressing that God does not exist,
> because all possibility of finding values in a heaven of ideas disappears
> along with Him; there can no longer be an *a priori* Good, since there is
> no infinite and perfect consciousness to think it. . . . and as a result man
> is forlorn, because neither within him nor without does he find anything
> to cling to. . . . if God does not exist, we find no values or commands
> to turn to which legitimize our conduct. So, in the bright realm of values,
> we have no excuse behind us, nor justification before us. We are alone,
> with no excuses.[9]

A recurring theme of Dostoevsky's classic *The Brothers Karamazov*
is that if there were no God, everything would be possible, at least
in the sense of being morally legitimate. For the atheistic Sartre,
there is no God and everything is, indeed, possible. In the world
of choices and moral commitments, "we are condemned to be free"
—free to do what we want and thus free to be what we want.

Sartre is not, however, a complete nihilist, that is, someone who
utterly rejects all value and meaning. Sartre simply shifts the *locus*
of value from the absent God to man himself. Because we can
no longer believe in God or some Platonic transcendent world of
pre-established essences in terms of which man and meaning can
be defined, we believe that "existence *precedes* essence:" Man first
exists and then, through his choices and commitments, defines his
own nature. In this "ethics of involvement," choices do matter. What
we decide, we decide for mankind; what we do, we make of mankind, for we are all involved in mankind, and each of us is, therefore, responsible for mankind. Like the artist, we on the ethical
plane are in a "creative situation," and the finished product, whatever it may be, will have to be judged in terms of the values evolved
along the way. (More of this in Chapter 9.)

[9] Jean-Paul Sartre, "Existentialism," tr. Bernard Frechtman, in *Existentialism and Human Emotions* (New York: Philosophical Library, 1957), pp. 22 f.

Rejection of the Rejection

The impression may have been given that the believer in the Moral Argument rests his case with an (unpersuasive?) appeal to some intuitive grasp of objective value. Some defenders of the argument may indeed be happy with such an appeal, and, after all, every argument must begin somewhere. Others, however, feel that the objective nature of moral value can be demonstrated by showing that alternatives such as those suggested above are ultimately impossible.

It may be argued, for example, that any moral judgment, such as "*x* is right" or "*x* is wrong," is unintelligible and empty unless it is believed that there is somewhere, somehow, something *in terms of which* the rightness or wrongness of *x* may be adjudged. Though we may not be always very articulate as to the nature of the objective source of moral value and may indeed change our minds from time to time as to what is really right or wrong, each time we make such judgments, or otherwise express (in our actions and choices) our moral commitments, we are implicitly affirming our belief in an external criterion of moral value. If we did not believe that there is an objective and unchanging foundation of moral values and ideals, then we would never bother to make such judgments, at least not seriously. On the contrary, that we continue to exercise moral judgment, not only in reference to ourselves but also to others, is clear evidence that we do, in fact, take such judgments as counting for something and as being ultimately and objectively significant. In this way, it may be argued, it is self-contradictory (practically speaking) to make judgments of moral value and to deny at the same time that there is any objective basis of morality. What can be more comical than someone who spends the day fanatically and passionately crusading for the eradication of certain evils, while in the evening he delivers cool lectures on the relativity of all ideals?

Gabriel Marcel, a contemporary Catholic existentialist who dislikes being called an existentialist, employs this same reasoning in his attack of Sartre's concept of freedom as the "baseless basis of value":

Sartre has announced that the third volume of his *Les Chemins de la Liberté* is to be devoted to the praise of the heroes of the Resistance.

Now I ask you in the name of what principle, having first denied the existence of values or at least of their objective basis, can he establish any appreciable difference between those utterly misguided but undoubtedly courageous men who joined voluntarily the Anti-Bolshevik Legion, on the one hand, and the heroes of the Resistance movement, on the other? I can see no way of establishing this difference without admitting that causes have their intrinsic value and, consequently, that values are real. . . . he quite often uses the words "good" and "bad," but what can these words possibly mean in the context of his philosophy?[10]

If there is no objective essence of man—something outside the individual in which his meaning is given—then there can be no real justification for any conception of man whatever, not even the one that Sartre urges us to actualize through our choices and commitments. The ideal of the Resistance fighter can claim no more legitimacy than that of the anti-Bolshevik.

It should be noted, incidentally, that Sartre himself accepts the Moral Argument in a kind of left-handed way. When he says that God does not exist, and therefore all possibility of finding objective values disappears, he is conceding that if there were such a thing as an objective moral order, then God would have to exist as its basis. Sartre accepts, then, the movement from an objective morality to its necessary source in absolute being; what he rejects is that any such morality is given to start with.

Still, what of the naturalistic interpretation of value? One of the most telling criticisms of ethical naturalism in general was levelled by G. E. Moore, whose *Principia Ethica* (1903) set in motion a debate that has not yet completely subsided. According to Moore, every attempt to ground morality in the properties and states of nature is guilty of the "naturalistic fallacy." This mistake comes of trying to derive *ought* from *is,* or concluding as Epicurus and Mill did, that because men do in fact desire something that they ought to desire it. It was Kant himself who first exposed this error (if it is an error) and insisted on a wholly non-empirical origin of moral concepts:

Is it not of the utmost necessity to construct a pure moral philosophy which is completely freed from everything which may be only empirical

10 Gabriel Marcel, *The Philosophy of Existentialism,* tr. Manya Harari (New York: Citadel Press, 1962), p. 87.

and thus belong to anthropology? That there must be such a philosophy is self-evident from the common idea of duty and moral laws. . . . the ground of obligation here must not be sought in the nature of man or in the circumstances in which he is placed, but sought a priori solely in the concepts of pure reason . . . .[11]

Notwithstanding the naturalistic fallacy, the reductionistic (or materialistic) version of ethical naturalism must at least face up to its implications for man's moral reason. Where is the contribution of reason more necessary than in relation to Kant's question, "What must I do?" It is in regard to questions of value and moral decision that we expect the most from man's critical reflection. But if moral judgments themselves reduce finally to statements of feeling and fact, then they can hardly be judgments *about* feeling and fact, so that here, where it is most needed, no contribution is forthcoming from man's reason. More specifically, if the statement "x is good" amounts to no more than my subjective feelings about x at the moment, then these unlikely consequences would follow: First, it would be impossible for me ever to be mistaken in my value-judgments, which seems absurd; second, because my feelings constantly change, my value-judgments could never mean the same thing twice; and third, no two people could ever, even in theory, intend the same thing in their value-judgments. It would appear patently impossible to reconcile these conclusions with any meaningful concept of morality and ethical discourse. As for the attempt to found morality in a communal state of mind, do we have to be reminded that in our time a whole nation ran amok and created a society in which the murder of 7 million Jews was considered by many to be moral?[12]

It may be objected, understandably, that false alternatives have been posed here, that it is not a matter of either a Kantian-type

[11] Immanuel Kant, *Foundations of the Metaphysics of Morals,* tr. Lewis White Beck (Indianapolis, Ind.: Library of Liberal Arts, 1959), p. 5. For a well-known discussion of the naturalistic fallacy (especially Moore's version of it), see W. K. Frankena, "The Naturalistic Fallacy," *Mind,* XLVIII (October, 1939).

[12] A development of this line of reasoning is provided in A. C. Ewing, *Ethics* (New York: Free Press, 1953), Ch. 7. For a survey and critique of the empirical and naturalistic approaches to the Moral Argument, see H. P. Owen, *The Moral Argument for Christian Theism* (London: George Allen & Unwin, 1965).

grounding of morality in a wholly non-empirical or transcendental source, *or* a reductionistic interpretation of moral awareness in purely physiological and psychological terms. The naturalist with a broader conception of nature will charge that neither transcendence-language nor physics-and-chemistry language have special priority over other ways of speaking about man. Human nature is a multi-faceted affair, the intersection of differing dimensions of reality, and there are, consequently, differing ways of picturing him, many kinds of languages in which he may be represented: physical, moral, religious, axiological, aesthetic, and so on. Dostoevsky's literary picture is very different from Watson's behavioristic one, and both of these are different from Milton's or Kant's; each, however, portrays something true and important about man. There is a form of naturalism, then, that would concur in the rejection of a purely physical or reductionistic theory of human nature and moral response.

Our discussion has given way, largely, to the question of objective morality, but that is because this is the *crux* of the Moral Argument. Obviously, many (including the present writer) are convinced that we cannot at any cost give up the idea of objective value, and that this in turn provides for the possibility of a Moral Argument for God. It might be added, though, that with respect to the real ethical problem the objectivists and absolutists can claim no monopoly on moral understanding. Those most enamored of reason and objective truth are often the first to sanction irrational and intolerant measures against their opponents. In a passage from St. Thomas' *Summa Theologica* (not frequently reproduced, under-standably), the Angelic Doctor defends the Church's Inquisition, arguing that heretics must be "shut off from the world by death." It is one thing to appeal to absolute truths and values; but, when that fails, to hand over the unbelieving soul to the executioner tends not to reflect too well on the first thing.

God's Will and the Good

Another question inevitably arises in relation to talk about God as the source of value. According to some, any attempt to make God the basis of value and morality presents us with this problem: Is *x* good because God wills it, or does God will *x* because it is good? Either alternative leaves much to be desired. If right and wrong, good and bad, is the result of God's unconditional fiat, then it would appear that all value is ultimately arbitrary. On the other hand, if goodness is something that exists outside God, then it turns out that there is something anterior even to God and to which he himself is subject. This problem, an old and vexing one, received perhaps its earliest statement in Plato: "Do the gods love piety because it is pious, or is it pious because they love it?"[13]

A scholastic like St. Thomas Aquinas or Duns Scotus would no doubt answer along the following lines. Of course the moral law proceeds from God's will; the divine will is the cause of all good, and anything is good from the mere fact that God wills it. But this answer does not, as it may seem, make the moral law or the good arbitrary because God, the supreme and perfect being, wills the greatest good necessarily. If in God there is no difference between his existence (that he is) and essence (what he is), then God's goodness (what he is) is, like his existence, underived and infinite. Furthermore, there can be no contradiction between what he is and what he wills; he can will neither more nor less than the greatest good (his own nature) without, in either case, ceasing to be God. The moral law, then, far from being arbitrary or capricious, is based upon the nature of things, indeed upon the highest nature.[14] On the other hand, it is not difficult to see how such reasoning has been passed off as merely a theological version of the naturalistic fallacy insofar as it identifies the good with what Is, though now with a capital "I."

Also related to this general problem is Mill's objection that a duty that derives from the command of a lawgiver does not qualify as *moral* obligation at all. Genuinely moral obligation "supposes something that the internal conscience bears witness to as binding in its own nature; and which God, in superadding his command, conforms to and perhaps declares, but does not create."[15] But at least two counter-observations may be proposed here. First, whereas moral obligation may not be enjoined upon me through the com-

[13] Plato, *Euthyphro*, 10A, in *Euthyphro, Apology, Crito*, tr. F. J. Church, rev. Robert D. Cumming (Indianapolis, Ind.: Library of Liberal Arts, 1956).

[14] See St. Thomas Aquinas, *Summa Theologica*, Part One, Qu. XIX, Arts. 2–4.

[15] John Stuart Mill, "Theism," in *Three Essays on Religion*, third ed. (London: Longmans, Green & Co., 1875), pp. 164 f.

mand of just any lawgiver, it may be different in the case of a lawgiver that can be shown to be wholly good and, in fact, the seat of all value. That is, my obligation to obey the law would seem to be a moral obligation if, for some reason, I am persuaded that the law originates in the will of a being who can only will what is good. Second, the shift from external commands to the data of "internal conscience" (or whatever) is irrelevant inasmuch as the most powerful version of the Moral Argument does not, as we have seen, proceed on the basis of particular rights and wrongs anyway but on the basis of the general moral consciousness that necessarily points beyond itself to an adequate source.

Scholastic distinctions and other scruples aside, surely there would be something strange about asking someone to abandon belief in an objective moral order because he cannot explain adequately the precise nature of its divine origin. It would be as absurd as informing someone that because he cannot give an articulate account of how the starry heavens came into being he ought therefore to give up his belief in them.

The Existence of God and Proof

As we have now completed our survey of the traditional theistic arguments, perhaps it is appropriate at this point to raise realistically the question of whether God's existence can be proved.

The answer depends on what one means by "prove." In one sense, proof has to do only with formal validity. In this sense an argument constitutes proof if it conforms to the rules of logical inference; in other words, if the conclusion follows logically from the premises. For example, any argument of the form

> If p, then q
> p
> Therefore, q

constitutes a formally valid proof no matter what may be substituted for p and q. There is a big difference, however, between validity and truth. The argument

All presidents have beards.
Hermes is a president.
Therefore, Hermes has a beard.

is a perfectly valid piece of reasoning (and in that sense is a proof), though not one of its propositions is true. In fact, any proposition whatsoever can be proved in this sense so long as one is willing to supply the appropriate premises. Although the notion of formal validity is obviously very important, it is clearly not this understanding of proof that concerns us at the moment.

Presumably, when we ask if God's existence can be proved, we are taking proof to be a presentation of evidence that gives rise to conviction. But now, proof in this sense is impossible for someone who does not share the same philosophical frame of reference. For example, the Moral Argument cannot compel assent for someone who does not accept the starting point of an objective moral order. Similarly, the Cosmological Argument can hold no force for someone who denies the principle of sufficient reason. All of the theistic arguments come to rest ultimately on certain givens. But this fact is hardly anything against these arguments inasmuch as it is equally true of every other argument. All reasoning and demonstration involves at one point or another some fundamental, indemonstrable affirmation of something, and the parties involved will have to agree on those basic assumptions or presuppositions concerning knowledge, language, and reality if the argument is to avoid a vicious regress and deliver any conviction. With this in mind, Aristotle comments that it is the mark of an uneducated man not to know that some things cannot be demonstrated.

Neither is proof in this sense possible for someone who does not share the same *psychological* frame of reference. Clearly, people have been known to accept the premises of an argument, agree that the premises imply the conclusion, and then reject the conclusion nonetheless. No one can be persuaded of something, whatever the evidence and however cogent the reasoning, if he does not want to be persuaded. For such a person the evidence does not elicit conviction, and therefore no proof has been provided. Thus, it is not possible to prove the existence of God (or anything else, for that matter) to someone who does not share the necessary epistemological and metaphysical assumptions and who does not approach the evidence with a certain openness.

Yet another matter remains. An objection frequently raised against the theist, especially the Christian theist, is that he believes as he does because he was born into a certain society, raised in a religious home, sent to parochial schools, and so forth. This objection commits the "genetic fallacy," the mistake of thinking that the truth of a person's position is somehow undermined by identifying its origins. Though the origins or causes of belief may be of some interest to psychologists or sociologists, they are completely irrelevant from a philosophical point of view. The philosopher is concerned not with the geographical, biological, environmental *causes* of a person's belief (all of them purely accidental) but with the *reasons* for it. What the skeptic must do is expose the inadequacy of a person's argument or reasoning. And for that matter, the skeptic's causal explanation works both ways—his own position can just as easily be explained.

The psychoanalytic critique of religion, such as Freud presents in his *The Future of an Illusion,* commits somewhat this same mistake though on a much larger scale. As Freud himself had to acknowledge, even if religious beliefs, and religion itself, could be explained psychoanalytically in terms of sublimated desires, projected father images, and Oedipus complexes, the question as to the *truth* of religion would still remain. And that is a philosophical question. Besides, someone has turned the tables on the psychoanalytic critique by observing that the hackneyed "Religion is a crutch" itself may spring from a neurotic refusal to admit that one is lame.

As for the general question before us, namely, what if anything may be accomplished by the traditional arguments for God, probably no better conclusion can be suggested than is provided in Job 26:14:

> Lo, these are but the outskirts of his ways;
> and how small a whisper do we hear of him!

A whisper that must no doubt be given full voice by revelation, but a whisper at least.

7

Religious Experience

We have concluded our survey of the four most important traditional arguments for the existence of God. As we indicated at the beginning, however, the rational approach to God is not the only one. There is an altogether different approach that some consider superior precisely because it transcends reason. Such is the position of the late theologian John Baillie:

We are rejecting logical argument of any kind as the first chapter of our theology or as representing the process by which God comes to be known. We are holding that our knowledge of God rests rather on the revelation of His personal Presence as Father, Son, and Holy Spirit. . . . Of such a Presence it must be true that to those who have never been confronted with it argument is useless, while to those who have it is superfluous.[1]

There is a tradition that even St. Thomas Aquinas enjoyed near the end of his life an experience such as to make all the discursive treatises that he had previously written seem as straw. This approach claims an immediate, direct, and personal confrontation with the divine.

---

[1] John Baillie, *Our Knowledge of God*, second ed. (New York: Scribner, 1959), p. 132.

Christian Experience

If someone perceives a fire burning in the fireplace, the most persuasive arguments and evidence to the contrary might not sway him an inch from his conviction. Indeed, if everyone in the world were to insist that there was no fire in the fireplace, he might rather judge that everyone else was somehow deluded than give up the truth of such clear and emphatic a testimony as his own immediate experience. Similarly, it is often futile to argue with someone who rests his case for theism on the self-authenticating evidence of religious experience.

There is a great variety of religious experience, but we can distinguish broadly three types: the Christian experience, the universal sense of a supernatural presence, and the experience of the mystic. Strictly speaking, Christian experience belongs properly to the sphere of revealed theology; it is conceived to be largely (if not from beginning to end) the work of God himself with man on the receiving end. But as this experience has played an important and sometimes central role in theological thinking it seems wise not to pass over it, even in a discussion concerned primarily with philosophical or natural theology.

The Christian experience of grace and faith, at least as it is understood in the Lutheran and Calvinist traditions, begins with a special revelation in which, it is believed, God has revealed both himself and man's need for salvation. The believer accepts the Biblical judgment concerning original sin and recognizes himself as fallen, estranged from God, and spiritually lifeless. But he accepts also God's gracious work in Christ his Son. In his humiliating death, Jesus Christ (on the traditional, orthodox view) made full atonement for sin; on the other hand, his righteousness is "imputed," or attributed vicariously, to the believer as he appropriates through faith God's gift of forgiveness and justification. The believer now stands before God freed from guilt, redeemed, justified, righteous: "For if while we were enemies we were reconciled to God by the death of his Son, much more, now that we are reconciled, shall we be saved by his life" (Rom. 5:10); again, "For our sake he made him to be sin who knew no sin, so that in him we might become the righteousness of God" (II Cor. 5:21). This understanding of

God's work on behalf of the sinner was given classic expression in Luther's brief essay, "Two Kinds of Righteousness," in which he distinguished the righteousness of Christ which has been freely bestowed upon us making us worthy of salvation before God, and the subsequent righteousness, wrought in our practical lives by the Holy Spirit, that we practice always imperfectly before man.

According to this interpretation it is through the atoning and mediating work of the God-Man that the Christian believer enjoys, by faith, the divine mercy and grace. Through the regenerating work of the Holy Spirit he becomes—to use Pauline expressions— a "new man" in Christ, and by "adoption," a son of God.

For the Christian all of this is considerably more than simply reading a book and following the instructions and considerably more than a mere theological doctrine. It may, in fact, take the form of a conversion experience with its overpowering sense of release and personal transformation. St. Paul seems to have in mind just this sort of decisive experience when he writes, ". . . if any one is in Christ, he is a new creation: the old has passed away, behold, the new has come. All this is from God, who through Christ reconciled us to himself . . . ." (II Cor. 5:17–18). For others, especially those born into a community of faith, this experience may reveal itself more quietly through a participation in the sacramental life of the Church and the buttressing fellowship of believers. Whatever form it may take, the Christian is one who has experienced not only contrition over sin, but also the joy of God's salvation; he has experienced, in one way or another, a divine operation in his own being; and he exclaims with St. Paul, "I have been crucified with Christ; it is no longer I who live, but Christ who lives in me; and the life I now live in the flesh I live by faith in the Son of God, who loved me and gave himself for me" (Gal. 2:20).

This whole way of talking must surely seem strange and foreign to many readers. On the other hand, a multitude of others (who can deny it?) in every period of the Christian tradition have claimed such an experience of the indwelling Christ, the forgiveness of sins, and the love of God shed abroad in their hearts. And for the certification of this they claim nothing more—nor less—than the *testimonium internum Spiritus Sancti.*

The "Numinous" and the "Thou"

Some would be quick to point out, however, that neither Christianity nor any other institutionalized religion has a monopoly on religious experience. The widespread "sense" of the divine may not be as dramatic as, say, the Christian experience, but it is, according to many, just as real and efficacious for a knowledge of God. Rudolf Otto (1896–1937), a German theologian and student of world religions, did much to explain and interpret those rare but real moments when the soul is rapt and swayed by an ineffable Something. Such an experience is almost universal; virtually everyone is introduced to it at some point in his life. Moreover, Otto asks us to consider whether this experience is not the innermost core of all religions worthy of the name.

To be sure, Otto was fully aware of reason's necessary contribution to religion. This awareness is clearly reflected in the full title of his influential book *The Idea of the Holy: An Inquiry into the Non-rational Factor in the Idea of the Divine and its Relation to the Rational,* and in his frequent reference to the rational and the non-rational as the "warp and woof" of religion. But he believed that the non-rational contribution had become lost in the shuffle of a prevailing intellectualist and rationalist interpretation of religion, and so he set out to emphasize and analyze "the *feeling* which remains where the concept fails" and to postulate a non-rational, *a priori* "faculty of divination" to be distinguished "from both the pure theoretical and the pure practical reason of Kant, as something yet higher and deeper than they."[2] Like the beauty of a musical composition, Otto says, this feeling defies complete analysis. (At one point he quotes Tersteegen's line, *Ein begriffener Gott ist kein Gott,* "A God comprehended is no God.") Nevertheless, he felt that an analysis was called for, and his 1917 publication *Das Heilige* (translated as *The Idea of the Holy*) was soon hailed as a classic of religious psychology.

What, then, is the nature and content of this experience? The expression "the sense of the holy" comes closest to capturing its essence. But the word "holy" has become so burdened with ethical overtones that it is not quite appropriate for the experience or sense

[2] Rudolf Otto, *The Idea of the Holy,* tr. J. W. Harvey, second ed. (New York: Oxford University Press, 1950), p. 114.

that Otto seeks to describe: "It is true that all this moral significance is contained in the word 'holy', but it includes in addition—as even we cannot but feel—a clear overplus of meaning, and this it is now our task to isolate."[3] In his attempt to identify this additional element in the meaning of "holy," Otto employs the word "numinous" (from the Latin *numen:* "divine will," "power," "presence") and speaks of a unique numinous category of value, the numinous state of mind, and the numinous feeling. We must not be misled by the latter and somewhat ambiguous locution. By "the numinous feeling" (*das numinose Gefühl*) Otto does not intend so much a subjective feeling (as in emotion) but rather a certain awareness of an object, a non-rational or supra-rational apprehension of something "out there." This experience of the numinous Otto describes as a feeling which

may at times come sweeping like a gentle tide, pervading the mind with a tranquil mood of deepest worship. It may pass over into a more set and lasting attitude of the soul, continuing, as it were, thrillingly vibrant and resonant, until at last it dies away and the soul resumes its 'profane,' non-religious mood of everyday experience. It may burst in sudden eruption up from the depths of the soul with spasms and convulsions, or lead to the strangest excitements, to intoxicated frenzy, to transport, and to ecstasy. It has its wild and demonic forms and can sink to an almost grisly horror and shuddering. It has its crude, barbaric antecedents and early manifestations, and again it may be developed into something beautiful and pure and glorious. It may become the hushed, trembling, and speechless humility of the creature in the presence of—whom or what?[4]

For the object of this wondrous experience, Otto says, there is only one appropriate name: *mysterium tremendum.* He then analyzes the *mysterium tremendum* into five aspects. The adjective *tremendum* involves at once the elements of Awefulness, Overpoweringness, and Urgency; the noun *mysterium* suggests a confrontation with the Wholly Other and the consequent captivation or Fascination.[5] All of this suggests the image of the soul, conscious of its creatureliness, shuddering and yet longing in the awe-inspiring and uncanny presence of the supernatural.

[3] *Ibid.*, p. 5.
[4] *Ibid.*, pp. 12 f.
[5] *Ibid.*, pp. 12 ff.

Some readers may recognize Otto's debt to the German theologian Friedrich Schleiermacher who, in the first parts of his *The Christian Faith* (1830), had developed a theory of religious consciousness based on the feeling of absolute dependence. But this debt does not detract from the originality of Otto's analysis which he himself regarded as more penetrating than Schleiermacher's in two important respects. Schleiermacher's "feeling of dependence" relativizes religious consciousness into a merely heightened form of a feeling (of dependence) that is experienced more or less in many contexts, whereas Otto's "creature feeling" suggests an experience without parallel, explicable only through itself. Second, in the feeling of dependence, the "feeler" is required to move inferentially from consciousness about himself to God as the cause of his feeling, whereas Otto insists that his creature feeling is inseparably bound up with and is cast like a shadow by an immediate consciousness of an Object. In these ways Otto is persuaded that his analysis has illuminated a more fundamental consciousness and has displayed the source of authentic religion.

Otto believed, it may be added, that his analysis explains, among other things, certain elements and motifs in artistic activity: The megaliths of Stonehenge, the Sphinx of Gizeh, the Chinese art of the T'ang and Sung dynasties, Gothic architecture, the liturgies of the Church, Bach's B minor Mass—all of these are man's artistic expressions of the numinous.[6] However, he finds the most striking witnesses to the numinous in the Bible, as when Abraham addressed God: "Behold, I have taken upon myself to speak to the LORD, I who am but dust and ashes" (Gen. 18:27); and especially Isaiah's vision of the Lord:

In the year that King Uzziah died I saw the Lord sitting upon a throne, high and lifted up; and his train filled the temple. Above him stood the seraphim; each had six wings: with two he covered his face, and with two he covered his feet, and with two he flew. And one called to another and said:

"Holy, holy, holy is the LORD of hosts;
the whole earth is full of his glory."

And the foundations of the thresholds shook at the voice of him who called, and the house was filled with smoke. And I said: "Woe is me! For

[6] *Ibid.*, pp. 65 ff. Or at least they bear a numinous imprint.

I am lost; for I am a man of unclean lips, and I dwell in the midst of a people of unclean lips; for my eyes have seen the King, the Lord of hosts;" (Isa. 6:1–5).

The Jewish philosopher Martin Buber (1878–1965) has provided still another account of our experience of the divine in his celebrated and oracular work *I and Thou*. For Buber it makes no sense to seek God, because there is nothing in which he is not present. To turn aside from this life in the pursuit of God is necessarily to miss him. But where, more specifically, is God to be found in this life? Certainly not in the world of space and time where mechanistic causality reigns unlimited, where things as mere objects are experienced, manipulated, observed, and used. This is what Buber calls the realm of the *It*. Rather, God is disclosed as *I* transcend the world of *It*, as *I* confront the spiritual dimension in something, as *I* meet, encounter, and enter into relation with it, as *I* address its *Thou*. In every authentic and spiritual relation with a being (not an *It*), "its *Thou* is freed, steps forth, is single, and confronts you."[7] And every particular *Thou* is a glimpse through to the eternal *Thou*, the Spirit, the absolute, illimitable Person, the *Thou* that can never become an *It*, the Being that is neither inferred nor expressed but addressed. Hence, the sanctity of the *I-Thou* relationship must be contrasted with the stultifying, stagnant, and oppressive character of the *I-It* relationship. Buber believes that his position represents an advance upon Otto:

> Of course God is the "wholly Other"; but He is also the wholly Same, the wholly Present. Of course He is the *Mysterium Tremendum* that appears and overthrows; but He is also the mystery of the self-evident, nearer to me than my *I*.
> If you explore the life of things and of conditioned being you come to the unfathomable, if you deny the life of things and of conditioned being you stand before nothingness, if you hallow this life you meet the living God.[8]

Both Otto and Buber have, however, at least this much in common: they do not, strictly speaking, argue for anything, rather

[7] Martin Buber, *I and Thou*, tr. R. G. Smith, second ed. (New York: Scribner, 1958), p. 78.
[8] *Ibid.*, p. 79.

they call attention to a kind of experience, revelatory and *sui generis*. Their contribution lies in their statements and analyses of the experienced *presence* of something.

Mystic Experience

In the history of both Oriental and Occidental thought one of the most dominant and persistent witnesses to the existence of a divine reality is the mystic tradition.

Unfortunately the words "mysticism" and "mystic" often give rise to all sorts of misconceptions. When someone hears these words he is apt to start thinking of astrology, Ouija boards, fortune tellings and other occult and pseudo-scientific affairs. If we are to appreciate what classical mysticism is, we must appreciate what it is not, and it most certainly is not any of these things.

We should also distinguish mysticism from the experiences of those who see visions and hear voices, and no doubt also from the "instant mysticism" of LSD, mescaline, and other hallucinogenic or mind-expanding drugs. We need not doubt that the latter type of experience does produce, on occasion, insight into something or other; one could hardly draw any other conclusion from, say, Aldous Huxley's accounts of his experiments with mescaline as he relates them in his well-known book *The Doors of Perception*. But whereas such experiences titillate and heighten the sensations of consciousness (Huxley speaks recurringly of dazzling sights, brilliant colors, and the like), the truly classical strain of mysticism, both Eastern and Western, seeks, as we shall see, to empty the consciousness and to transcend all sensations and ideas.[9] As for visions and voices, it should be enough that many of the great mystics themselves have cautioned us not to mistake those phenomena for the mystical state and have, in fact, generally regarded them as impediments to the achievement of genuine mystic consciousness.

[9] Huxley's *The Doors of Perception* (New York: Harper & Row, 1954) represents only one approach to the question of artificially induced "mystical" states. A beginner would do himself a serious injustice if he did not compare the Huxley-type approach with the alternative understanding of, say, R. C. Zaehner as he presents it in the first two chapters of his *Mysticism: Sacred and Profane* (Oxford, England: Clarendon Press, 1957).

What, then, is mysticism? It is the belief that God, or the Divine, or the Good, the One, the Void, the Absolute, or whatever one may choose to call it, .can be known, apprehended, or grasped, in a direct, transcendent, and ecstatic experience.

Though all mystics claim a union with the divine, there are striking differences in their accounts of their experiences. For some it is the consummation of a prolonged and torturous preparation; others seem to be grasped by it in a spontaneous and rapturous flash. Some mystics claim to apprehend an impersonal "ultimate"; to others the experience discloses the three persons of the Holy Trinity. Nevertheless, certain overlapping features are more or less common to all mystical experiences. First, the mystic experience is completely *transcendent,* beyond all consciousness of space and time. Second, it is *ineffable,* an inexpressible experience that transcends even the concepts and categories of language; it defies expression or description. Third, it is characterized by an element of *passivity.* It is true that the mystic may make certain preparations and actively set upon his quest, but once in the grip of the mystical experience itself (at least in its highest stages) the mystic is oblivious to all else and can only respond passively to the divine revelation. Fourth, the experience is attended by an *ecstatic* quality ("ecstasy" means, literally, a standing outside oneself) in which the soul is buoyed up to God in a state of joyous and blissful exaltation. Finally, there is a *noetic* aspect to the experience. The mystic claims to know something otherwise unknowable; he beholds and loves a Truth that lies beyond the limits of sense-experience and discursive reasoning.[10]

The distinction is sometimes drawn between introverted and extroverted mysticism. The goal of the mystic is to penetrate to the underlying Unity of all things and to become one with it. The extroverted mystic claims to apprehend the essential Unity as it is radiated through the external world of sensible things transfigured by the mystic consciousness. The introverted mystic discovers the Divine, or the One, or the Absolute, by turning away from sense-experience to the world of his own consciousness and self. Insofar

[10] This list is somewhat of a variation of William James' "four marks" of the mystic experience, in his influential *The Varieties of Religious Experience* (New York: Modern Library, reprint 1929), pp. 371 f., which in turn should be compared with Evelyn Underhill's four criteria in her classic study *Mysticism* (London: Methuen, 1911), pp. 80 ff.

as the distinction between these two types of mystical experience is legitimate at all, it is clearly introverted and introspective mysticism that has been the more dominant and influential.

The Ascent of the Soul

In the Christian tradition, this form of mysticism is exemplified in the writings of St. Augustine, Pseudo-Dionysius, St. Francis of Assisi, St. Bonaventure, Meister Eckhart, St. Teresa, St. John of the Cross, and others. These mystics inherited (more or less) the Platonic idea that only that which is absolutely One and Immutable is wholly real and true. God is to be apprehended only by turning away from multiplicity and change, and by turning toward unity and immutability.

The world of sense-experience must therefore be abandoned as a distraction from our highest pursuit. But withdrawing into ourselves and closing out all sense-experiences, we find ourselves yet in possession of what is often called the "sensory consciousness," pervaded by impressions and images drawn from sense-perception. So we must move beyond the sensory consciousness with its distracting multiplicity and change. Withdrawing even further into ourselves, we discover that even the "intellectual consciousness" is characterized by multiplicity and change; the pure *a priori* operations of the intellect ("If *A*, then *B*; *A*, therefore *B*") involve a plurality of concepts and movement of the mind. We must, then, transcend even our own thoughts. Having stripped away all sensations, passions, desires, and ideas, and having abandoned all our faculties, we confront finally the ego or self, the very principle of our being. And the soul, thus withdrawn into its own unity, is prepared for union with the Absolute, the One, or God.

The following passage from Pseudo-Dionysius (c. 500) is an excellent statement of the introverted and transcendent nature of the mystic experience:

Thou then, my friend, if thou desirest mystic visions, with strengthened feet abandon thy senses and intellectual operations, and both all non-being and being; and unknowingly restore thyself to unity as far as possible, unity of Him Who is above all essence and knowledge. And when thou hast transcended thyself and all things in immeasurable and absolute purity of mind, thou shalt ascend to the superessential rays of divine shadows, leaving all behind and freed from ties of all.[11]

There transcending all distinction, all plurality, all movement, the mystic enjoys ecstatic union with the Divine. This pilgrimage of the self from its involvement in the world of sense-experience to beatific union with the One (a progress often requiring extraordinary discipline) has been called, appropriately, the mystical ascent of the soul.

One of the most gifted of Christian mystics was St. John of the Cross (1542–1591) whose poetry is regarded as among the most accurate and eloquent expressions of the mystical life. Employing one of the favorite motifs of mystic writers, he developed the concept of the "dark night of the soul," the title of his most important poem and attending commentary. In this state all sensations, images, and ideas have been blotted out, all desires eclipsed and extinguished, and the soul thus darkened is prepared to pass from the purgative stage of the mystical ascent to the dazzling and resplendent light of the illuminative stage, and finally to the ecstatic and utterly transcendent unitive stage in which the soul is at last rendered completely transparent to the divine will.

John's poem *Verses Written After an Ecstasy of High Exaltation*[12] emphasizes the "darkness" as well as other features of the mystic experience as conceived in terms of Christian theology:

> I entered in, I know not where,
> And I remained, though knowing naught,
> Transcending knowledge with my thought.
>
> Of when I entered I know naught,
> But when I saw that I was there
> (Though where it was I did not care)
> Strange things I learned, with greatness fraught.

[11] Pseudo-Dionysius, quoted in St. Bonaventure, *The Mind's Road to God,* tr. George Boas (Indianapolis, Ind.: Library of Liberal Arts, 1953), p. 45. This latter work is itself an instructive account of the several stages leading to the mystical union with God from the standpoint of a scholastic mystic of the thirteenth century.

[12] St. John of the Cross, *Poems,* tr. Roy Campbell (Baltimore, Md.: Penguin Books, 1960), pp. 46 ff.

Yet what I heard I'll not declare.
But there I stayed, though knowing naught,
Transcending knowledge with my thought.

Of peace and piety interwound
This perfect science had been wrought,
Within the solitude profound
A straight and narrow path it taught,
Such secret wisdom there I found
That there I stammered, saying naught,
But topped all knowledge with my thought.

So borne aloft, so drunken-reeling,
So rapt was I, so swept away,
Within the scope of sense or feeling
My sense of feeling could not stay.
And in my soul I felt, revealing,
A sense that, though its sense was naught,
Transcended knowledge with my thought.

The man who truly there has come
Of his own self must shed the guise;
Of all he knew before the sum
Seems far beneath that wondrous prize:
And in this lore he grows so wise
That he remains, though knowing naught,
Transcending knowledge with his thought.

The farther that I climbed the height
The less I seemed to understand
The cloud so tenebrous and grand
That there illuminates the night.
For he who understands that sight
Remains for aye, though knowing naught,
Transcending knowledge with his thought.

This wisdom without understanding
Is of so absolute a force
No wise man of whatever standing
Can ever stand against its course,
Unless they tap its wondrous source,
To know so much, though knowing naught,
They pass all knowledge with their thought.

This summit all so steeply towers
And is of excellence so high
No human faculties or powers
Can ever to the top come nigh.
Whoever with its steep could vie,
Though knowing nothing, would transcend
All thought, forever, without end.

If you would ask, what is its essence—
This summit of all sense and knowing:
It comes from the Divinest Presence—
The sudden sense of Him outflowing,
In His great clemency bestowing
The gift that leaves men knowing naught,
Yet passing knowledge with their thought.

Every line in this poem suggests something important about the mystic experience. For example, when John says, "I know not where," and "I know not when," he is emphasizing that this experience cannot be localized in space or time inasmuch as the soul has been purged of all sensible perception. "The solitude profound" suggests that state in which, transcending both external and internal multiplicity, the soul has completely withdrawn into its own unity in anticipation of the divine and gracious infilling. The picture of the mystic "stammering" in the presence of the "secret wisdom" may be taken as a clue to the ineffability of the experience. The fourth stanza attempts to describe the indescribable ecstasy, a rapture unlike any other that the soul can know. The line "The farther that I climbed the height" is an image of the soul's struggling progress from darkness and estrangement to illumination and union with the divine. And the recurring "knowing naught" signifies the soul's withdrawal from all images and ideas; this is actually, therefore, a claim to know All, an All that lies beyond the grasp of experience and reason and thus beyond all knowledge in the ordinary sense.

As a whole, the poem is an example of the way in which the mystic seeks through indirect, poetic, and often paradoxical expression to point the reader in the direction of something that cannot, in fact, be argued or even expressed. It is, as it were, an invitation to the reader to come and see for himself, or, as the Psalmist says, "O taste and see that the LORD is good" (Ps. 34:8).

Mysticism East and West

It is often observed that Western thought is characteristically academic and rational whereas the outlook of Eastern thought is essentially mystical and religious, and it is sometimes heard that there is no such thing as Eastern "theology." One must be careful not to exaggerate this point. Eastern literature, as well as Western, includes vast tomes of discursive treatises and even a counterpart to St. Thomas' Five Ways can be found. On the other hand, it is true, generally, that Eastern philosophical and theological investigations should be viewed in the context of a larger setting wherein the highest truth is revealed in a non-discursive and mystical way.

In light of what has been said above concerning Christian mysticism, one might compare two representative passages from the literature of Hinduism. The first, from the *Bhagavad-Gita* (often called the Gospel of Hinduism), is suggestive of the universal mystic interest in the subjugation of the senses and the elimination of all sensible distractions. Krishna (an incarnation of the god Vishnu, and one of whose epithets is "subduer of the senses") is instructing Arjuna (Everyman) in Sankhya-Yoga (the Way of Knowledge):

> The wind turns a ship
> From its course upon the waters:
> The wandering winds of the senses
> Cast man's mind adrift
> And turn his better judgment from its course.
> When a man can still the senses
> I call him illumined.
> The recollected mind is awake
> In the knowledge of the Atman
> Which is dark night to the ignorant:
> The ignorant are awake in their sense-life
> Which they think is daylight:
> To the seer it is darkness.[13]

[13] *The Bhagavad-Gita,* tr. Swami Prabhavananda and Christopher Isherwood (New York: New American Library, 1951). Otto cites also the eleventh chapter of the *Gita* (where Krishna reveals himself in all of his glory to Arjuna) as yet another remarkable expression of the feeling of the numinous; in fact, he calls this "one of the perfectly classical passages for the theory of Religion" (*op. cit.,* p. 62, n. 1).

The second passage, from the *Mandukya Upanishad* (part of the oldest extant mystical literature) is an exhaustive summary of the unity of the mystic experience:

> The Fourth [and highest aspect of the Self], says the wise, is not subjective experience, nor objective experience, nor experience intermediate between these two, nor is it a negative condition which is neither consciousness nor unconsciousness. It is not the knowledge of the senses, nor is it relative knowledge, nor yet inferential knowledge. Beyond the senses, beyond the understanding, beyond all expression, is the Fourth. It is pure unitary consciousness, wherein awareness of the world and of multiplicity is completely obliterated. It is ineffable peace. It is the supreme good. It is One without a second. It is the Self. Know it alone![14]

There is, however, one especially fundamental difference between the Christian and the Eastern (at least the Upanishadic Hindu) conception of mystic union: the difference between a monistic and a theistic conception. According to Upanishadic Hinduism, for example, all reality, unconscious and conscious, is an appearance or manifestation of the absolute Reality called Brahman, the primordial ground and essential unity of all things. The mystic seeks through the various *yogas* ("yokings" or "Ways" of enlightenment) to rise above *maya* (the present illusory world) and achieve *moksha* (liberation from the cycle of change) and *nirvana*, that blissful state in which the soul is completely reabsorbed into the impersonal unity of Brahman. Actually, the being of Brahman and the being of the mystic (as well as of all other things) is believed to be one and the same, and enlightenment is the realization that one *is* Brahman, a matter of overcoming an illusory cleavage or estrangement within a self-identical reality.

In the Western tradition, mystic union is conceived very differently, operating as that tradition does with a very different theology. Jewish, Christian, and Islamic theologies all teach as one of their central doctrines the essential difference between the being of God and the being of creatures. Man's being is not the same as God's since God did not make the world and man out of himself (either through a Platonic emanation or any other means) but *ex nihilo*, "out of nothing." Union with God can never mean, therefore, union

14 *The Upanishads*, tr. Swami Prabhavananda and Frederick Manchester (New York: New American Library, 1957), p. 51 (my bracketing).

with the One-in-the-All, but rather with the One-above-the-All. It can never mean a unity of being or substance, but rather a complete conformity of the mystic's will to the divine will, a complete infilling of the divine love. To use a metaphor from St. John, it means a complete cleansing of the mirror of the self so that the divine being and light and love may be wholly reflected without distortion or blemish.

The above serves to emphasize that there are important differences in the ways in which mystics interpret their experiences, and that these differences are the products of divergent philosophical and theological positions. Nonetheless, the important point remains. Any mystic tradition would appear, from a cosmopolitan point of view, to be a particular expression of a universal and timeless phenomenon.

Religious Experience and Proof

But what good is religious experience as a proof or demonstration of God's existence? The answer is, None. That people do have such experiences is undeniable. The question, rather, is whether their experiences have anything to do with God. Many have argued that such experiences may be explained quite simply through purely natural causes such as sublimated sexual desires or even physiological disorders! William James contemptuously attacks the latter sort of explanation, which he calls "medical materialism," as one that

finishes up Saint Paul by calling his vision on the road to Damascus a discharging lesion of the occipital cortex, he being an epileptic. It snuffs out Saint Teresa as an hysteric, Saint Francis of Assisi as an hereditary degenerate. George Fox's discontent with the shams of his age, and his pining for spiritual veracity, it treats as a symptom of a disordered colon. Carlyle's organ-tones of misery it accounts for by a gastro-duodenal catarrh.[15]

Whether such explanations beg more questions than they answer may be left for the reader to decide. As for those who relegate mysticism to the study of abnormal psychology, the simple fact is

[15] James, *op. cit.*, p. 14.

that the classical mystics appear no less sane than most of us. But even so, it is sometimes observed that perhaps those who are slightly cracked are those in whom the light shows through more easily—an observation that just may be as insightful as it is clever.

Philosophically, a yet more important matter must be raised. If someone says, "There is a fire burning in the fireplace," it would not normally occur to me to doubt that he really does *perceive* a fire in the fireplace. On the other hand, I might at that very moment observe that there is, in fact, no fire in the fireplace. But there is a big difference between saying, "There is a fire burning in the fireplace," and saying, "I have had an experience with the divine." The difference is, of course, that I can go and see for myself whether there is a fire in the fireplace, whereas there is no possible way to verify or confirm, say, mystical experience; such a claim is by its nature subjective and private. But perhaps it is a bit too strong to say that all notions of verification or falsification are wholly inappropriate to the mystic's claim, or to say with one philosopher, that "in describing his vision the mystic does not give us any information about the external world; he merely gives us indirect information about the condition of his own mind."[16] This of course may be true in a way, but it must be admitted that the mystic's is a most extraordinary and interesting state of mind; in fact, so interesting as to constrain us to reflect seriously upon it and to ask what might possibly account for it. And in any event it would not be the only instance of our inference of the existence of something unseen on the basis of something seen.

Though there may be no way to verify or falsify the veracity of actual mystic experiences, it is not difficult to verify at least the fact of the mystic tradition and that this tradition continues to be a dominant, forceful, historical reality. Perhaps, then, the mystics considered collectively constitute a universal and historical witness that skeptics have never quite explained and probably never will. Of course none of this kind of talk is of much interest to the mystic himself, for he does not claim to *prove* the existence of God or anything else. He rests his knowledge of God on a private certainty that carries its own guarantee. For the rest of mankind, he who sees, sees, and he who does not see, does not see.

[16] Alfred Jules Ayer, *Language, Truth and Logic*, second ed. (London: Gollancz, 1946), p. 119.

8

Faith and Reason

The question of God's existence, as we have already emphasized, occupies a central position among the concerns of philosophical theology. There is, nevertheless, a multitude of related issues that must also be considered if our survey is to be complete. One of the most important and obvious of these is the problem of faith and reason.

Rational and Non-Rational

The word "faith" is usually associated with religion and the Bible, and the problem of faith and reason immediately suggests a theological or religious issue. The issue involved in faith and reason, though, is actually a general epistemological problem, a problem concerning knowledge, and a real problem for every thinking individual, not only the theologian or the religious person.

If we use the word "reason" to denote the mind's logical, rational, discursive activity, then many would insist that there is more to knowledge than what is contributed by reason alone. For example, someone might appeal to creative imagination as playing an essential role in our intellectual life. Another might suggest the necessity for intuition, a direct apprehension of truth, unmediated either by sense-experience or logical deduction. There are always those who claim that certain kinds of truths can be derived from feeling—can be felt. We have already seen that various religious experiences can have a cognitive significance. The religious man, further, may distinguish what he knows through natural reason from the knowledge he attains through sacred writings. In one way or another we thus tend to analyze our knowledge into two elements: the *rational* and the *non-rational*. I suggest that the problem of faith and reason, when reduced to the real issue, represents just this distinction between the rational and the non-rational elements of our understanding and the difficulty of estimating, weighing, and relating their respective contributions. (It should be apparent that we are presently regarding faith as a cognitive activity, that is, as a way of knowing something. Admittedly, this would be disagreeable to those who take faith as having to do not so much with our knowledge of something as with our trust in something. This latter opinion may, in fact, be a richer understanding of faith, at least from a religious point of view.)

Though the problem of faith and reason can be construed in this way as a general philosophical problem, it is no accident that it has been treated by and large as a theological or religious one. "Faith" is not necessarily a religious word; certainly the Greek πίστις ("belief," "faith") suggested nothing particularly religious or theological in antiquity, and even we speak of our faith in scientific laws or our belief that tables and chairs are still there even though no one is observing them. For those in the Christian tradition, however, "faith" is in fact heavily weighted with religious overtones because of the New Testament emphasis on "believing" and, more specifically, the Pauline doctrine of justification by faith. Moreover, for nearly 2,000 years theology has been juxtaposing revealed and natural knowledge, and the Christian has been insisting on the centrality of revelation and religious experience. Clearly, in our own Judeo-Christian tradition, the religious expressions of faith have been sifted out from the other expressions as the most consequential—witness, for example, the ragings in past years over the supposed conflicts between science and the Bible. The religious problem of faith and reason is, then, only one version of the larger philosophical problem concerning the relation of the rational to the non-rational aspects of our knowledge, but it is, at the same time, the most obvious and most important version.

Athens or Jerusalem?

Nearly all Christian thinkers agree that we have a supernatural knowledge revealed by God, though they are not at all agreed (as we saw in Chapter 2) about the contribution of natural knowledge. The problem of faith and reason (in its Christian version) has therefore amounted to this question: Inasmuch as God has revealed himself in a supernatural self-disclosure, to what status shall we assign natural reason in the theological sphere? Two ancient Church Fathers, Tertullian of Antioch (*c.* 160–230) and Clement of Alexandria (*c.* 150–215), reflect that from the beginning of Christian theology there existed two radically different answers to this question. Of course, something important is already betrayed by the fact that Antioch was an early stronghold for the literalist interpretation of the Bible, whereas in cosmopolitan, intellectualist Alexandria the Old Testament had been translated into Greek, Philo Judaeus had synthesized Platonic and Jewish thought, and Christian theologians were pursuing the allegorical method of Biblical interpretation. It should not be surprising that very different approaches to the question of faith and reason should arise from these two centers of early theology.

Tertullian took as his point of departure St. Paul's declaration that

Jews demand signs and Greeks seek wisdom, but we preach Christ crucified, a stumbling block to Jews and folly to Gentiles, but to those who are called, both Jews and Greeks, Christ the power of God and the wisdom of God. For the foolishness of God is wiser than men, and the weakness of God is stronger than men (I Cor. 1:22–25).

Armed with this, as well as with Paul's warning, "See to it that no one makes a prey of you by philosophy . . . ." (Col. 2:8), Tertullian set out to vindicate the divine foolishness of Christianity while denouncing philosophy as the demon-inspired mother of heresies. No better evidence is found for Tertullian's contempt for philosophy and vain reason than his rhetorical challenge, "What has Jerusalem to do with Athens, the Church with the Academy?", and his famous outburst concerning the death and resurrection of Christ, "I believe because it is absurd; it is certain because it is impossible!"[1] For

---

[1] Tertullian, *Prescription Against Heretics*, 7; *On the Flesh of Christ*, 5.

Tertullian, it is sufficient that God himself has spoken. The Scriptures must be our only guide and standard in all matters pertaining to faith and doctrine, and we must be on constant guard against those who seek to ensnare us with sophistical reasonings and to corrupt the pure and simple Christian teachings. After all, does not St. Paul warn us that "Satan disguises himself as an angel of light" (II Cor. 11:14)? Tertullian concludes that the Christian knows through revelation all that he needs to know; beyond that, it would be better to remain ignorant than to risk falling into the evil clutches of philosophy and heresy.

Clement of Alexandria, on the other hand, was an early representative of those who saw in pagan philosophy a direct benefit for Christian faith. According to Clement, Christ is the *Logos*[2], the instructor of all humanity. We should therefore expect that even the pagans have apprehended something of God's truth. More specifically, Clement taught that philosophy was perhaps even a divine gift directly bestowed upon the Greeks, just as St. Paul taught (Gal. 3:24) concerning the Law given to the Jews, as a preparation for Christianity. Philosophy lifted and turned the Hellenic mind toward Christ and helped to set the stage, historically and culturally, for the advent of the Gospel. Indeed, Clement documents his own writings profusely from Greek culture, in which he sees many anticipations of Christian ideas. Further, God's will is that the believer should, as much as possible, *know,* and philosophical activity equips him in his progress from faith to understanding or genuine *gnosis*.[3] Thus, Clement calls philosophy the "handmaid of theology," one of the ways in which God has made the world responsive to the Gospel and a useful tool through which Christian understanding is cultivated and established.

Clement supports his position, too, with numerous passages from

---

Actually, Tertullian never said, *Credo quia absurdum;* what he said was, *Credibile est, quia ineptum est.*

[2] *Logos:* a Greek word (λόγος) applied to Christ by the writer of the Fourth Gospel (John 1:1 ff.) and understood by Clement to mean "Reason," one of its several possible meanings.

[3] *Gnosis:* a Greek word (γνῶσις) meaning "knowledge" that Clement borrowed from the heretical Gnostics who professed a kind of secret wisdom concerning things divine.

the Scriptures (often allegorized to his advantage), drawing especially upon the Wisdom literature of the Old Testament. For example:

"Now," says Solomon, "defend wisdom, and it will exalt thee, and it will shield thee with a crown of pleasure" (Prov. 4:8–9). For when thou hast strengthened wisdom with a cope by philosophy, and with right expenditure, thou wilt preserve it unassailable by sophists. The way of truth is therefore one. But into it, as into a perennial river, streams flow from all sides. It has been therefore said by inspiration: "Hear, my son, and receive my words; that thine may be the many ways of life. For I teach thee the ways of wisdom; that the fountains fail thee not. . . ." (Prov. 4:10–11).[4]

And concerning St. Paul's warning against philosophy (Col. 2:8), Clement explains that the full statement reveals Paul's true intent: "See to it that no one makes a prey of you by philosophy and empty deceit, according to human tradition, according to the elemental spirits of the universe, and not according to Christ." That is, according to Clement's exegesis, Paul is not denouncing philosophy as such, but rather the return to philosophy by one who has already passed through its elemental, rudimentary, and preparatory counsels; once having served its preparatory function in the life of the believer, human philosophy should be left behind for the higher knowledge (Paul often uses the word ἐπίγνωσις: "super-knowledge," or "full knowledge") that is given by God. As for the wisdom of this world that is foolishness with God (I Cor. 1:18 ff.), Clement assures us that Paul had in mind only the materialistic Epicurean philosophy. Not even Clement claimed that all philosophy is divinely inspired.[5]

Tertullian and Clement represent, in this way, extreme positions on the question of faith and reason. Nevertheless, many, if not most, Christian thinkers also incline to one or the other of these poles, so there arises the distinction between the fideists (from the Latin *fides:* "faith") who affirm the exclusive sufficiency of faith, and the rationalists or intellectualists who embrace also the contribution of reason.

---

[4] Clement of Alexandria, *Stromata*, I, 5, tr. William Wilson, *Ante-Nicene Christian Library*, IV (Edinburgh: T. & T. Clark, 1884).

[5] *Ibid.*, I, 2 ff.; VI, 5 ff.; and *passim.*

Faith in Search of Understanding

It would clearly be a mistake to think of St. Thomas Aquinas, and even more of a mistake St. Augustine, as Clement-types or extreme rationalists in theology. Nevertheless, they do represent a strain of thinkers within the Christian tradition who, though acknowledging the final authority of revelation, theologize with a distinctly intellectualist bent. Their theologies are classic examples of *fides quaerens intellectum*, "faith in search of understanding." Of course, we have already seen this principle at work in the birth of St. Anselm's Ontological Argument.

St. Thomas inherited from Greek philosophy an interest in man as a rational being. According to that tradition, and especially Plato and Aristotle, there is implanted in all men a natural appetite for knowledge, and it is by virtue of his reason that man is elevated above all other creatures. Everything has its proper good or end, and man's proper end is rational activity. Contemplation and the pursuit of knowledge actualizes, enhances, and perfects man's essential nature and happiness. It is clear that Thomas adopts this understanding of man when he says, "Among all human pursuits, the pursuit of wisdom is more perfect, more noble, more useful, and more full of joy."[6] More specifically, he derived his doctrine from the Aristotelian conception of reality that came finally to exert so much influence over the entire Thomistic system. God, the highest reality, is pure form or actuality; in him there is no matter or unrealized potency. This means, in a word, that God is pure intelligence. Now insofar as man is possessed of intelligence, he partakes, says Aristotle, in the life of the gods. Thomas agrees with Aristotle that the ancient poets were simply wrong when they insisted,

> It ill befits a mortal
> To think immortal thoughts.

It behoves us, rather, to soar as high as our intellect can take us, thereby realizing and exercising as much as possible the divine element within us.

With respect to Christian truth specifically, we have seen ear-

---

[6] St. Thomas Aquinas, *Summa Contra Gentiles*, I, 2, tr. Anton C. Pegis (Garden City, N.Y.: Image Books, 1955).

lier that Thomas insisted on the necessity of a special revelation. Even the knowledge about God that lies within reach of natural, unaided reason would, due to the difficulty of the subject and the weaknesses of human nature, be grasped by only a few, and after a long time, and with the admixture of many errors. Indeed, "if the only way open to us for the knowledge of God were solely that of the reason, the human race would remain in the blackest shadows of ignorance."[7] And if revelation is required for an adequate knowledge of the truths that reason can know, how much more is it required for a knowledge of those truths that would otherwise lie forever beyond the reach of all human understanding? Still, though many divine truths utterly exceed our ability to understand (such as the truth of the Trinity), some knowledge of God is yet attainable, however imperfectly, through the natural light of reason (such as knowledge of His existence and many of His attributes). This is the Thomistic concept of the "twofold mode of truth."

Now the Christian man ought, as much as possible, to pursue philosophical knowledge concerning the divine since he, being a man, possesses a natural desire and proper inclination to understand what he already accepts on faith. Reason, moreover, is necessary for the clarification and explanation of revealed doctrines, the refutation of opposing and erroneous teachings, and for the apologetic purpose of reasoning with those who do not accept the authority of the Scriptures. With respect to this last motivation, Thomas reminds us that St. Paul himself (as is recorded in Acts 17:28) documented one of his sermons from a Stoic philosopher, showing that he was willing to meet the pagan thinkers on their own ground.[8]

St. Augustine (who antedated Thomas by nearly nine centuries) also follows this approach, though with an important difference. Both Thomas and Augustine recognized as their foes certain intellectualists whose positions excluded Christian faith and revelation. Thomas, preoccupied with the possibilities of reason, was inspired to show against the Averroists that the truths of revelation could be harmonized with the truths of philosophy. Augustine, on the other hand, who was more interested in the interior life of the soul and who composed no systematic *Summas*, sought to vindicate the

---

[7] *Ibid.*, I, 4.
[8] *Ibid.*, I, 2 ff.; St. Thomas Aquinas, *Summa Theologica*, Part I, Qu. 1, Art. 8.

necessity of faith before understanding, and wrote an instructive little book entitled *The Advantage of Believing* directed at the Manichaean heresy that a saving knowledge should be attained through reason apart from revelation.

Augustine's position on the role of faith pervades his entire philosophy, though he draws together his central reasoning for it in the above-mentioned work. His argument is that no understanding is possible to a person who willfully persists in skepticism and unbelief. It is easy to support this position from ordinary experience. Friendship, for example, would be impossible apart from a willingness to entrust oneself to another. What would become of parental discipline if the child is not required to believe what he does not yet himself understand? In fact, what would be left of society if we refuse to act save on knowledge and certainty, and if the fool refuses to trust the wise? The principle applies *a fortiori* in the context of religion where the distance between the fool and the wise is often much greater than in everyday affairs, and the consequence of mistakes and disobedience is infinitely greater. Let us therefore begin, says Augustine, by believing the religious authorities and God himself; the Gospel then purifies the natural intellect, disposes it toward God, and leads it into full wisdom and understanding. Augustine's position is aptly summarized in his famous exhortation, ". . . understanding is the reward of faith. Therefore do not seek to understand in order to believe, but believe that thou mayest understand."[9] It is important to note, however, that Augustine understood faith to consist not only in *assensus* ("intellectual assent") but also in *fiducia* ("trust").

Augustine was not in any way an anti-intellectualist. The emphasis of the famous dictum *Credo ut intelligam* is that "I believe *in order that* I may understand." Faith is not the termination of reason but the prerequisite and beginning of reason. We know, furthermore, that God is the author of all truth and illumination and that the Logos is "the true light that enlightens every man . . . ." (John 1:9). Augustine was, in this way, much interested in the potential contribution of philosophy to faith: ". . . I have broken and cast away from me the odious bonds by which I was kept back

[9] St. Augustine, *Homilies on the Gospel of St. John*, XXIX, 6, tr. John Gibb and James Innes, *Nicene and Post-Nicene Fathers*, VII (Edinburgh: T. & T. Clark, 1888).

from the nourishing breasts of philosophy through despair of attaining that truth which is the food of the soul."[10] He did, in fact, draw heavily upon Platonic philosophy (as we saw earlier and will see again) with its conception of a transcendent and spiritual realm, insisting that the Christian understanding of reality was to be found there even if the doctrine of the Incarnation was not.

Kierkegaard: The Leap of Faith

Very different from either St. Thomas or St. Augustine are those who believe that in the presence of divine revelation the natural intellect should be abandoned, at least in the sphere of theological and spiritual wisdom, because it contributes little or nothing, or may even hinder knowledge of the truth. This attitude, which recalls Tertullian, recurs throughout the Christian tradition, especially in Protestantism. Martin Luther believed strongly in the *Deus Absconditus,* the "hidden God," unknown except through his supernatural self-disclosure in Christ. John Calvin emphasized that the effects of original sin extended even to the natural intellect, blinding and distorting it such that it cannot, by itself, make an adequate approach to divine truth. As we have already remarked, the late Karl Barth, stressing in his earlier writings the wholly-otherness of God, announced a resounding "Nein!" to natural theology and philosophy: The great gulf fixed between God and man is bridgeable only through acceptance of God's gracious act in Christ. For Thomas and Augustine, it is possible to move from pre-rational faith to genuine (if incomplete) understanding; but for these other thinkers, spiritual truth by its very nature cannot be attained through the categories and concepts of reason—ever.

An example *par excellence* of this fideist approach is the Danish philosopher and writer, Sören Kierkegaard (1813–1855). Kierkegaard is usually regarded as the founder of modern existentialism, a philosophy that (among other things) tends to repudiate rationalism and speculative philosophy as academic, superficial, and irrelevant. Kierkegaard himself regarded intellectual approaches to the highest truth as ludicrous. He rejected virtually a whole tradition of speculative philosophy with its abstractions, proofs, and

[10] St. Augustine, *Letters,* I, 3, tr. J. G. Cunningham, *Nicene and Post-Nicene Fathers,* I (Edinburgh: T. & T. Clark, 1886).

eternal verities, and was especially annoyed by the prevailing Hegelian concept of truth as a synthesis of opposite states that dissolves the existing individual into the evolving universal. All of this, says Kierkegaard, has contributed to a gross misunderstanding of the nature of Christian truth and faith.

According to Kierkegaard, most people blunder into thinking that Christianity is some sort of philosophical system and that faith is a rational assent to it, a kind of signing intellectually on the dotted line. This misunderstanding in turn produces the weekly comedy of vast numbers of people rising from their pews like machines to recite the Apostles' Creed and thinking that they therefore have faith. In fact, "every misunderstanding of Christianity may at once be recognized by its transforming it into a doctrine, transferring it to the sphere of the intellectual."[11] This distorted view of Christianity, says Kierkegaard, is the product of the long succession of philosophers and thinkers for whom truth means *objectivity*. For them, truth—even Christian truth—is something "out there," like tables and chairs, common to all of us, such that with enough intellectual effort and the right methodology we should be able to grasp it, systematize it, and demonstrate it.

For Kierkegaard, the objective approach may be appropriate for scientific, mathematical, or other trivial and inconsequential truths, though it is most certainly not the appropriate approach to existential truths, that is, those truths that bear immediately on my own existence and meaning. In the case of the objective inquirer, thought is turned away from the thinking subject and is directed to an object outside himself; he is not as Kierkegaard says, "infinitely and personally and passionately interested on behalf of his own eternal happiness for his relationship to this truth."[12] Truth, at least the kind that ought to concern us most, is not a matter of objectivity but *subjectivity*. This truth cannot be grasped through philosophical, scientific, or historical methods, but only when through the passion of infinite concern the existing individual abandons himself to the Teacher in a "leap of faith." This leap occurs in the decisive Moment in which the individual surmounts the infinite, qualitative difference between time and eternity and

11 Sören Kierkegaard, *Concluding Unscientific Postscript*, tr. David F. Swenson and Walter Lowrie (Princeton, N.J.: Princeton University Press, 1941), p. 291.
12 *Ibid.*, p. 23.

grasps (or is grasped by) God. There is, then, a kind of inverse proportion between the existential urgency of a truth and the mind's ability to come to terms with it. As for Christian truth, which concerns us most, human reason finds itself at a complete loss: "There is only one proof of the truth of Christianity and that, quite rightly, is from the emotions, when the dread of sin and a heavy conscience torture a man into crossing the narrow line between despair bordering upon madness—and Christianity."[13] Becoming a Christian involves an either/or decision, rationally groundless but existentially necessary.

(Some writers speak of Kierkegaard's "subjectivism," but this invites a great misunderstanding. By "subjectivity" Kierkegaard does not mean that the individual subject becomes the source or standard of truth, but that the highest truth, which yet remains objective in some sense, can be discovered only in inwardness or subjective consciousness. His doctrine is not a variation of Protagoras' relativistic principle, "A man is the measure of all things," but of Socrates' introspective "Know thyself." It would be best to avoid altogether any reference to subjectivism and to speak instead of Kierkegaardian subjectivity.)

Christianity, for Kierkegaard, is not a doctrine, and faith is not a refuge for the feeble-minded. Christianity is a Person: Jesus Christ, the God-Man, a Paradox to reason (I Cor. 1:18 ff.). And faith is not an intellectual assent to some proposition or other. Faith is passion, inwardness, infinite concern, and assimilation. Kierkegaard provides his own definition of (subjective) truth and faith: "*An objective uncertainty held fast in an appropriation-process of the most passionate inwardness* . . . .[14] Genuine faith is not a what but a how; its certification lies not in its object but in its intensity. It follows that from an intellectual, objective standpoint faith necessarily involves an element of risk and uncertainty. It follows also that faith is not something exercised once and for all. The existential individual lives continually in dread of the meaningless dread that can be assuaged only by a continued and renewed commitment to Christ. In this sense one never *is* a Christian but is always *becoming* one.

[13] Sören Kierkegaard, *The Journals,* sec. 926, ed. and tr. Alexander Dru (London: Oxford University Press, 1938).

[14] Kierkegaard, *Concluding Unscientific Postscript, op. cit.,* p. 182.

Without risk there is no faith. Faith is precisely the contradiction between the infinite passion of the individual's inwardness and the objective uncertainty. If I am capable of grasping God objectively, I do not believe, but precisely because I cannot do this I must believe. If I wish to preserve myself in faith I must constantly be intent upon holding fast the objective uncertainty, so as to remain out upon the deep, over seventy thousand fathoms of water, still preserving my faith.[15]

Christian faith is, furthermore, an acutely personal matter. It is a decision, born of an individual's pain and crisis, in which he chooses to stand in fear and trembling alone before God: "Christianity proposes to endow the individual with an eternal happiness, a good which is not distributed wholesale, but only to one individual at a time."[16] (Kierkegaard suggested for his epitaph, "That Individual.")

The faith that springs from despair and rests continually in the intensity of personal commitment is not the superficial faith of institutional "Christendom." Toward the end of his career, Kierkegaard (who had resolved early to raise trouble everywhere) vented a fiery outburst against Christian society like that of his native Denmark with its official state church. In such a society it is not required of one that he be contemporary with Christ and suffer with him. Indeed, in such a society to be a Christian is the acceptable thing. It is easy to be a Christian and everyone is a Christian. *But in such a society no one is a Christian.* There is no existential concern, no real appropriation of grace, no anguish, no suffering, no passion, no faith. An example of Kierkegaard's stinging indictment of the pseudo-church is his comment: "In the magnificent cathedral the Honorable and Right Reverend Geheime-General-Ober-Hof-Prädikant, the elect favorite of the fashionable world, appears before an elect company and preaches *with emotion* upon the text he himself elected: 'God hath elected the base things of the world, and the things that are despised'—and nobody laughs."[17]

---

15 *Ibid.*

16 *Ibid.*, p. 116.

17 Sören Kierkegaard, *The Instant, No. 6,* "Short and Sharp," 2, in *Attack Upon 'Christendom,'* tr. Walter Lowrie (Princeton, N.J.: Princeton University Press, 1944).

The *crux* of Kierkegaard's conception of existential truth is the following. The mainstream of traditional, speculative philosophy (culminating for Kierkegaard in Hegel) rendered the world rational or intelligible by subordinating particulars to universal concepts and general laws. Kierkegaard, on the other hand, located the highest truth, and genuine faith, not in uninteresting universal ideas ("All men are mortal") but in the passion of individual existence ("I too must die!"). In this state of subjectivity the existential man is enabled to transcend both the aesthetic level with its interest in immediate enjoyment, as well as the ethical level with its interest in conformity to general principles, and approach God on a truly religious plane wherein ethical principles are suspended and the individual stands before God in a unique relation. The Kierkegaardian categories of individuality and particularity (the opposite of universality) resist, of course, the very sort of rational manipulation that traditional philosophers glorified, and shift our attention from the domain of objective, intellectual observation to the sphere of subjective, passionate assimilation, from the approximation-process to the appropriation-process. The supreme object of this appropriation is the event of the God-Man, an event characterized by its utter uniqueness and particularity, incapable of being subsumed under any general principle and for that reason a scandal to the intellect. From this it follows, as was suggested above, that the greater the existential import of a truth, the less does that truth fall within the grasp of the objectivizing intellect. But what is lost to the objective way is precisely what is recovered and preserved in the subjective way—the existing Individual.

In all of this may be seen a Christian expression of what Jean-Paul Sartre called the common ground of all existentialism, the principle that "existence precedes essence," and it is difficult to miss the Kierkegaardian sound of Sartre's charge that philosophy's tragic sin lies in its ability to drain man of his lifeblood and turn him into a pale abstraction.

Among the possible criticisms of Kierkegaard is the charge that he was insane. One writer castigates Kierkegaard for a rejection of reason that borders on perversion, maintaining that his obsessions, self-centeredness, and other neuroses qualify him as a dubious guide for training in Christianity. That writer concludes that the less we have of this kind of faith the better.[18] No doubt, Kierkegaard's relation to his father and ill-fated love affair with Regina Olsen left their imprint on his works, it is true that he was in fact a deeply subjective person, and it was not for nothing that he was called "the melancholy Dane." But to judge that he was really sick may be a bit much. And in any case, one might prefer that kind of sickness to the spurious life of the detached and dispassionate spirit who turns aside from the crisis of concrete and conscious existence. Kierkegaard proclaims, rightly, that authentic philosophy is not a fantasy speculation concerning fantasy people; the philosopher addresses himself to *human beings.*

James: The Will to Believe

Another variation on the subordination-of-reason-to-faith theme is William James' concept of "the will to believe," a concept that must be understood against the backdrop of the American philosophy known as Pragmatism and to which James (1842–1910) was a chief contributor. For this philosophy, workability or the satisfaction of needs is the criterion of truth: A proposition is true if it works, that is, if it is profitable or expedient (either intellectually or practically) to believe it. As James expresses it, Pragmatism is *"the attitude of looking away from first things, principles, 'categories,' supposed necessities; and of looking towards last things, fruits, consequences, facts. . . . The true is the name of whatever proves itself to be good in the way of belief, and good, too, for definite, assignable reasons."*[19] It is no wonder that James himself called Pragmatism the philosophy of "cash value."

James' pragmatic point of view is given specific shape in his well-known essay "The Will to Believe," directed against William K. Clifford, an English mathematician and thorough-going rationalist. Clifford himself had written an essay entitled "The Ethics of Belief" in which he argued that it is immoral and harmful, both for the individual and for society, to affirm the truth of something

[18] H. J. Paton, *The Modern Predicament* (London: George Allen & Unwin, 1955), pp. 75, 120.

[19] William James, *Pragmatism* (New York: Longmans, Green & Co., 1907), pp. 54 f., 57.

that lacks complete intellectual justification: ". . . it is wrong always, everywhere, and for anyone, to believe anything upon insufficient evidence."[20] According to James, however, it often turns out that an important decision may have to be made even though the rational evidence for the decision be insufficient on either side. In such a situation the only intelligent thing to be done is to make a decision or judgment in light of its practical consequences; in other words, *to will* something to be true. James called himself a radical empiricist, and he believed that at best God lay on the "fringe" of experience, hardly an object of scientific knowledge. On the other hand, he believed also that there may be just such a practical value, a pragmatic truth, in the theist position. He summarizes his thesis against Clifford: *"Our passional nature not only lawfully may, but must, decide an option between propositions, whenever it is a genuine option that cannot by its nature be decided on intellectual grounds . . . ."*[21]

It is important to emphasize that James in no way seeks to skirt the possible contribution of reason; of course we must be as reasonable and as evidenced in our positions as possible. But in those situations where no dictate is forthcoming, then James offers his principle as both applicable and necessary. Further, his principle does not work for just any dilemma but only for those involving a "genuine option," that is, an option that is living, forced, and momentous. Whether the choice between believing or not believing in God cannot be made on rational grounds is, of course, an individual matter and only the reader knows whether reason is successful in tipping the scale one way or the other. Be that as it may, for most readers the decision does constitute at least a genuine option; living (not dead), forced (not avoidable), and momentous (not trivial).

It is a *living* option inasmuch as both theism and atheism (or agnosticism) commend themselves to us as real possibilities. A decision between, say, Jesus as the Son of God or Krishna as an incarnation of Vishnu would be for most westerners a dead option since belief in Krishna simply does not fit and cohere with our general view of things. We must, after all, begin where we

[20] William Kingdon Clifford, *Lectures and Essays,* ed. Leslie Stephen and Frederick Pollock (London: Macmillan, 1886), p. 346.
[21] William James, *The Will to Believe and Oher* (New York: Longmans, Green & Co., 1905), p. 11.

find ourselves, with whatever frame of reference we happen to enjoy and with whatever tools happen to be at hand. To believe or not believe in God is, further, a *forced* option. Of course, many decisions may be avoided by refusing to choose at all; the decision to prepare my Greek lesson or read a novel may be avoided by simply going to a movie. But in the present case, like many others, it is quite different; it is not possible not to choose, the issue demands from us a decision one way or the other, the option is a forced one: "We cannot escape the issue by remaining skeptical and waiting for more light, because, although we do avoid error in that way *if religion be untrue,* we lose the good, *if it be true,* just as certainly as if we positively chose to disbelieve."[22] Finally, the issue is a *momentous* one. Many questions, such as whether Sirius is 8.7 light years away, may strike us as fairly inconsequential, leaving us completely indifferent and unmoved; they make no intellectual or practical demand on us. There are, however, other issues that make a difference, perhaps a great difference. For many of us, the existence of God and the truth of Christianity are two such issues. They press themselves upon us as urgent questions and we recognize that we stand possibly to lose something if we judge wrongly.

There may be, therefore, a *prima facie* attractiveness about the rationalist ideal of objectivity and suspense of judgment in the face of inadequate evidence, but it quickly goes bankrupt in the face of the concrete and practical decision-situations portrayed by James. After all, what kind of a principle is it that would prevent me from believing in the truth if the truth were actually there? And if the point of it all is to be, as James says, "on the winning side," why is dupery through fear of being wrong to be preferred to dupery through hope of being right? "In truths dependent on our personal action, then, faith based on desire is certainly a lawful and possibly an indispensable thing."[23] (It may be of interest to note that just a few years before, John Stuart Mill had predicted that more attention would be given to the imaginative and pragmatic consideration of the theist position: ". . . the indulgence of hope with regard to the government of the universe and the destiny of man after death, while we recognize as a clear truth that we have no ground for more than a hope, is legitimate and philosoph-

[22] *Ibid.,* p. 26.
[23] *Ibid.,* p. 25.

ically defensible. The beneficial effect of such a hope is far from trifling."[24])

James' voluntarism (so-called because of the primacy of volition or will) has, understandably, been severely criticized by those who see in it only an egotistic concern for saving one's skin at any cost. But it may be doubted whether such critics have always appreciated the full force of this reasoning. If there were *no* other reason to believe, what could possibly be a better reason than to save one's skin? In fact, what could be more intelligent than to want to be right, to attain the good, to be saved, to escape evil, and to act accordingly? And as for the suggestion that God could hardly honor any faith thus motivated, it might be countered that presumably God honors also the prudent man over the fool. Furthermore, can it be believed that God esteems faith only in proportion as it is evidenced, rationalized, and certified? If so, many believers will be found sadly wanting. A better criticism, perhaps, is the following. Is such a belief in God as James proposes really a belief? A child can really believe in Santa Claus, but an adult cannot, not even if he recognized some advantage in really believing. Likewise, there is a difference between believing in God and believing that there is a pragmatic advantage in believing in God. Still, one must not be too hasty, even in this indictment. James himself stresses that it is a misapprehension to regard faith as did the schoolboy who defined it as "believing what you know ain't true." Neither the hypothesis of Santa Claus nor any other can be an object even of pragmatic belief unless it is a *live* hypothesis.

All of this reminds one, of course, of the famous Wager of the French thinker Blaise Pascal (1623–1662) upon whom James draws more than once in his own argument. Pascal urged the unbeliever to believe, for consider: Would you not wager without hesitation against high stakes if you stood to lose nothing? "Let us weigh the gain and the loss in wagering that God is. Let us estimate these two chances. If you gain, you gain all; if you lose, you lose nothing. Wager, then, without hesitation that He is."[25] Obviously, this reasoning gains even more force when it is realized that if we fail

[24] John Stuart Mill, "Theism," in *Three Essays on Religion,* third ed. (New York: Longmans, Green & Co., 1875), p. 249.

[25] Blaise Pascal, *Pensées,* No. 233, in *Pensées and the Provincial Letters,* tr. W. F. Trotter and Thomas M'Crie (New York: Modern Library, 1941).

to wager, or if we wager that God does not exist and it turns out that He does, then we lose everything! Actually Pascal's voluntarism goes further than James' for he taught that in this matter one ought to wager *no matter what may be the rational evidence.* If there is but one chance in an infinite number that reason may be mistaken and that God may exist, we still stand possibly to gain something and certainly to lose nothing by betting on God. Thus reason must be renounced if it may mean the preservation of our souls. Pascal goes further than James also in another respect. He believed that just as seeing comes through looking, so for many it is only by participating in Christianity that they may come to recognize its truth. For James it was a matter of making a decision in view of its practical value and then hoping for the best. For Pascal there is a sense in which the truth discloses itself through and in the willing of it. Thus he urges the skeptic to act as if he believed, to take holy water and have masses said: "Even this will naturally make you believe and deaden your acuteness."[26]

A further note. Pascal is often considered an eloquent spokesman for the non-rational approach to religious truth and rightly so. Strewn throughout his celebrated *Pensées* ("Thoughts") are warnings against overintellectualizing the faith. For example, he distinguishes the God of the philosophers from the God of Abraham, Isaac, and Jacob; and he correctly emphasizes that the writers of the Bible never attempted to prove the existence of God. Pascal's best statement on this subject is his well-known comment, "The heart has its reasons, which reason does not know. . . . It is the heart which experiences God, and not the reason. This, then, is faith: God felt by the heart, not by the reason."[27] (For Pascal "heart" does not mean anything akin to emotional feeling; reason is *above* sense and feeling, and "the order of charity," where the heart operates, is above reason.) But though he sees clearly that there is a decidedly non-rational aspect to Christian faith, and even appears to be preoccupied with it, he does not deny that reason has also a necessary role to play. In one remarkable passage, Pascal emphasizes the necessity of *both* the rational and the non-rational contributions to religious truth: "If we submit every-

---

[26] *Ibid.*
[27] *Ibid.*, nos. 277–278.

thing to reason, our religion will have no mysterious and supernatural element. If we offend the principles of reason, our religion
will be absurd and ridiculous."[28]

Importance of the Problem

It can hardly be denied that the non-rational (whether understood as a transcending religious experience, feeling of the "numinous," acceptance of divine authority, willing appropriation, or
whatever) is a central and distinctive ingredient of religion, if not,
as Otto insisted, its very core. On the other hand, any religious
position that is represented to the world by means of concepts and
language (and what religion isn't?) must be rendered both intelligible and credible. Even St. Paul, though he met the living God
face to face on the road to Damascus, did not shy away from
his intellectual responsibility. It becomes evident that any adequate
position on religious truth will have to do justice both to its rational and to its non-rational dimensions.

We emphasized at the beginning of this chapter that the problem of faith and reason is not, after all, merely a religious or theological problem. Everyone, including the non-religious person, must
decide if he is going to acknowledge at all the presence of the
non-rational in his understanding of the world, and if so what its
source and authority is. The problem of faith and reason is, therefore, a general philosophical problem, one that must be confronted
by anyone who attempts to interpret human knowledge.

But there is something further. Though it was suggested in
Chapter 2 how the problem of God is, in a way, foundational to
all the questions of philosophical theology, it is now apparent that
in another way the problem of faith and reason is most basic. The
British philosopher John Locke judged that the failure to settle
first the "measures and boundaries" of faith and reason has certainly led to disputes and perhaps to grave errors as well. He
concludes,

till it be resolved how far we are to be guided by reason and how far by
faith, we shall in vain dispute, and endeavour to convince one another in

[28] *Ibid.*, no. 273.

matters of religion. . . . This ought to be the first point established in all questions where faith has anything to do.[29]

We are not allowed to make up the rules after the game has gotten under way. Similarly, it may be suggested that we cannot properly begin to theologize until we have made it clear to ourselves whether theoretical knowledge is even possible, and have established the role of special revelation, reason, sense-experience, the "heart," and so forth. Whether or not that is strictly true (not everyone would agree that theology rises or falls with epistemology), it does appear that at least in some sense the problem of faith and reason is fundamental to all the others. And that is why in both of St. Thomas Aquinas' massive works, the *Summa Theologica* and *Summa Contra Gentiles,* the first question he considers is the question of faith and reason.

[29] John Locke, *An Essay Concerning Human Understanding,* ed. Alexander Campbell Fraser (Oxford, England: Clarendon Press, 1894), II, 415 f.

9

The Problem of Evil

Another problem for philosophical theology is posed by the existence of evil, both moral perversity and innocent suffering. This problem, however, possesses, an element of immediacy and urgency that distinguishes it from all others. Many philosophical and theological debates may appear, after all, rather academic and out of touch with the real world; evil and suffering, on the other hand, sooner or later touch every man. It has been said that the Psalmist who announced (Ps. 37:25),

> I have been young, and now am old;
> yet I have not seen the righteous forsaken
> or his children begging bread.

must have been either very lucky or very blind.

Statements of the Problem

Obviously, the problem of evil (also called the problem of "theodicy," meaning, literally, "justification of God") is not a concern of religious people only. Any sensitive person, whether religious or not, is sure to be troubled by the presence of evil and pain in the world. At the same time it should also be evident why it is in a religious or theological context that this problem receives its most forceful expression. The religious man or the theologian is always talking about how good God is. But how is the hideous reality of evil—both the *natural* evil that is produced by nature's calamities and the *moral* evil that springs from man's own will—to be reconciled with the theologian's omnipotent and benevolent God? John Stuart Mill delivers the challenge in this way:

every kind of moral depravity is entailed upon multitudes by the fatality of their birth, through the fault of their parents, of society, or of uncontrollable circumstances, certainly through no fault of their own. Not even on the most distorted and contracted theory of good which ever was framed by religious or philosophical fanaticism can the government of nature be made to resemble the work of a being at once good and omnipotent.[1]

Goethe puts the matter more passionately:

> Wer nie sein Brot mit Tränen ass,
> Wer nie die kummervollen Nächte
> Auf seinem Bette weinend sass,
> Der kennt euch nicht, ihr himmlischen Mächte.
>
> Ihr führt ins Leben uns hinein,
> Ihr lasst den Armen schuldig werden,
> Dann überlasst ihr ihn der Pein:
> Denn alle Schuld rächt sich auf Erden.
>
> ———————
>
> Who never ate his bread with tears,
> Who never the sorrowful nights
> Sat weeping on his bed,
> Knows you not, you heavenly powers!
>
> You lead us off into life,
> You let the wretch incur guilt
> Then abandon him to his torture:
> For all guilt is avenged on earth.[2]

The simplest and most famous statement of the problem of evil is probably that of David Hume who, rephrasing an ancient ques-

[1] John Stuart Mill, *Utility of Religion*, in *Nature and Utility of Religion*, ed. George Nakhnikian (Indianapolis, Ind.: Library of Liberal Arts, 1958), pp. 26 f.
[2] Johann Wolfgang von Goethe, *Harfenspieler* (my translation).

tion, asked: "Is he willing to prevent evil, but not able? then is he impotent. Is he able, but not willing? then is he malevolent. Is he both able and willing? whence then is evil?"[3] The theologian's inability to supply the skeptic with a straightforward and satisfying answer to this challenge has made evil, no doubt, the biggest single stumbling block to belief in a God of love.

The Goodness of the Whole

Nevertheless, many thinkers, persuaded of the ultimate intelligibility of things and of reason's ability to grasp it, have made important attempts to come to grips philosophically with evil in hopes of reconciling it with belief in an omnipotent and benevolent deity, or at least a rational universe, or both.

A striking example of this confidence is found in the seventeenth century German philosopher G. W. Leibniz who, in his tightly reasoned *Theodicy*, deduced that this is the "best of all possible worlds" on the grounds that it would be impossible for God, infinitely wise and good, to have chosen any other. His vindication of the presence of evil in the world proceeds along several lines, all of which have been suggested in one form or another both before and after him.

One of these arguments asserts that it is logically impossible to have a world devoid of evil. Leibniz, who had formulated his own version of the Cosmological Argument, reasoned that God, who is absolutely perfect, cannot create a second God, for the second just by virtue of having been created would possess contingent existence and for this reason would lack something of the perfection and goodness of the first. It is *logically* required, therefore, that creation manifest some degree of imperfection or evil. Another of Leibniz's arguments, and otherwise known as the *ad maiorem gloriam Dei* ("to the greater glory of God") solution, portrays God as using sin and evil as a kind of foil by which he magnifies and enhances his own grace and glory. The reasoning is that if God had not permitted sin, then he would have been prevented from displaying his benevolent mercy, thus frustrating

[3] David Hume, *Dialogues Concerning Natural Religion*, ed. Henry D. Aiken (New York: Hafner, 1948), p. 66.

the manifestation of the divine glory as well as the greater good for man attained through divine grace. Another view, sometimes called the "therapy theory of evil," finds men emotionally matured and strengthened in character through the experience of suffering: Evil often turns out to be a godsend for our own well being. Finally, it has been suggested that evil (both natural and moral) is necessitated by the richness of life's complexity. Just as a painting requires contrasting hues and a musical composition some dissonance, so does the fullness of life and the diversity of experience require some dark moments and flaws. As Leibniz observes, it would be very dull to own a thousand well-bound Vergils and to eat nothing but partridges.

Such explanations will appear to many as forced and superficial. Large consolation to a man racked with cancerous pain to be assured that into every life a little rain must fall, or to be assured that his experience will count for much personal enrichment—if he survives! We are reminded of Voltaire's satirical novel *Candide* in which the hapless Candide falls from one outlandish and ridiculous evil into another, smiling all the while and maintaining that "this is the best of all possible worlds." There are, however, two explanations of evil which, though overlapping in some ways with the above, are worthy of greater attention. Though we will present them in terms of historical figures or movements, it should be noted that in every age many have found them persuasive and helpful.

The first of these may be called the "aesthetic" or "totality" theory of evil, the idea of the goodness of the whole. According to this theory, evil (both moral and natural) is something that appears to exist only from our limited, finite, distorted point of view. If we could survey history and the universe *sub specie aeternitatis* ("under the aspect of eternity") or from the standpoint of the whole, we would see that ultimately all things are interconnected and related so as to produce the greatest possible harmony, beauty, and good. This understanding of good and evil probably received its most articulate expression in the ancient Greek philosophy known as Stoicism. Central to this philosophy was its conception of a divine Logos, or Reason, that directs the unfolding of the cosmos and history, a divine reason and purpose that encompasses all that exists.

Cleanthes' *Hymn to Zeus* (c. 250 B.C.) outlines succinctly the important features of Stoicism, including its belief in the ultimate unity, harmony, and goodness of the universe[4]:

Most glorious of immortals, many-named, omnipotent ever,
King of Nature, Zeus, who steer all things by Law,
Hail! for it is right that all mortals too address thee.
For we are sprung from thee, allotted the image of God,
We alone of mortal things that live and creep upon the earth.
Thus shall I praise thee and sing thy power always.

By thee the whole heaven, spinning 'round the earth,
Is guided where you lead, and willingly is ruled by thee.
In thine hand invincible you wield the aweful tool:
The forked and fiery everliving thunderbolt.
For Nature's every work advances by that blow
By which you guide the universal Reason, ranging over all,
Mingling with celestial lights both great and small. . . .

[How greatly born, thou King supreme forever!]
No deed is wrought upon the earth apart from thee, O God,
Nor down the divine aethereal sky, nor in the sea,
Save what the wicked do in their own unthinking.
But you know how to set excess aright,
To order things disordered, and the not-fair are fair to you.
Thus have you harmonized all into one, the evil with the good:
And the Reason of all is made one, eternal.

But this the wicked of mortals abandon, fleeing.
Ill-fated, these, ever bent on possession of goods,
Perceive not nor obey God's universal Law,
Which wisely trusting in they'd find a noble life.
But they, fools, rush each one to a different evil:
Some with contentious zeal for glory,
Some in reckless pursuit of profit,
Others to license and delights of the body.
. . . borne along from one to another,
In search of a goal opposite their end.

But Zeus! all-giving cloud-wrapt thunderer,
Deliver men from ruinous ignorance.
Dispel it from their souls and grant them, Father, to find

---

[4] Cleanthes, *Hymn to Zeus* (my translation). It is suspected that a lacuna follows line 13 and that line 14 is spurious. Reconstructions of line 30 have been attempted but the text is so mutilated that such attempts are dubious.

Knowledge, wherein trusting you steer all things with justice
That honored thus by thee we may honor thee in turn,
Singing ever of thy works, a fitting thing for a mortal.
For greater blessing there is not, for mortals or for gods,
Than justly to sing the ever universal Law.

In the Stoics' view, everything is governed by divine reason and law, and everything contributes, ultimately, to the ordered unity and goodness of the whole. The judgment that there is evil in the world follows simply from our ignorance of the whole, from our barbarous insensitivity to the rationality and purpose present to all things. From the standpoint of the all-embracing knowledge of God, on the other hand, all things are good and beautiful, all things reflect an ultimate order and purpose, even what from our limited points of view appears disgusting and pernicious. It behoves one, then, to attune his soul to the divine Logos, to appreciate the ultimate harmony of things, to cultivate a divine perspective. Such a man is freed from the anxiety and fear that plague the ignorant, for he has seen and has confidence in the rule of Reason. In this sense, knowledge is salvation. Of course, there follows from all of this the well-known Stoic doctrine of resignation to one's allotted role. This idea received eloquent expression in Epictetus, a later Stoic:

Remember that you are an actor in a drama of such sort as the Author chooses—if short, then in a short one; if long, then in a long one. If it be his pleasure that you should enact a poor man, or a cripple, or a ruler, or a private citizen, see that you act it well. For this is your business—to act well the given part, but to choose it belongs to another.

And he urges us always to have ready at hand this short piece by Cleanthes:

Conduct me, Zeus, and thou, O Destiny,
Wherever your decrees have fixed my lot.
I follow cheerfully; and, did I not,
Wicked and wretched, I must follow still.[5]

---

[5] Epictetus, *The Enchiridion*, 17, 51, tr. Thomas W. Higginson, (Indianapolis, Ind.: Library of Liberal Arts, 1948). Copyright © 1948 by The Liberal Arts Press, Inc. Reprinted by permission of The Liberal Arts Press Division of The Bobbs-Merrill Company, Inc.

It may be no small problem for some readers to maneuver themselves into a Stoic view of things with its optimism about the world's nature and outcome, and certainly an unqualified denial of evil would have to be judged as either utterly naive or the product of philosophical psychosis. Further, viewing the matter from a Christian standpoint, one might find it impossible to accept any theodicy that subordinates personal good to an impersonal aesthetic scheme. This is to say nothing of the problem of reconciling a pervasive determinism (even a divine determinism) with the moral necessity of free will, a problem never satisfactorily resolved by the Stoics or by anyone else.

Nonetheless, this position reminds us that aside from Mill, Hume, Goethe, and all those who seem bent upon exalting the problem of evil, there are others who find themselves overwhelmed by the balance of harmony, beauty, and goodness in the world; and any religion teacher will testify that in the classroom the least suggestion of Original Sin is shouted down with humanistic cries affirming the basic goodness of man. There are some, then, for whom it is not so much a problem of evil as it is a problem of goodness. Mill's outrage quoted above may in fact be restated without any loss of its original force: Not even on the most distorted and contracted theory of evil which ever was framed by atheistic fanaticism can the government of nature be made to resemble the work of a being who is unconcerned about the well being of his creatures. And is not the question "Whence is love, good will, harmony, and beauty?" every bit as interesting and deserving of an answer as is Hume's "Whence is evil?" Why is it any easier to account for goodness without God than it is to account for evil with him? That the problem of evil generates more fury than the problem of goodness may be more a matter of psychology than philosophy. At any rate, the Stoics represent a long tradition of reflective people who have felt constrained to opt for a Logos, God, or some such, rather than an inconceivable abandonment of the world and experience to a malevolent irrational.

Evil as Privation of Good

Another influential explanation of evil is that evil is nothing at all, being but a privation or absence of being and goodness.

The most important version of this position derives from Platonism. According to Platonic and Neo-Platonic thought, reality is conceived as a continuum extending from absolute being to non-being. All things have being in varying degrees, depending on their proximity to their common source, the One or the Good. Just as the rays of the sun, shining into the surrounding darkness, become more and more dispersed and diluted with increasing distance from their source, so the being and goodness (one and the same thing) of this world, being an emanation of the divine, represent a falling away from or diminution of the absolute being and goodness, which means the inevitable presence to the world of a degree of non-being and evil, that is, the absence of being and goodness. Platonically understood, the relative non-being and evil in the world manifests itself as multiplicity and mutability, a kind of distortion and fragmentation of the divine unity and immutability; this distortion in turn produces the vicissitudes of nature resulting in human misery and perturbations of the soul resulting in moral evil. For Platonism, then, the One or the Good is responsible for the relative being of the world, not its non-being; it is responsible for the degree of goodness in the world, not the evil.

To state this more simply, and in terms that recall one of Leibniz's arguments: Even an omnipotent God cannot do that which is *logically* impossible; he cannot make a rock so big that he cannot lift it, he cannot make four-sided triangles, he cannot make things both to be and not to be at the same time and in the same respect, and he cannot create something that possesses the full power of being that he himself possesses. Anything that God creates is by its conception dependent upon him for its being and is therefore a relative being, not an absolute being. And since the being of creation is only relative, not absolute, it is lacking also in complete goodness; in other words it is imperfect. This "metaphysical" evil is, then, necessarily attendant upon creation and is the ultimate source of all natural and moral evil. Conceivably, one might blame God for creating a world in the first place (another problem), but he cannot blame God for creating a world with evil in it—a created order that possesses God's own measure of being and goodness would be a logical absurdity.

In the Christian Platonism of St. Augustine (354–430) we find a variation on the Platonic theory of evil, though conceived quite differently. The Christian believes (as was mentioned in an earlier discussion) that God created the world not through an emanation of his own being but out of nothing, which means that the being of the world is fundamentally different from God's being. Evil in the world does not, therefore, reflect a diminution of God's being, but the diminution of a thing's *own* being brought about by sin, a concept foreign to pagan Platonism. Augustine's position on the nature of evil is a classic one in the history of philosophy and theology; let us consider it further.

Before Augustine's conversion to Christianity he was a disciple of Manichaeism, a later version of the old Persian Zoroastrianism. The Manichaeans, like their Zoroastrian predecessors, held to an absolutely dualistic and materialistic conception of reality. There are two primordial realities, Light and Darkness, or Good and Evil, both conceived as material substances. The world and the souls of men are the battlefields of these eternal powers which are engaged in an endless struggle for supremacy. In time, however, Augustine became disenchanted with this crude materialism and especially with the Manichaeans' failure to explain the nature of good and evil, a problem that preoccupied him from his youth. After rejecting Manichaeism, Augustine discovered Platonism which lifted his mind to incorporeal reality. As he testifies in his *Confessions,* addressing God, " . . . having then read those books of the Platonists, and thence been taught to search for incorporeal truth, I saw Thy invisible things, understood by those things which are made."[6] According to the Platonism that Augustine knew (actually the Neo-Platonism of Plotinus, a third century Greek philosopher), this world is, as we have seen, suspended midway on a ladder of reality extending from being to non-being. This world is but an imperfect likeness of a transcendent realm of ideal realities, presided over by the absolute One, the cause of all being, truth, and goodness.

Understandably, Augustine interpreted his discovery of Platonic philosophy as a providential preparation for his own reception of the Gospel. And it was in this spiritual view of reality that Augustine found a satisfying philosophical solution to the problem of evil: Evil is simply a privation or absence of being and goodness.

In any Platonic-type philosophy, being, truth, and goodness are viewed as commensurate, or more precisely, different aspects of the

---

[6] St. Augustine, *The Confessions,* VII, tr. Edward B. Pusey (New York: Modern Library, 1949), p. 140.

same thing; that which is greatest in being is, therefore, greatest in truth and goodness. It follows for the Christian Platonist that God, the supreme being, the one who says, "I AM WHO I AM" (Ex. 3:14),[7] is the absolute and supreme good as well. Now because everything in the universe exists through the creative act of God (Augustine would be apt to neo-Platonize this as the inevitable overflowing of God's creative fecundity), everything by the sheer fact of its existence (and this includes even the Devil) possesses some trace of God's own being and goodness. We naturally think of the recurring judgment in Genesis 1, "And God saw that it was good," and Augustine concludes, "All things that exist, therefore, seeing that the Creator of them all is supremely good, are themselves good." It must be noted, however, that though the natural world is good in its own way, it is only derivatively good and not supremely good. Augustine continues,

But because they are not, like their Creator, supremely and unchangeably good, their good may be diminished and increased. But for good to be diminished is an evil, although, however much it may be diminished, it is necessary, if the being is to continue, that some good should remain to constitute the being. For however small or of whatever kind the being may be, the good which makes it a being cannot be destroyed without destroying the being itself.[8]

Still, because the world is *created,* its being and goodness are contingent, or mutable, or able not-to-be. This ability not-to-be is not itself evil, nor does it necessitate evil, it merely renders evil possible. The actual defection of the creature from God and the consequent vitiation of the creature's own nature is what Augustine understands by evil. This defection, in the case of man, is an act of free will whereby he incurs guilt; hence Augustine calls it *malum culpae* "evil of guilt." (More commonly, the original defection, embracing all men in its unhappy lot, is referred to as the Fall). Free will is a gift of God that enables man to be a moral agent: ". . . no

---

[7] Actually, this important text (in the Septuagint, ἐγώ εἰμι ὁ ὤν; in Augustine's Latin version, *Ego sum qui sum*) may be translated, "I AM THE ONE WHO IS," or "I AM WHO AM," and was understood by Augustine and other medieval and scholastic thinkers as a self-designation of the Self-Subsistent Being.

[8] St. Augustine, *The Enchiridion on Faith, Hope and Love,* 12, tr. J. F. Shaw (Chicago: Henry Regnery, 1961).

righteous act could be performed except by free choice of the will
. . . God gave it for this reason."[9] Sin, on the other hand, is the
abuse of free will, the failure to will what is right, a rebellious
turning aside from God's goodness:

The will . . . commits sin when it turns away from immutable and common goods, toward its private good, either something external to itself
or lower than itself. It turns to its own private good when it desires to
be its own master; it turns to external goods when it busies itself with
the private affairs of others or with whatever is none of its concern; it
turns to goods lower than itself when it loves the pleasures of the body.
Thus a man becomes proud, meddlesome, and lustful.[10]

The evil will has, as Augustine describes it, not an efficient but a
"deficient" cause.

Malum paenae, "evil of suffering," follows *malum culpae;* it is
the punishment consequent upon the creature's voluntary fall from
its source and good. The generation and corruption of the created
order is now experienced by the fallen creature in the form of
suffering: plagues, famines, disease, accidents, and the like. *Quae
causa infirmitatis nisi iniquitas?*, "What is the cause of infirmity
but iniquity?" What is the cause of *iniquity* remains an unanswered
question. Although Augustine has explained (if he has) the *nature*
of evil, he concedes that its ultimate *cause* is a mystery that lies
hidden forever in man's inscrutable free will. Nonetheless, with
his conception of evil as a privation of goodness, St. Augustine
was confident that both moral and natural evil could be reconciled with the goodness and justice of God.

It must not be concluded from all of this talk about evil as the
privation and absence of goodness, that evil is for Augustine somehow *unreal.* Few men have been more sensitive to the terrible
reality of evil, sin, and suffering than Augustine. What is being
denied, rather, is that evil has a positive existence or is, in Augustine's language, a substance. This philosophical understanding of

[9] St. Augustine, *On Free Choice of the Will*, II, 18, tr. Anna S. Benjamin
and L. H. Hackstaff (Indianapolis, Ind.: Library of Liberal Arts, 1964). Augustine's move here is a variation on what is known in modern parlance as the
"free-will defense." For an important contemporary defense of the more or less
traditional free-will defense, see Alvin Plantinga, *God and Other Minds* (Ithaca, N.Y.: Cornell University Press, 1967), Ch. 6.

[10] *Ibid.*, II, 19.

evil does not at all lessen its existential urgency. Furthermore, the fact that the natural world and the human will represent only imperfectly the goodness of the Creator should give no occasion for blaming God. We ought rather, says Augustine, to marvel at the way in which God is able through suffering and evil to work his divine purposes and display his goodness in an even greater measure. The crucifixion of God's Son was at once both the epitome of evil and the occasion of God's greatest blessing on men. Even the Fall turns out to be something over which the believer may exult: *O felix culpa!*, "O happy fault!"

The Augustinian solution (if that is the correct word) to the problem of evil raises, of course, one big question, namely, the truth of the Platonic metaphysics on which it is founded. Though a simple-minded rejection of this theory of reality would be out of place, it may not be the only one amenable to Christian theodicy. In any event, we are reminded again that particular positions on the issues in this book are often intimately bound up with holistic views of reality and cannot be fully appreciated apart from a full understanding of those views. More specifically, one might have problems with Augustine's doctrine of the Fall which functions so decisively in his explanation of evil. Whatever else Augustine might have thought about the Garden episode of Genesis 1, he clearly saw the Fall as a historical (if not literal) event. Whether we, reflecting on the Fall in light of recent historical, paleological, and Biblical criticism can accept a historical, before-and-after interpretation, and if not, whether the Augustinian position can be reconciled with some such theory as Paul Tillich's interpretation of the Fall (suggested later) as a transhistorical symbol of man's abiding existential estrangement, are further questions worth raising.

Even more specific is the observation that man's sin must have been predetermined inasmuch as God in his omniscience had foreknowledge of the Fall. But this involves a common misunderstanding. Although it follows, according to theologians like St. Augustine and St. Thomas, that if God foreknows x, then x will happen, it does not follow that x will necessarily happen because God foreknows it. In the case of the Fall, what God foreknows (by virtue of his immediate and eternal presence to all of history) is that man *in his freedom* chooses to sin. The Fall is no more determined by

God's foreknowledge than it is by his postknowledge, or even by ours, for that matter.

Related to the foreknowledge problem is John Hick's complaint that

if He chose to make creatures who are bound sooner or later to fail (even though they do so without external compulsion), He cannot reasonably complain when they do fail. He must have foreseen that they would fail if He made them, and He must nevertheless have decided to make them. This consideration points to a fatal contradiction within the Augustinian-Thomist theodicy.[11]

It probably doesn't. Hick's reasoning turns on the principle that "what can fail sometimes does," and concludes that due to the "metaphysical weakness" in Adam's nature he was bound to sin sooner or later. But against this two questions must be raised. First, the principle involved should be spelled out more fully, "What can fail sometimes does, *if you wait long enough.*" And though it is true that given an infinite number of throws of the dice a seven must turn up, and that given an infinite number of temptations Adam must sin, neither Augustine, Thomas, nor the Bible suggest that the amount of time available to Adam was sufficient to insure the inevitability of his fall, namely, an infinite amount. Second, neither Augustine, Thomas, nor the Bible would concede any "metaphysical weakness" in Adams's original state. It has already been mentioned that the Biblical emphasis is on the goodness of creation, and certainly both Augustine and Thomas view Adam's free will as a divinely bestowed good and the exercise thereof as wholly his own, independent of any compulsion *whatsoever*. The contradiction lies not in Augustine or Thomas but in Hick's misrepresentation of their positions.

Concerning the remaining question as to why God created men knowing full well that they would (whether inevitably or not) sin, Augustine's main response has already been given in the reference to *O felix culpa!*—a response that might or might not satisfy the contemporary, non-Biblically oriented man.

Before concluding this section yet another attempt to rationalize the reality of evil might be mentioned to show that positions conceived to be entirely different may sound strikingly similar in their

[11] John Hick, *Evil and the God of Love* (New York: Harper & Row, 1966), p. 197.

conclusions. We have already encountered F. R. Tennant's concept of the wider teleology, and now it will be seen that he has also a wider theodicy to go with it. Tennant rejected both the goodness-of-the-whole idea (on the grounds that if evil is an illusion then the illusion is evil) and the Augustinian privation-theory (on the grounds that through a linguistic sleight-of-hand it translates the concrete and positive manifestations of evil into an abstraction) and turns, as we might guess from our earlier discussion, to a thoroughly scientific and empirical analysis of evil.

We have seen that the several strands of natural processes, especially evolutionary development, are regarded by Tennant as divine instruments for the realization of man. Such processes, however, necessarily involve certain mishaps, accidents, and other unfortunate occurrences, otherwise the natural world would not be a created order but would be (for the third time now) God himself. Natural evils are inevitable by-products of a created order inhabited by finite beings and characterized by natural processes. Moreover, are not the calamities and sufferings produced by nature often conducive to the purification and elevation of human values? As for moral evil, Tennant observes that there can be no moral goodness in a clock inasmuch as there is no moral goodness apart from autonomy and the possibility of evil. Thus free will is requisite to man (the moral being) as well as the full possibility of his misuse of that freedom resulting in sin. Both the natural and moral spheres converge, therefore, even with their imperfections and evils, upon the production of man's developing moral consciousness, and thus upon the best of all possible worlds.[12]

Evil and the Absurd

Not everyone shares this confidence in the ultimate intelligibility of things—even evil—and some have seized upon evil (especially suffering) as a reflection, rather, of the ultimate irrationality and absurdity of existence. This approach is characteristic of existentialism, at least in its atheistic variety. Space does not permit a full exposition of atheistic (or humanistic) existentialism, but

[12] F. R. Tennant, *Philosophical Theology* (Cambridge, England: University Press, 1928–30), II, Ch. 7.

neither is it possible to present the existentialist position on evil without at least a cursory consideration of some of the central concepts of this philosophy.

Most of these thinkers are agreed in their rebellion against the more or less traditional idea that all of history and life takes place, as it were, in a big box with its stable sides, top, and bottom providing fixed points of reference. According to one dominant strain of traditional philosophy, an existing thing is determined to be what it is by something outside and anterior to it. We might distinguish the existence of a particular paper cutter from its essence or essential nature which somehow determines and explains the particular existing paper cutter: why it is shaped thus, why it has a flat surface, a blade, and so on. In this way, essences are prior to their particular existing embodiments. This view of reality is most obvious in Platonic philosophy with its belief in a transcendental world of ideal and eternal "Forms" or essences or archetypes which cause and order all existing things, though it is true generally of all those philosophies that seek in one way or another to impose a rational structure on the world.

According to the existentialist Jean-Paul Sartre, whom we have encountered already in Chapter 6, there is no God, all things are possible, and the responsibility for the universe falls to man himself. There is no God, no big box, no ultimate frame of reference, no absolute and eternal truths, no anterior essences—only individual, existing men, doomed to pick their way through an ambiguous and meaningless existence, doing what they can to give it some essence or meaning. In this way, "existence precedes essence," the closest statement in existentialism to an official doctrine. To put it another way, as Sartre himself did, "subjectivity must be the starting point."[13] The point of departure for all authentic philosophizing must be the existing individual, cast into a world that is, on the face of it, meaningless and absurd.

The idea of the absurd figures strongly in existentialist literature. It suggests, of course, something more profound than the observation that life seems at times to be no more than a dull and pointless routine. It suggests, rather, that existence itself is meaningless. Any attempt to explain the universe must be in terms

[13] Jean-Paul Sartre, "Existentialism," tr. Bernard Frechtman, in *Existentialism and Human Emotions* (New York: Philosophical Library, 1957), p. 13.

of existence. But existence, the fundamental category, is absurd. Therefore the confrontation with existence and the discovery of oneself as an existing being is, as the German existentialist Martin Heidegger expresses it, "forlornness," or to use the title of one of Sartre's novels, "Nausea." It is despair. Thus the existentialist preoccupation with Nothingness (Heidegger: *das Nichts;* Sartre: *le néant;* Tillich: Non-being) is not so much an ontological or metaphysical concept as it is a value concept expressive of the existentialist's sense of isolation and powerlessness in the midst of an alien universe.

Closely related is the existentialist rejection of the view that the human mind resembles a big machine and all we have to do is drop in a nickel and grind out the answers to all the philosophical problems of the ages. For the existentialist, most traditional philosophical thinking, with its elaborate proofs and scholastic distinctions, is academic and irrelevant. Though not usually considered an existentialist, Robert Frost in his poem *A Masque of Reason* reflects the ludicrous element in a man's presumptuous attempt to grasp intellectually the enigma of suffering. At one point in the poem, which is a satire on Job's suffering, Job asks God why he has been allowed to suffer, to which God replies,

> I'm going to tell Job why I tortured him
> And trust it won't be adding to the torture.
> I was just showing off to the Devil, Job,
> As is set forth in chapters One and Two.

In other words, ask a stupid question and you get a stupid answer. Or, as Job himself responded to God,

> 'Twas human of You. I expected more
> Than I could understand and what I get
> Is almost less than I can understand.[14]

The traditional formulas are dead. The philosophers' attempts to explain evil have proved empty. The universe is absurd.

But what then shall we do? Sartre urges us to meaningful de-

[14]From "A Masque of Reason" from *The Poetry of Robert Frost* edited by Edward Connery Lathem. Copyright 1945, © 1969 by Holt, Rinehart and Winston, Inc. Reprinted by permission of Holt, Rinehart and Winston, Inc.

cision and commitment, for only in responsible commitment can authentic living be found and an essence of man evolved. Albert Camus represents a variation on this Sartrean theme. He asserts, in a way, that the solution to the problem of evil is to see that it has no solution, and he shifts our attention rather to the question how or in what manner we are to live in view of this fact. In his essay "The Myth of Sisyphus," Camus thus directs himself to the most urgent of issues, the meaning of life, and asks the ultimate existential question, namely, whether suicide is not perhaps a legitimate response to absurdity. The answer is, No:

One of the only coherent philosophical positions is . . . revolt. It is a constant confrontation between man and his own obscurity. It is an insistence upon an impossible transparency. It challenges the world anew every second. . . . That revolt gives life its value. Spread out over the whole length of a life, it restores its majesty to that life. To a man devoid of blinders, there is no finer sight than that of the intelligence at grips with a reality that transcends it. The sight of human pride is unequaled. . . . It is essential to die unreconciled and not of one's own free will. Suicide is a repudiation. The absurd man can only drain everything to the bitter end, and deplete himself. The absurd is his extreme tension, which he maintains constantly by solitary effort, for he knows that in that consciousness and in that day-to-day revolt he gives proof of his only truth, which is defiance.[15]

Camus says, in effect, that whatever we do in the face of absurdity we must not yield to the temptation of suicide, for that is exactly what it wants us to do. We must not give in. On the contrary, we must struggle against it with all the passion we can muster, thereby letting it know that it has not conquered us. (One cannot help but note with what frequency such words as revolt, challenge, confrontation, struggle, and defiance occur in Camus' writings.) It turns out, then, that while the point is to live without resignation to the absurd, without illusion, and without hope, Camus concludes, paradoxically, that precisely therein lies our hope. The dignity and meaning of man lie in his unyielding resolve against the absurd. Camus' is a life-affirming pessimism.

In this way, " 'The Myth of Sisyphus' . . . attempts to resolve

---

[15] Albert Camus, *The Myth of Sisyphus and Other Essays,* tr. Justin O'Brien (New York: Vintage Books, 1955), pp. 40 f.

the problem of suicide . . . without the aid of eternal values," it "declares that even within the limits of nihilism it is possible to find the means to proceed beyond nihilism," and it invites us "to live and to create, in the very midst of the desert." For as in the case of the mythological Sisyphus who was doomed by the gods to spend eternity rolling a huge stone up a hill only to have it roll back down, "the struggle itself toward the heights is enough to fill a man's heart."[16] Or as Dr. Rieux, a character in Camus' novel *The Plague,* says,

". . . since the order of the world is shaped by death, mightn't it be better for God if we refuse to believe in Him and struggle with all our might against death, without raising our eyes toward the heaven where He sits in silence."

Tarrou nodded.

"Yes. But your victories will never be lasting; that's all."

Rieux's face darkened.

"Yes, I know that. But it's no reason for giving up the struggle."

"No reason, I agree. Only, I now can picture what this plague must mean for you."

"Yes. A never ending defeat."

. . .

"Who taught you all this, doctor?"

The reply came promptly:

"Suffering."[17]

But it is crucial to appreciate that if Sisyphus and Rieux are existential heroes it is because they are, as Camus says, *conscious.* They live in full awareness of their wretchedness before the absurd. This consciousness is quite opposite to the everyday sleep of the everyday man who, caught up in the wheel of everyday trivia, is oblivious to the malignant absurdity that engulfs his existence, and it is a consciousness that issues in action and involvement.

In all of this it is clear that, for Camus, life may be lived all the better if there is no meaning, no Logos, no God, no box. For one thing, the existential man will refuse to be indifferent to evil

[16] *Ibid.,* pp. v, 91.

[17] Albert Camus, *The Plague,* tr. Stuart Gilbert (New York: Modern Library, 1948), pp. 117 f.

and suffering. Camus himself said as much in his brief comment to a group of Dominican monks: "I share with you the same revulsion from evil. But I do not share your hope, and I continue to struggle against this universe in which children suffer and die."[18]

The Biblical Synthesis

We have mentioned several solutions (or at least responses) to the problem of evil, and have seen that these can be reduced, generally, to two fundamental though essentially different approaches. First, there are those who, dominated by an optimistic intellectualism, believe that if only we concentrate our critical faculties we can grasp the nature of evil and reconcile it with the idea of a benevolent God or at least a rational universe. On the other hand, there are those who, struck by the unintelligibility of existence, choose to relegate evil to the domain of the enigmatic and irrational. Each of these approaches, proffered in every generation, probably reflects something very important about the human psyche: its desire for meaning and intelligibility, and its frustration with its own limits.

What is the consensus of man? From the epic of Gilgamesh to the tragedians of Greece to Shakespeare to Dostoevsky, man's confidence in the good has not been eclipsed by the mystery of evil. Certainly this is the position of the Bible which has dominated the thinking of the Judeo-Christian culture.

The writers of the Bible do not shrink from treating evil nor do they entertain any illusions about it. The most scathing indictments of human nature in all of its perversity and depravity are found in the Holy Scriptures, and, of course, the perennial problem of innocent suffering receives classic expression in the book of Job. Yet, for all of its desperation over evil, the Bible delivers no coherent, articulate, and ready-made solution. Even though God finally speaks, in the book of Job, he never answers the question, "Why do the righteous suffer?" Rather, he contrasts the learned discourses of Job and his friends with the authority that shrouds his own divine majesty:

[18] Albert Camus, *Resistance, Rebellion, and Death,* tr. Justin O'Brien (New York: Modern Library, 1960), p. 53.

> Then the LORD answered Job out of the
> whirlwind:
> "Who is this that darkens counsel by words
> without knowledge?
> Gird up your loins like a man,
> I will question you and you shall declare to me.
>
> "Where were you when I laid the foundation
> of the earth?
> Tell me, if you have understanding.
> Who determined its measurements—surely you know!
> Or who stretched the line upon it?
> On what were its bases sunk,
> or who laid its cornerstone,
> when the morning stars sang together,
> and all the sons of God shouted for joy?
>
> "Or who shut in the sea with doors,
> when it burst forth from the womb;
> when I made clouds its garment,
> and thick darkness its swaddling band,
> and prescribed bounds for it,
> and set bars and doors,
> and said, 'Thus far shall you come, and no farther,
> and here shall your proud waves be stayed'?"
> . . .
> And the LORD said to Job: "Shall a faultfinder
> contend with the Almighty?
> He who argues with God, let him answer it."
> (Job 38:1–11, 40:1–2).

Throughout the Bible there is recurrent emphasis on the divine transcendence and mystery. Moses was not permitted to look upon the face of God. Again,

> ". . . my thoughts are not your thoughts,
> neither are your ways my ways, says the LORD.
> For as the heavens are higher than the earth,
> so are my ways higher than your ways
> and my thoughts than your thoughts."
> (Isa. 55:8–9).

And St. Paul exclaims, "O the depth of the riches and wisdom and knowledge of God! How unsearchable are his judgments and how inscrutable his ways!" (Rom. 11:33). On the other hand, for the writers of the Bible mystery never gives way to despair. They are possessed of an unshakable confidence in the ultimate purposefulness of the universe and of history, a confidence born of their conviction that

In the beginning was the Logos, and the Logos was with God and the Logos was God. The same was in the beginning with God. All things were made by him, and apart from him not one thing was made. That which has come about through him was life, and the life was the light of men. The light shines in the darkness, and the darkness has not overcome it. . . . And the Logos became flesh and lived with us, full of grace and truth (John 1:1–5, 14).[19]

And the same Paul who speaks of the unsearchableness of God's judgments also writes, "We know that in everything God works for good with those who love him, who are called according to his purpose" (Rom. 8:28). Even Job himself, though consumed with suffering, cried out his faith:

> ". . . I know that my Redeemer lives,
>   and at last he will stand upon the earth;
> and after my skin has been thus destroyed,
>   then without my flesh I shall see God,
> whom I shall see on my side. . . ."
>   (Job 19:25–26).

It may be noted, in conclusion, that whereas the few positive disproofs of God's existence have usually been based on evil (most attacks are in fact levelled against the theistic arguments rather than God himself), it would appear that none have succeeded in showing an actual *formal* or *logical* contradiction between the essential tenets of theism and the reality of evil. This failure sug-

[19] My translation, reading at vss. 3–4 . . . χωρὶς αὐτοῦ ἐγένετο οὐδὲ ἕν. ὃ γέγονεν ἐν αὐτῷ ζωὴ ἦν. . . . "Logos" (λόγος), used here as an appellation for Jesus the Christ, may reflect the "Word-Wisdom" tradition of the Old Testament, or it may be drawn from the Greek philosophical tradition in which case it probably means "Reason," or the author of the Fourth Gospel may be writing for several traditions or communities at once. The source and significance of the Johannine Logos is a complex question, but at the very least it would seem to suggest the intelligibility of all things.

gests, of course, that like other issues we have encountered the problem of evil vs. God cannot be decided on purely rational, deductive, or scientific grounds but is, for the atheist no less than the theist, bound up with a general way of reading the world, a total confrontation, interpretation, and feeling for the whole of things. As we observed in an earlier context, surely there is a lesson in the fact that so many intelligent and insightful men disagree about the most obvious facts of experience.

10

The Soul and Immortality

Almost everyone has, at one time or another, experienced the anguish and the hope of Job's question: "If a man die, shall he live again?" (Job 14:14). For many the idea of finality is a torment, and, as Pascal says, "The immortality of the soul is a matter which is of so great consequence to us, and which touches us so profoundly, that we must have lost all feeling to be indifferent as to knowing what it is."[1]

Plato or Paul?

Before the rise of philosophy (about 600 B.C.) the Greeks had only a vague, pessimistic idea of the hereafter. In Homer, for example, the soul is a shadowy something that leaves the body at death and is transported across the gloomy river Styx to the House of Hades where it will squeak and flit about indefinitely in the dank darkness of the underworld. No wonder Achilles, when visited by Odysseus in the underworld, lamented,

[1] Blaise Pascal, *Pensées,* no. 194, in *Pensées and the Provincial Letters,* tr. W. F. Trotter and Thomas M'Crie (New York: Modern Library, 1941).

> I would rather as a hireling serve
> A needy man without much wealth,
> Than rule all the perished dead.[2]

The Old Testament Sheol (place of the departed) appears little better than the Greek Hades.[3] But in time all of this underwent radical reformulation, and the picture of the soul and the hereafter which we in turn have inherited is (more often than not) a confused mixture of elements drawn both from Greek philosophy and the New Testament.

The classical Greek concept portrays the soul as something essentially different from the body and superior to it. This dualistic idea is reflected already in Hesiod's *Theogony*, it was passed along by the Orphics and the Pythagoreans, and received, finally, an eloquent philosophical expression in Plato's *Phaedo*. In this Platonic dialogue, which ostensibly relates the last moments of Socrates with his disciples before his execution, Socrates explains that he does not fear death but, in fact, desires it. The reasoning is that the highest and most essential activity of the soul is the pursuit of knowledge, though as long as the soul is imprisoned in the body it is continually distracted from its proper pursuit by the requirements of the body and the distracting cares of this life. Furthermore, in this life knowledge is only imperfectly accessible, owing to the deficiency of the senses. Only in the hereafter, when the soul is released from the body into the presence of absolute truth, can it enjoy complete knowledge and uninterrupted happiness. Socrates concludes,

It seems that so long as we are alive, we shall continue closest to knowledge if we avoid as much as we can all contact and association with the body, except when they are absolutely necessary; and instead of allowing ourselves to become infected with its nature, purify ourselves from it until God himself gives us deliverance.[4]

Very different from the Platonic conception of immortality of the soul is the Pauline doctrine of the resurrection of the body.

---

[2] Homer, *Odyssey*, XI, 489 ff. (my translation).

[3] Though one should note Jesus' use of the Old Testament in connection with his belief in the resurrection in Mark 12:18–27.

[4] Plato, *Phaedo*, 67A, tr. Hugh Tredennick, in *The Last Days of Socrates* (Baltimore, Md.: Penguin Books, 1954).

This latter receives its fullest treatment in the fifteenth chapter of I Corinthians where, among other things, St. Paul says (vss. 42–44, 51–55):

What is sown is perishable, what is raised is imperishable. It is sown in dishonor, it is raised in glory. It is sown in weakness, it is raised in power. It is sown a physical body, it is raised a spiritual body. . . . Lo! I tell you a mystery. We shall not all sleep, but we shall all be changed, in a moment, in the twinkling of an eye, at the last trumpet. For the trumpet will sound, and the dead will be raised imperishable, and we shall be changed. For this perishable nature must put on the imperishable, and this mortal nature must put on immortality. When the perishable puts on the imperishable, and the mortal puts on immortality, then shall come to pass the saying that is written:

> "Death is swallowed up in victory."
> "O death, where is thy victory?
> O death, where is thy sting?"

The radical difference between the New Testament idea of the resurrection of the body and the Greek idea of the immortality of the soul reflects their very different concepts of creation and man.[5] The Greek debasement of the body and elevation of the soul follows from a more or less dualistic understanding of reality: The body belongs to the mundane, corporeal, dark, and evil sphere, eternally juxtaposed to the sphere of the intelligible and spiritual world of light, the proper home of the spiritual soul and the place to which she seeks desperately to make her escape. The Bible, on the other hand, represents the world as a good creation of God, and the body, not a thing to be despised, is called by St. Paul "a temple of the Holy Spirit" (I Cor. 6:19). Death is the consequence of sin and represents a hostile invasion of evil into the good and natural sphere; it is not a natural and friendly thing to be embraced with Socratic equanimity, but rather a horror and a

---

[5] It strikes me that the difference between the Greek and New Testament ideas on the future life (and all that difference implies) is extremely important both in itself and for an understanding of subsequent development, especially the medieval synthesis. For an excellent treatment of this question from a Protestant Biblical standpoint, see Oscar Cullmann's brief but influential *Immortality of the Soul or Resurrection of the Dead?* (New York: Macmillan, 1958). In the present discussion I am greatly indebted to Cullmann.

tragedy that causes one to sweat, as it were, great drops of blood. Yet death is an enemy that will be finally defeated in God's gracious gift of a new creation (when the perishable puts on the imperishable and all things are made new) which has already been anticipated and indeed made possible in the resurrection of Jesus Christ. It is important to emphasize that the resurrected body is not a body like that of the raised Lazarus (John 11), resuscitated only to die once more, but a body like the resurrected Christ's—changed, reconstituted, recreated, and glorified.

Closely related to this is the Bible's unwillingness to separate body and soul. It is true that the New Testament writings emphasize that there is something more to a man than his body (in one passage St. Paul distinguishes between body, soul, and *spirit*—as if we did not already have enough problems), but any honest reader must concede that the primary emphasis in St. Paul and throughout the New Testament is upon the unity of man: body and soul, outer and inner, both created by God, both good, and both together constituting full humanity.

St. Paul's notion of a "spiritual body" is in itself no easy concept to grasp, and the Biblical idea of the eventual re-creation and glorification of the body is hardly a subject for philosophical speculation and demonstration. When St. Paul called the resurrection a "mystery" (echoing the mystery-religions of Greece and Rome), he meant that it was a divine secret revealed to the "initiates," something that could be appreciated only in light of the total Biblical teaching concerning God's sovereignty and purposes. Nevertheless, the Christian idea of resurrection has had a widespread and profound influence in every age; its inspiration is, for example, apparent in John Donne's famous lines:

> At the round earths imagin'd corners, blow
> Your trumpets, Angells, and arise, arise
> From death, you numberlesse infinities
> of soules, and to your scattered bodies goe,
> All whom the flood did, and fire shall o'erthrow,
> All whom warre, dearth, age, agues, tyrannies,
> Despaire, law chance, hath slaine, and you whose eyes
> Shall behold God, and never tast deaths woe.[6]

[6] John Donne, *Holy Sonnets*, VII.

Traditional Proofs for Immortality

Aside from the question of resurrection, the Greco-Christian view that a man somehow survives death and lives on in the hereafter has occupied a fairly secure position in Western thought. The list of philosophers, scientists, and poets who have affirmed the soul's immortality is impressive indeed, perhaps bearing out Cicero's observation, ". . . somehow or other, there is inherent in the mind a forecast of times to come, and this is especially the case and most readily exhibits itself in the highest characters and the loftiest souls."[7] Even the skeptic Voltaire, who set out to destroy Christianity, could not but admit that we are profoundly indebted to the New Testament for its teaching concerning the future of the soul. And though the idea of immortality, like the idea of God, grasped men even before they were able to devise arguments for it, they did not hesitate to devise the arguments when they were finally able. Three different approaches are apparent in Plato, St. Augustine, and Kant.

Actually, Plato offered a whole series of proofs for the immortality of the soul. He argues, for example, that in the sphere of things that come into being and pass away every state is generated out of its opposite: the small from the great and the great from the small, the weak from the strong and the strong from the weak, the cold from the hot and the hot from the cold, waking from sleep and sleep from waking. It would seem to follow, then, that just as death is generated out of life, so likewise life must be generated out of death, otherwise in this one instance nature will be, as Socrates says, limping or lopsided. Furthermore, were not all things generated out of their opposite states, all natural processes would eventually cease altogether, including the phenomenon of life—something quite incompatible with the observed fact of a continuing cycle of living and dying.

Plato observes, again, that even in this life we discover in our minds such concepts as absolute equality. Where do we get these concepts? Surely not from this world, because there is not a single instance in the entire sensible world of absolute equality or abso-

---

[7] Cicero, *Tusculan Disputations,* I, 15, tr. Robert Black, in *The Basic Works of Cicero,* ed. Moses Hadas (New York: Modern Library, 1951).

lute anything: Everything grasped through sense-experience is at best relative, a fluctuating approximation of its absolute and immutable essence. Plato answers that we must have acquired the idea of equality, for example, in a former state wherein the soul existed, prior to its embodiment in this world, in the immediate presence of the absolute essences or Forms; this knowledge was "forgotten" at birth but later "recollected" through a kind of association of ideas when the soul, peering out through prison bars, is confronted with sensible and relative counterparts of the Forms. Plato believed that only on the hypothesis of the pre-existence of the soul could innate knowledge be explained.[8]

Neither of these, however, should be mistaken for Plato's main proofs, spread out over many pages of the *Phaedo* and revolving around his belief in the soul's immateriality. Given the difference between the body and the soul, and given the spiritual nature of the soul, it is not possible that the soul could ever die. By "death" we usually mean the dissolution of a thing or the scattering of its parts. A flower is said to die when it wilts, fades, and crumbles into dust; a man is said to die when his soul is separated from his body; the body is said to die when it is corrupted and its elements dispersed. But how can the soul die? It is not physical, it has no parts, there is nothing to be dissolved. The soul cannot die for it is by its nature simple, noncomposite, spiritual: If, through the practice of philosophy, the soul has kept itself pure from the contaminations of the body, then it "can have no grounds for fearing that on its separation from the body it will be blown away and scattered by the winds and so disappear into thin air, and cease to exist altogether."[9] Also, life is an essential attribute of the soul. That is, it is of the very nature of the soul to live just as it belongs to the essence of three to be odd. And since life is eternally incompatible with death, the soul can no more die than three can admit evenness. But though there can be no such thing as a dead soul, can't the soul perhaps simply cease to exist at the approach of death? The answer is that if the soul cannot admit death, then it is deathless or immortal and thus also imperishable. The soul, then, is a spiritual reality, and its essence

[8] Plato, *op. cit.*, 69E ff.
[9] *Ibid.*, 84B.

is to live. From this it follows, says Plato, that the soul is inde-structible.[10]

Another classical proof for the soul's immortality was provided by St. Augustine. Augustine, too, was enamored of incorporeal truth, abiding above both our mutable senses and minds, an abso-lute and unchanging light to which all rational men assent and by which the truth or falsity of all judgments may be (and will be in the end) illuminated. In fact, he devoted the whole of his *Against the Academicians* to variations of the *reductio ad absur-dum* that one cannot even deny the reality of truth without pre-supposing it, as when the skeptic asserts, "There is no truth," thereby implying that his own statement, at least, is true. Augustine further stressed the eternal necessity of some truths, for example, mathematical truths: At all times and in all places it is absolutely true that three plus seven equals ten—something even a fool could hardly deny. From the inexorable givenness of such truths Augus-tine believed that it is possible to prove both the existence of God and the immortality of the soul.

Briefly stated, his argument for God is that unless eternal truths are purely subjective and relative (which by their conception is impossible), there must exist for them an eternal *locus* from which they derive, namely, the infinite mind of God who is the Eternal Truth itself.[11] One may recognize in this *a priori* reasoning an epistemological counterpart to Rashdall's version of the Moral Ar gument; we might, in fact, call it the Epistemological Argument for God. Augustine believed also that from the reality of truth it is possible to formulate a demonstration of the soul's immortality. For if knowledge "exists anywhere, and cannot exist except in that which lives; and if it is eternal, and nothing in which an eternal thing exists can be non-eternal; then that in which knowledge ex-ists lives eternally."[12] The body belongs to the sensible world and is, eventually, corrupted along with everything else in it. But the mind's activity lies in the intelligible world, its aim is incorporeal truth. And since the mind must share in the nature of that which

[10] *Ibid.*, 102A ff.

[11] St. Augustine, *On Free Choice of the Will*, II, 12 ff.

[12] St. Augustine, *On the Immortality of the Soul*, 1, in *Concerning the Teacher and On the Immortality of the Soul*, tr. George G. Leckie (New York: Appleton-Century-Crofts, 1938).

actualizes it, the mind must be, like truth and knowledge, itself immaterial, spiritual, and eternal. Augustine's debt to Platonic philosophy should be obvious.

A very different proof is offered by Immanuel Kant. As we have seen, Kant rejected all of the traditional theistic arguments on the grounds that the "theoretical reason" has no application beyond what is given in experience, and he presented a new argument, the Moral Argument, according to which it is necessary to postulate God as a condition of moral experience. Now we may add that the immortality of the soul is also, for Kant, a postulate of moral experience, built right into moral experience as one of its conditions.

According to Kant, in a moral universe the actualization of the *summum bonum,* "the highest good," must be a real possibility. No single rational being (the only kind of being capable of moral experience) nor all collectively are able to achieve the highest good. Such an achievement requires the complete conformity of our will to the moral law, but this would involve a degree of holiness of which we limited beings are totally incapable, as we know only too well. All that is possible for limited beings like ourselves is an endless progress from a lower to a higher worthiness to receive the *summum bonum.* And an infinite progress is possible for us only if we possess an infinitely enduring existence, and thus, Kant reasons, our souls must be immortal. There is a further matter. In a truly moral universe all goodness must sooner or later be rewarded and evil punished, something that obviously does not happen in this life. It follows that rational beings must somehow survive death, for only on that supposition is possible the complete actualization (at least as seen from the standpoint of the Infinite Being who grasps our enduring progress as completed) of the happiness or misery which Kant believed inevitably follows upon keeping or breaking the moral law.

In this way, immortality is required if morality (as it displays itself in this life) is to be rational or consistent with itself. Apart from immortality, the moral law either (1) is degraded by indulging our personal desires and convenience, winking at our moral failures and achievements, or (2) it becomes a suffocating impossibility, an unattainable and therefore an unreal ideal. Kant concludes: ". . . the highest good is practically possible only on the supposition of the immortality of the soul, and the latter, as inseparably bound to the moral law, is a postulate of pure practical reason."[13] Thus again what we could not attain through the "theoretical reason" we can attain through the "practical reason."

These proofs rest plainly on important assumptions. Whether a contemporary will find such arguments persuasive may depend on his ability to free them from their particular cultural expressions, but certainly it will depend on his own philosophical mood and frame of reference. Proofs inspired by Plato can hardly hold any force for someone unwilling to accept the hypothesis of absolute and incorporeal truth, or for that matter, unwilling to acknowledge any non-empirical reality whatsoever. Kantian proofs clearly rest on the belief in objective value, but we have seen already that this itself is a subject of philosophical debate and the source of a major split among philosophers.

More specifically, traditional arguments for immortality have been challenged along the following lines. First, from a physiological standpoint, it would appear that what we call the mind is intimately and causally bound up with bodily functions, especially those of the brain. Some hold, in fact, that the *self* is just the continuity of one's thoughts and memories (if neither my mind nor my memory survive, what would make me think that *I* as a distinct personality have survived?), and that these are exclusively a matter of stimuli, brain cells, and chemical reactions. Second, the idea of the self as simple, distinct, and continuing may be incompatible with psychological and psychoanalytic findings concerning mental disintegration and the phenomenon of multiple personalities. Finally, and more philosophically, the charge is made that the concept of a disembodied soul makes for linguistic difficulties. Person-words (for example, "I," "you," "he," "someone") are intelligible insofar as they refer to concrete embodiments of physical and mental characteristics, personal histories, and so on. A disembodied soul, on the other hand, is not an object that may be pointed out: It neither wears a tie nor shakes hands, and is otherwise radically different from anything that "he" or "someone" usually refers to. What could "disembodied soul" *mean?*

Nevertheless, many contemporary thinkers appear to have no trouble identifying with traditional metaphysical systems, nor do

[13] Immanuel Kant, *Critique of Practical Reason*, tr. Lewis White Beck (Indianapolis, Ind.: Library of Liberal Arts, 1956), p. 127.

they seem much troubled by physiological, psychological, or analytic challenges such as the above. One example is Jacques Maritain, a present day scholastic. Maritain first rejects that noble but uninspiring view of immortality according to which we shall all live eternally in the contribution we have made to posterity. It would be, Maritain says, a supreme delusion to seek in this concept of immortality "any adequate fulfillment of that irrepressible aspiration to survival which inhabits the depths of our substances."[14] He then proceeds to fashion his own version of the Platonic-Augustinian proof. In order for there to be genuine knowledge at all, the intellect must be capable of rising above the purely material or sensible dimension of things and grasping their immaterial essences, for the knowable is that which abides unchangeably, unconditioned by the imperfections and relativities of matter. This means that the intellect too, commensurably with its object, must be immaterial or spiritual in nature; because the intellect is a faculty of the soul, the soul too must be spiritual; and from the spirituality of the soul, Maritain deduces its immortality:

A spiritual soul cannot be corrupted, since it possesses no matter; it cannot be disintegrated, since it has no substantial parts; it cannot lose its individual unity, since it is self-subsisting, nor its internal energy, since it contains within itself all the sources of its energies. The human soul cannot die. Once it exists, it cannot disappear; it will necessarily exist forever, endure without end.[15]

It would appear, then, that in some philosophical and theological circles at least some of the traditional proofs for immortality continue to be very much alive.

The Evidence of Psychical Research

Others, products of our scientific age, have become disenchanted with philosophical proofs for immortality and have sought instead a more empirical evidence for their belief in the soul and the afterlife. Such evidence has been more and more forthcoming from

[14] Jacques Maritain, *The Range of Reason* (New York: Scribner, 1952), p. 54.
[15] *Ibid.*, p. 60.

the investigations sponsored by "psychical research." Understandably, there has been widespread suspicion of psychical research
because it is so often associated with the occult, including weird
things such as ghosts and séances. The days are gone, however,
when one could scoff and sneer at talk about phenomena such as
extrasensory perception and perhaps even disembodied spirits. The
Society for Psychical Research, founded in London in 1882 and
presided over by an impressive list of notable people including
psychologists, philosophers, and scientists, has done much to make
these subjects both prominent and respectable. In recent years,
psychical research has become a center of serious scientific study
and will clearly have to be taken more seriously in the future.

According to believers in ESP (extrasensory perception) and
PK (psychokinesis, literally "mental movement"), one mind can
operate upon or move another mind, thing, or event (or vice versa)
without any aid whatever from the five senses. Telepathy, clairvoyance, and precognition are examples of ESP. In telepathy one
mind is said to communicate certain ideas to another mind through
mental activity alone; clairvoyance is the ability to perceive things
not present to the senses; and precognition is the ability to perceive and predict future events. One notable pioneer in this area,
J. B. Rhine, has published extensive accounts of his telepathic experiments (conducted at Duke University) including results that
reflect staggering odds against chance-occurrences.[16] The results
of other experimenters are equally spectacular. Of course such
findings have come under the scrutiny of skeptics, and the inevitable statistical questions have been raised. Nevertheless, the grow-
ing consensus of responsible researchers is that the evidence for
ESP and PK is overwhelming.

The question of otherworldly spirits (a second concern of psychical research) is, at this stage, more dubious. But even here one
should be cautioned against a premature and out-and-out rejection.
C. D. Broad, a well-known philosopher of science, wrote in 1924
of his confidence in the psychical evidence for survival:

I do presuppose that the careful work of the Society for Psychical Research has elicited a mass of facts which may fairly be called "super-
normal," in the sense that they cannot, if genuine, be explained on the

---

[16] J. B. Rhine, *Extra-Sensory Perception* (Boston: Society for Psychical Research, 1935).

usual assumptions of science and common-sense about the nature and powers of the human mind. And I do assume that a great many of the facts that come up to the extremely high standard of evidence required by the Society are "genuine," in the sense that they have been correctly reported and that they are not simply due to fraud or self-deception. I assume this on the basis of a fairly careful study of the literature; of a knowledge of the kind of persons who have controlled the policy of the Society and taken part in its investigations; and of some investigations of my own.[17]

It may be of interest, further, to quote an account of a recent, first hand experience by the celebrated Biblical translator, J. B. Phillips. Phillips, who describes himself as "incredulous by nature, and as unsuperstitious as they come," ventures his encounter with the late C. S. Lewis:

C. S. Lewis, whom I did not know very well and had only seen in the flesh once, but with whom I had corresponded a fair amount, gave me an unusual experience. A few days after his death, while I was watching television, he "appeared" sitting in a chair within a few feet of me, and spoke a few words which were particularly relevant to the difficult circumstances through which I was passing. He was ruddier in complexion than ever, grinning all over his face and, as the old-fashioned saying has it, positively glowing with health. The interesting thing to me was that I had not been thinking about him at all. I was neither alarmed nor surprised nor, to satisfy the Bishop of Woolwich, did I look up to see the hole in the ceiling that he might have made on arrival! He was just *there*—"large as life and twice as natural." A week later, this time when I was in bed, reading before going to sleep, he appeared again, even more rosily radiant than before, and repeated to me the same message, which was very important to me at the time.[18]

For the present writer what is most striking about this account is that it was sworn by a man of such integrity and unquestioned good sense.

The evidence of psychical research is, of course, especially agreeable to those who would like to meet the scientist on his own empirical ground. Some have insisted, for example, that inasmuch as psychical research has scientifically established the reality of

---

[17] C. D. Broad, *The Mind and Its Place in Nature* (London: Kegan Paul, Trench, Trubner & Co., 1925), p. 514.

[18] J. B. Phillips, *Ring of Truth* (New York: Macmillan, 1967), p. 117.

such things as ESP and disembodied spirits, it has overthrown the materialist theory of human personality. Others hesitate at this point, for they see that the sword is two-edged: The materialist may argue just as forcefully from the same evidence that his materialism is simply more pervasive and subtle than he had expected. At any rate, the statistical analyses and testimonials of parapsychology and psychical research are subject to the same incompleteness and tentativeness that plague all scientific theories and evidence. Further, is the picture of the soul being painted by psychical researchers really a relevant one from a *religious* point of view? Most theologians would probably balk at any attempt to ground the reality, personality, and survival of the soul in the obscure evidence drawn from this kind of approach. Still, who questions that there are, after all, more things in heaven and earth than are dreamt of in our philosophy?

Mind and Body

Most people are convinced that they have a body, and that they have a soul (though they may prefer to call it by some other name), and that these are essentially different from one another. The body is thought to be physics and chemistry, whereas the soul is conceived as transcendent and spiritual, incapable of being weighed or dissected or in any way grasped by the senses. Of course, the belief that the soul transcends the space-time world is for many people closely related to the idea of life after death. If, after all, the soul is independent of the body, why should it not survive the death of the body?

This persistent view of the soul and its survival has its roots in René Descartes who argued more emphatically than anyone else in the history of philosophy that mind (he used "mind," "soul," "spirit," and "self" interchangeably) is one thing and that matter is another. Beginning with his celebrated intuition, *Cogito ergo sum* ("I think, therefore I am"), Descartes believed that through a kind of introspective immediacy he could grasp directly his own enduring mind or soul:

I concluded that I was a thing or substance whose whole essence or nature was only to think, and which, to exist, has no need of space nor of any material thing or body. Thus it follows that this ego, this mind, this soul, by which I am what I am, is entirely distinct from the body and is easier to know than the latter, and that even if the body were not, the soul would not cease to be all it now is.[19]

According to Descartes, the first thing of which I can be absolutely certain is that I exist and that I am a "thinking substance." He then proceeds to reduce the existence of another kind of reality, matter, or "extended substance." These two substances underlie all reality; everything in the cosmos, including man, is reducible to mind and matter.

With his dualism of mind and matter Descartes laid the foundation for many modern philosophies, but he also posed a most vexing problem: the mind-body problem. If we believe with Descartes that the mind is one thing and that the body is another, essentially different substances, then how do we get them back together again? And we must get them back together again if we are to explain their obvious causal relation to one another. Clearly, our mental states depend on our bodily states as, for example, when we become depressed by being repeatedly beaten over the head. Similarly, psychosomatic illnesses show that bodily states may be caused by mental states. But how can there exist such a causal relation between body and mind if they are two absolutely different substances with nothing in common?

Descartes' immediate successors inherited from him the mind-body problem and found themselves hard pressed to provide a solution. Malebranche, another French thinker, suggested occasionalism, the doctrine that on the occasion of a physical sensation God causes the appropriate idea to occur in the mind, and vice versa. In this way there is always an appropriate and predictable correspondence between mental and physical states. Whereas Malebranche attributed the agreement between mind and body to the immediate intervention of God, Leibniz's doctrine of a pre-established harmony declares that God so ordained mind and matter from the beginning that thoughts and sensations would always agree, just as two clocks, wound up and synchronized, would always tell the same time. More likely is the double aspect theory of the Dutch

---

[19] René Descartes, *Discourse on Method*, IV, in *Discourse on Method and Meditations*, tr. Laurence J. Lafleur (Indianapolis, Ind.: Library of Liberal Arts, 1960), p. 25.

philosopher Spinoza. According to this view, mind and matter are "attributes" of a single underlying substance, providing through parallel mental and physical states two manifestations of the one reality.

One of the most obvious moves is that of the materialist who simply denies that the mind exists as anything different from matter. The only thing that really exists is matter in motion, and mind turns out to be a configuration of energy or, at best, an "epiphenomenon," a mere by-product of physical and chemical processes. The idealist, on the other hand, reverses this position when he says that mind is the only reality and all sensible things are in some way ideas or configurations of mental activity.

Probably the most common solution (even at the present) is interactionism. This position (which was Descartes') holds that though the mind and body are essentially different from one another, there must be, nevertheless, some kind of necessary though obscure causal relation between them. Descartes had said that the mind must be intimately joined to the body, and he even identified the exact place where matter and mind are transformed into one another—the pineal gland! Aside from Descartes' questionable physiology, this explanation simply begs the question by pushing it a step backwards. In fact, any version of interactionism ultimately poses all over again the very difficulty that it attempts to explain, namely, how two different substances with no common *nexus* can interact.

All in all, however, interactionism may not be quite as tenuous a position as one might at first think. The interactionist does have a problem explaining the causal relation of mind and matter (whether in the pineal gland or elsewhere), but then we have already seen that *any* causal relation is a far from simple matter and the critic may be wise not to push this objection too far lest it backfire. Further, the image of some sort of unbridgeable chasm fixed forever between mind and matter is itself probably misleading. It suggests that the mind is another "thing" standing in a kind of spatial relation to the body, which is exactly what the mind-matter dualist denies—there can hardly be a gap between two things if one of them does not even occupy space. On the other hand, not even the interactionist denies that there is *some* sense in which the mind, whatever its nature, exists in time and is localized in space: I am very sure that my mind exists now rather than 200 years ago and that it is present in this room rather than down the hall someplace.

Or am I? David Hume believed that we have no knowledge of our own minds whatever, at least no rationally derived knowledge. We saw in Chapter 4 that for Hume there can be no knowledge of reality except what is disclosed through the data of sense-experience, and that this in turn led him to abandon causality as a metaphysical principle. Now we must prepare for the collapse of a second pillar of traditional philosophy, the concept of *substance*.

Philosophers like Descartes and Locke were certain that just as there must be some material substance (from the Latin *substantia:* literally, "that which stands under") upholding the physical qualities of sensible objects, so must there be a mental substance—mind —that underlies mental activities such as thinking, doubting, willing, and remembering. After all, they reasoned, qualities and activities can no more exist apart from a substance than a predicate can exist without a subject. But according to Hume's phenomenalism, there is no reason for thinking that there is anything more to the table than its perceived qualities: rectangular, brown, smooth-on-top, and so on. There is no evidence or necessity for some mysterious, underlying material substance; the table is merely a collection of sensible qualities, or at least that is as much as we can know. Hume applies the same reasoning to mental substances as well. He characterizes the position of his opponents:

There are some philosophers, who imagine we are every moment intimately conscious of what we call our SELF; that we feel its existence and its continuance in existence; and are certain, beyond the evidence of a demonstration, both of its perfect identity and simplicity. . . . To attempt a farther proof of this were to weaken its evidence; since no proof can be deriv'd from any fact, of which we are so intimately conscious; nor is there anything, of which we can be certain, if we doubt of this.[20]

But, as we should expect by now, Hume does doubt it. He argues that it is simply not possible to plumb the depths of consciousness and confront at last an underlying self or "I." At least it was not possible for Hume:

If any one upon serious and unprejudic'd reflexion, thinks he has a different notion of *himself*, I must confess I can reason no longer with him.

[20] David Hume, *A Treatise of Human Nature*, ed. L. A. Selby-Bigge (Oxford, England: Clarendon Press, 1888), p. 251.

All I can allow him is, that he may be in the right as well as I, and that we are essentially different in this particular. He may, perhaps, perceive something simple and continu'd, which he calls *himself;* tho' I am certain there is no such principle in me.[21]

All that can be discovered introspectively is a passing parade of perceptions: love, hatred, pain, pleasure, hot, cold, and so forth. In fact, says Hume, in an important statement, a man *is* simply a "bundle or collection of different perceptions."[22] With Hume's analysis, the concept of substance vanishes into thin air, and all possible talk about mental substance or the soul vanishes with it.

Still another and more contemporary view rejects altogether such talk about mental substances as involving a "category-mistake," a concept introduced by the analytic philosopher Gilbert Ryle. A category-mistake is the mistake of applying a concept within a conceptual system to which it is inappropriate. For example, says Ryle, if a visitor comes to the university campus and asks to see the library, it is a simple matter to point to the library and say, "There it is"; or, if he asks to see the administration building, to point to it and say, "There it is." But if the visitor then asked to see the *university,* it would be clear that he mistakes a university for something like a library or science building, something that can be pointed out, rather than an organization of colleges and schools. According to Ryle's logical geography of mental concepts, the traditional dogma of the "ghost in the machine" rests on the same kind of a mistake: "It represents the facts of mental life as if they belonged to one logical type or category (or range of types or categories), when they actually belong to another."[23]

Though the origins of the category-mistake antedate Descartes, it was he, says Ryle, who foisted it upon the modern mind. Himself a man of science, Descartes was naturally influenced by the concepts of Galileo's mechanics. And though he contended for the real difference between mind and matter, he understood both of these within the selfsame framework, namely, the categories of thing, stuff, attribute, state, process, change, cause, and effect. Ryle represents Descartes' thinking: "Minds are things, but different sorts of things from bodies; mental processes are causes and effects, but

21 *Ibid.,* p. 252.
22 *Ibid.,* p. 190.
23 Gilbert Ryle, *The Concept of Mind* (London: Hutchinson, 1949), p. 16.

different sorts of causes and effects from bodily movements. And so on."[24] Ryle believes that our troubles began when Descartes called mind a "thing" or "substance." The mind-body problem is a pseudo-problem, a problem of language rather than reality.

Man a Machine?

Notwithstanding the mind-body problem, a great many thinkers are convinced that there must be something about man that eludes the laws of physics and chemistry, something about him that somehow transcends the conditions of space and time. A purely materialistic or naturalistic conception of man may solve some difficulties, but the cure is worse than the disease.

Some have argued that one of the corollaries of materialism (in all of its forms) is the belief in a complete causal determinism, the belief that anything that happens can be explained entirely by means of antecedent causes or conditions. This would mean that a man's mental states and decisions, as well as his physical make-up, may be explained in terms of factors over which he has ultimately no control, and that he is, therefore, merely an elaborate machine.[25] Now we do not hold machines morally responsible for their actions. We may kick them and curse them, but we do not blame or punish them. Similarly, if man is a machine, however complicated and sophisticated, then the idea of moral responsibility becomes meaningless. If, then, we take moral experience seriously, we must believe that something in man (or about him) transcends the mechanism and determinism of purely empirical processes. He must have *free will*. It is difficult to give a positive account of just what is involved in the concept of free will or indeterminism, but no one means by

24 *Ibid.*, p. 19.

25 Most philosophers would distinguish between determinism and the more extreme mechanistic determinism. Mechanistic determinism conceives of the universe as a gigantic machine governed by a fixed and finite number of causal laws such that if one could know the exact condition of every detail in the universe at any point in time, he could, theoretically, predict the exact condition of the whole universe for anytime in the future. Many claim that whereas mechanism is incompatible with teleology or purpose, determinism pure and simple is not. Nevertheless, any version of determinism holds that a man's choices and decisions are completely determined, and for our purposes that is the important point.

it that the will can operate in a vacuum or independently of conditions. What is denied is that given a set of conditions, a *certain* decision must be made; a particular choice may be caused, and yet not be determined.

The idea that there can be no genuine morality apart from free will is a very old one and not without its modern defenders. Maritain, for example, represents the case in this way:

If human actions were mere events of nature, resulting from the interaction of the constellations of causes at work in the world, there would be only the universe of nature—there would be no ethical universe, no universe of morality. But human actions are introduced into the world as the result of a free determination, as something which depends on an initiative irreducible to the causal connections at play in the whole world, and taken by another whole which is my self, my own person, in such a way that I am responsible for it, I myself am the author of my action, be it good or bad.[26]

Kant, too, believed that freedom of the will must be postulated in order to account for moral experience. We saw previously that Kant was a firm believer in the "moral law within," a fundamental sense of duty or "ought." He now emphasizes that the implementation of the moral law requires that the will somehow rise above the morally blind determinism of the natural world, for "ought implies *can*." Of course, it will have to be admitted that all scientific research favors (more accurately, presupposes) a complete causal determinism, even though physics has abandoned the billiard-ball model of things and causality in science is not what it used to be. But for Kant the data of moral experience are as real and undeniable as the data of sense-experience, and we are driven, therefore, to the conclusion that there must be more to reality than what appears in the phenomenal world. To accept a complete causal determinism extending even to thinking and willing would be to exclude oneself from the world of moral discourse and responsibility.[27] Kant's famous trilogy of moral postulates is now complete: God, Immortality, and Freedom.

Of course, the "self-determinist" turns this reasoning upside down

[26] Jacques Maritain, *The Responsibility of the Artist* (New York: Scribner, 1960), pp. 27 f.

[27] Immanuel Kant, *Foundations of the Metaphysics of Morals,* tr. Lewis White Beck (Indianapolis, Ind.: Library of Liberal Arts, 1959), pp. 64 ff.

when he insists that a man can be held morally responsible for his actions only if they are determined—determined by the man's own character. If someone were suddenly seized by a momentary and uncontrollable spasm of his arm and struck you in the face, you would not hold him morally responsible for the act for it hardly reflected his intention or attitude. On the other hand, you would most certainly hold him morally responsible if you judged that his act was the product of his real character, that is, was caused by his deliberation, disposition, and intention. According to self-determinism, then, I can be held morally accountable for my acts only if they reflect the person that I am, only if they are determined by my character. Though there is on the surface a plausibility about this position, two rather obvious questions may be raised. First, has not the self-determinist simply defined the problem away when he identifies genuine freedom with self-determinism and then announces that freedom is compatible with determinism? Second, is it not the case that those features of our own character (choices, desires, attitudes, interests) are themselves the product of external causes over which we have no control? Are we not who we are because of biological constitution, religious training, education, and innumerable other factors? Upon closer examination, then, the self-determinist appears to take back with one hand what he gives with the other, and the real problem of determinism and morality remains.

Rational or cognitive activity is often cited as still further evidence for man's transcending nature. We observed a moment ago that we do not blame machines or hold them morally responsible; similarly, though we plug them in and we program them, we do not reason with them. (A person who seems to be reasoning with a computer is, of course, actually reasoning with the computer's logical system which is the invention of human intelligence.) The possibility of knowledge and meaningful discourse suggests that cognitive experience also transcends the contrived and blind responses of the causally determined: There is an obvious difference between the reasons for a position and its causes. Thus the doctrine of the determinist is even self-refuting. For he intends that his statement, "All things are causally determined," should be taken as a piece of meaningful discourse, but if all things are indeed causally determined, then that statement too is causally determined and therefore of no more cognitive significance than if uttered by a drugged man who was out of his head. In sum, if man is a truly rational and moral being, he cannot be reduced to a mere bundle of inclinations being bounced about in an environmental pin-ball machine.

It might be objected, as in our discussion of the Moral Argument, that neither physics-and-chemistry-language *nor* transcendence-language are adequate to the full, manifold, and complex nature of man, that they pose false alternatives, that both languages plus many others represent equally real and important dimensions of human nature. But whatever may follow from this broader conception of human nature, it remains that we are compelled to acknowledge a dimension of man's experience that cannot wholly be explicated by the categories employed by the behavioral or physical sciences. And this, if nowhere else, is the point at which a philosophical discussion of the soul may begin. On the other hand, we seem now to be a long way removed from Donne's religious certainty:

> One short sleepe past, wee wake eternally,
> And death shall be no more; death, thou shalt die.[28]

---

[28] Donne, *op. cit.*, X.

11

Religious Language

It is frequently remarked that the task of the theologian nowadays is not to show that the statement "God exists" is true, but to show that it is even intelligible. Of course, not all religious language is problematic. There is, for example, nothing more or less troublesome about the statement in the Nicene Creed that "he suffered under Pontius Pilate" than about many other statements. Nevertheless, religious language does have, in many respects, its peculiar problems. The Scripture says "the Lord's hand is not shortened, that it cannot save," but God does not have hands does he? We read that the serpent in the Garden beguiled Eve to sin, but do we take that story seriously? The answer is probably both Yes and No. When we say that God is good, do we mean that he is good like this or that or anything in this world? Would not the Christian continue to assert "God loves us" even in spite of evidence all to the contrary? And some, though they ordinarily strain to free themselves of contradiction, nonetheless have no trouble affirming (as the *Augsburg Confession* expresses it) that Christ "took on man's nature in the womb of the blessed virgin Mary. So there are two natures, divine and human, inseparably conjoined in the unity of his person, one Christ, true God and true man . . . ."[1] Clearly, there is something very special about a kind of discourse that cultivates and even thrives on such paradoxes and ambiguities. It should cause

[1] *Augsburg Confession,* III, in *The Book of Concord,* tr. and ed. Theodore G. Tappert (Philadelphia: Fortress Press, 1959), p. 29.

no wonder that religious language constitutes still another problem that has long preoccupied philosophical theologians.

The Via Analogiae

One of the most influential interpretations of religious language was suggested by St. Thomas Aquinas. Having demonstrated the existence of God, Thomas sought then to establish certain of the divine attributes, an enterprise that fills long sections of his *Summa Theologica* and *Summa Contra Gentiles*. But how is it possible to know or to say of a reality that infinitely surpasses us that it is one, incorporeal, good, and wise? In fact, how is it possible to say anything at all about it? The answer (at least for a long line of Christian thinkers) lies in the *via negativa* and the *via affirmativa,* the "way of negation" and the "way of affirmation."

Negative theology has always been regarded by theologians, especially those of a mystic bent, as an effective means to a knowledge of the divine nature. According to the way of negation (sometimes called the way of remotion), it is possible to ascend to a knowledge of some things about God by stripping away or removing from the concept of God all that is inappropriate to it. Approaching God (as Thomas says we must) indirectly through sense-experience, we can never know the divine substance as it is in itself, but we can at least know what it is not and therefore through systematic remotion approximate more and more to a positive (though ever incomplete) knowledge of what it is:

Now, in considering the divine substance, we should especially make use of the method of remotion. For, by its immensity, the divine substance surpasses every form that our intellect reaches. Thus we are unable to apprehend it by knowing *what it is.* Yet we are able to have some knowledge of it by knowing *what it is not.* Furthermore, we approach nearer to a knowledge of God according as through our intellect we are able to remove more and more things from Him.[2]

We can establish, for example, that God must be infinite (not finite), immutable (not changeable), incorporeal (not material), and

---

[2] St. Thomas Aquinas, *Summa Contra Gentiles,* I, 14, tr. Anton C. Pegis (Garden City, N.Y.: Image Books, 1955).

simple (non-composite). Whereas the *via negativa* in this way moves our knowledge of the divine nature forward by denying to it certain features found in sensible reality, the *via affirmativa* allows us to predicate of God other features, such as wisdom and goodness, positively and affirmatively.

This brings us to a crucial (if not the essential) doctrine of Thomistic philosophy, the doctrine of the *analogia entis*, the "analogy of being." Reflecting again the influence—if not the terminology—of Aristotle, Thomas explains that our positive talk about God is neither "univocal" nor "equivocal," but "analogical."

We speak univocally (literally, naming in one way) when we apply a word with the same meaning to different things. Thus when we say, "Peter is a man, and James and John also," we predicate exactly the same thing of James and John as we do of Peter. Here we are using the word "man" univocally. But when we say, "God is good," are we predicating "good" univocally of both God and created things? Obviously not. God cannot be good in exactly the same way that Peter, James, and John are good. Any good with which we are acquainted here in this world is at best a pale reflection of the infinite goodness of God. And because there is a great gulf fixed between the Creator and created things, concepts like being, goodness, and wisdom cannot bear exactly the same meaning, or be used univocally, in reference to both God and creatures.

Then is all talk about God equivocal? We speak equivocally (literally, naming in like ways) when we employ a single word but intend completely different meanings, as when we use the word "pen" to mean at one time an instrument for writing and at another time a place for pigs. (And thus in logic the "fallacy of equivocation" is the fallacy of shifting the meaning of a word or phrase in the course of an argument.) Whereas it may be true that when we say, "God is good," we do not intend that he is good in exactly the same way that we are good, we surely do not intend either that his goodness is wholly unlike and completely unrelated to our own. Though there may be a great gulf fixed between God and his creatures, it is not that great. If God so transcends our concepts that they have no application to him at all, then all knowledge of God and discourse about him would be impossible. In this way, our concepts like being, goodness, and wisdom do not apply to

God and creatures entirely equivocally, or in an altogether different way.[3]

We speak about God, therefore, neither univocally nor entirely equivocally, but analogically. The creature is the effect of the Creator. The world stands in a real relation to God and bears his imprint, as every effect necessarily bears something of the perfection of its cause. Thus, however imperfectly represented in space and time, something of the divine nature is preserved and reflected in the natural world. Thomas summarizes both sides of this situation when he says,

Sensible things, from which the human reason takes the origin of its knowledge, retain within themselves some sort of trace of a likeness to God. This is so imperfect, however, that it is absolutely inadequate to manifest the substance of God. For effects bear within themselves, in their own way, the likeness of their causes, since an agent produces its like; yet an effect does not always reach to the full likeness of its cause.[4]

The natural world, and we ourselves, may not be wholly like God, but neither is it wholly unlike him. Creatures, by the fact that they *are*, resemble God who is Being Itself, and analogical predication is based on just this resemblance. Thomas believed that we can acquire, through experience of God's creation, ideas of perfections such as being, goodness, and wisdom. Moreover, we can by analogy affirm these perfections of God:

whatever is said of God and creatures is said according as there is some relation of the creature to God as to its principle and cause, wherein all the perfections of things pre-exist excellently. Now this mode of community is a mean between pure equivocation and simple univocation. For in analogies the idea is not, as it is in univocals, one and the same; yet it is not totally diverse as in equivocals; but the name which is thus used in a multiple sense signifies various proportions to some one thing . . . .[5]

Certainly, therefore, when Thomas speaks of "analogy" he does not mean likeness pure and simple, nor does he have in mind the

[3] *Ibid.*, 32 f.
[4] *Ibid.*, 8.
[5] St. Thomas Aquinas, *Summa Theologica*, Part I, Qu. 13, Art. 5, in *Basic Writings of St. Thomas Aquinas*, ed. Anton C. Pegis (New York: Random House, 1945), I.

use of metaphor wherein there is no real likeness at all. When we say, metaphorically, that God is a fortress, we do not mean that God is really a fortress, but when we say that God is good, we mean that he is really good. That is, Thomas' idea of analogy involves a real metaphysical relation and resemblance of creatures to God. Even so, this idea is a bit more complicated than one might at first think. Actually, there is considerable discussion concerning the exact nature of Thomas' doctrine of analogy, though it appears that the most fundamental meaning of analogy in Thomas is that of "proportion." The perfections that exist in the sensible world divided and multiplied exist in God supereminently or most excellently, and the predication of perfections is necessarily relative to the subject's mode of existence: As we are good in a finite way, so is God infinitely good; as we are wise in a finite way, so is God infinitely wise. In this way, creatures exhibit relatively and proportionately the perfections that exist infinitely in God. It should be noticed, however, that what is epistemologically prior is metaphysically posterior. The term "good" as we *know* it applies first to creatures and second to God, whereas in *fact* goodness exists primarily in God and only derivately or secondarily in creatures.

It should not be thought that the predication of many attributes to God (such as one, simple, good, and wise) does violence to the divine simplicity. We identify and label the divine nature in a plurality of ways because we necessarily approach God through the world of nature in which the being of God is, as it were, refracted and seen under different and varying lights; something of the divine being is reflected in the goodness that we creatures know, in the wisdom that we know, and so on. If we were able to know God as he is in himself (which is impossible), then we would, of course, see that the divine attributes converge into one, identical with the simple and divine nature that is God.[6]

Thomas' doctrine of analogy is more than a conception of language. It is a metaphysical doctrine of the unity of God and the world in terms of a proportion between the being of the Creator and the being of creatures. Nonetheless, the doctrine does illuminate also the meaning of religious discourse. Though it does not allow us to say anything more or anything less about God than

---

[6] St. Thomas Aquinas, *Summa Contra Gentiles*, 31, *op. cit.*

we did before, it does clarify *what* we are saying—and are not saying. On the other hand, it should be noticed that since Thomas' *via analogiae* depends upon a real likeness between creatures and God resulting from God's creative causality, it therefore depends upon the success of his Cosmological Proof.

Theology as Meaningless

At the opposite extreme from St. Thomas is the view (born of a modern climate) that discards theology entirely, claiming that we can say nothing about God and related matters because all such talk is, quite literally, meaningless.

This is the position of Logical Positivism, a philosophical movement that had its roots in the Vienna Circle, a group of thinkers who banded together in the 1920s with a common interest in a new and radical empiricism seasoned with a strong dash of linguistic analysis. These thinkers (Moritz Schlick, Rudolf Carnap, Herbert Feigl, Kurt Gödel, Frederick Waismann, and others) saw themselves as following in the tradition of David Hume who, as we have seen recurringly, rejected metaphysical knowledge as groundless, reducing all knowledge to self-evident analytic truths and empirically derived synthetic truths:

> If we take in our hand any volume; of divinity or school metaphysics, for instance; let us ask, *Does it contain any abstract reasoning concerning quantity or number?* No. *Does it contain any experimental reasoning concerning matter of fact and existence?* No. Commit it then to the flames: for it can contain nothing but sophistry and illusion.[7]

Another empiricist having somewhat to do with the shaping of Logical Positivism was the French philosopher and sociologist Auguste Comte who over the years 1830–1842 published a work entitled *The Positive Philosophy*. Comte's thesis was that several evolutionary stages are discernible in the history of philosophy, and that just as the mythological stage gave way to the theological and the theological to the metaphysical, so now must the metaphysical stage yield to the scientific. Philosophy, if it is to enjoy

[7] David Hume, *An Enquiry Concerning Human Understanding*, ed. L. A. Selby-Bigge, second ed. (Oxford, England: Clarendon Press, 1902), p. 165.

the same kind of advance and unanimity in its inquiries that the sciences have achieved, must abandon its speculative or metaphysical concerns and adopt a thoroughgoing empirical methodology. Philosophy must, in other words, become scientific. The Vienna Circle bore also the imprint of Ludwig Wittgenstein who, along with Russell and Moore, contributed much to the shaping of British analytic philosophy. Wittgenstein himself worked out an empirical-analytic rejection of metaphysical problems as linguistic bubbles, concluding his *Tractatus Logico-Philosophicus* with the quasi-mystical aphorism, "What we cannot speak about we must consign to silence."[8]

Out of the Vienna Circle came the celebrated "Verification Principle," the watchword of Logical Positivism. The Verification Principle has been variously expressed and many times modified, but its essence is this: A statement has literal meaning if and only if it is either analytic or (at least in principle) empirically verifiable. Or, to express it otherwise, a proposition is meaningful, that is, possesses truth-falsity status, only if one knows what kinds of situations would have to exist in order for its truth or falsity to be shown. If a statement is not even in theory empirically verifiable (the only kind of verification the logical positivists allow), then it is cognitively vacuous and meaningless. The Verification Principle reflects at once an interest in linguistic analysis, a radically empirical criterion of meaningfulness, the judgment that speculative philosophy and metaphysics have been the source of philosophical confusion, and a desire to recover philosophy from its traditional abortive state.

Where does this leave propositions like "God exists?" For the logical positivist, such statements are *meaningless*. This is not to say that "God exists" is simply irrelevant or unimportant as in "That was a meaningless experience." Instead the statement "God exists" is, for the logical positivist, literally without meaning, literally nonsensical, it holds no more cognitive significance than "Creech creech." And so it is with all traditional speculative or metaphysical statements such as "The soul is immortal," "The world had a beginning in time," and "Everything that exists is an imperfect copy of an archetypal ideal."

---

[8] Ludwig Wittgenstein, *Tractatus Logico-Philosophicus*, tr. D. F. Pears and B. F. McGuinness (London: Routledge & Kegan Paul, 1961), p. 151.

This position was given classic expression in A. J. Ayer's influential *Language, Truth and Logic* (first edition, 1936), the first chapter of which bears the revealing title "The Elimination of Metaphysics." He begins, as he says, "by criticising the metaphysical thesis that philosophy affords us knowledge of a reality transcending the world of science and common sense."[9] Specifically on the question of God, Ayer argues that it is not even possible to be an atheist. The atheist says, in effect, "The statement 'God exists' is meaningful, that is, it is either true or it is false, and I happen to think that it is false." For Ayer, however, the statement "God exists" is neither true nor false, because there is not even in principle any way of verifying it. The statement is cognitively empty and nonsensical. The same is also true of the agnostic. He cannot say, "I do not know if the statement 'God exists' is true," without assuming that it may be true, whereas according to Ayer it can be neither true nor false. The whole of theological discourse is, in this way, relegated to the realm of meaninglessness and nonsense.[10]

Furthermore, Ayer argues, even if such statements *were* meaningful, we still could not provide any demonstration of God's existence in the manner of traditional philosophers like St. Thomas or Descartes. The reason is that the Verification Principle with its purely empirical criterion of meaningfulness excludes any possibility of synthetic *a priori* propositions, that is, propositions whose truth is known independently of sense-experience but which inform us, nonetheless, about reality. This means, echoing Hume, that every meaningful statement is either an analytic tautology (like "All barking dogs bark") or an empirical generalization (like "All swans are white"). Thus the premises of any theistic argument must be either analytic or empirical. And because we can get no more out of a conclusion of an argument than is already contained in the premises, the conclusion, too, must be either analytic or empirical. If the conclusion is analytic, it is an uninformative tautology; and if the conclusion is empirical, its truth can only be probable. In either case, the existence of God cannot be proved with demonstrative certainty.[11]

[9] Alfred Jules Ayer, *Language, Truth and Logic*, second ed. (London: Gollancz, 1946), p. 33.
[10] *Ibid.*, pp. 115 f.
[11] *Ibid.*, p. 114 f.

The critics of this position immediately saw that it was self-refuting: The Verification Principle itself cannot be empirically verified and is, therefore, meaningless on its own showing—something the logical positivists could never quite get over. (Similarly, Hume's own principle, quoted above, should be committed to the flames inasmuch as it fails its own criterion of meaningfulness!)

In the introduction to the second edition of *Language, Truth and Logic*, Ayer, who did not want his Verification Principle to be construed as either an empty tautology or mere empirical generalization, answered rather feebly that it was intended as a "definition" and a "methodological principle." Others responded that we should no more expect the Verification Principle to judge its own meaningfulness that we would expect a weighing machine to weigh itself. Of course both of these defenses played into the hands of the critics, for both admit that there is at least one statement (the Verification Principle itself) that is non-tautologous and non-empirical, and yet cognitively meaningful. John Wisdom notes: "The fact is, the verification principle is a metaphysical proposition—a 'smashing' one if I may be permitted the expression."[12] Smashing aside, the logical positivists' intent to pigeonhole meaningful knowledge exclusively in terms of empirical verification was even more philosophically intolerant than the traditional approaches they sought to reject.

A more popular criticism charges that Logical Positivism is, perhaps, both arbitrary and unimaginative from an epistemological standpoint. As one philosopher observes, ". . . it seemed extraordinary to have to exclude a vast area of language from what could be admitted as meaningful and significant; and even odder that people still continued to use 'meaningless' jargon."[13] Certainly it is misguided from an existentialist standpoint. Whereas positivistic or "scientific" philosophy emphasizes that the only meaningful questions are those that fall within the domain of the scientific method and empirical investigation, the existentialists, on the other hand,

[12] John Wisdom, *Philosophy and Psychoanalysis* (Oxford, England: Blackwell, 1953), p. 245. For one of the very earliest criticisms along the above lines, see A. C. Ewing's important article, "Meaninglessness," *Mind*, XLVI (July, 1937). It should be noted that Ayer made several adjustments in his position in the Introduction of the second edition of *Language, Truth and Logic*.

[13] Ian T. Ramsey, *Religious Language* (New York: Macmillan, 1957), p. 13.

insist that the most meaningful and urgent questions are those that lie *beyond* the domain of the scientific method. (We see, however, that these are two very different conceptions of meaningfulness, the former cognitive and the latter existential.) Kierkegaard has already warned us that the more "objective" a truth is, the less interest does it hold for the subjectively existing individual, and Paul Tillich charges that although Logical Positivism "can be interpreted as the justified distrust of an interference of emotional elements with cognitive statements," it may also be interpreted as "the desire to escape problems which are relevant to human existence."[14]

The Falsification Debate

Notwithstanding the success or failure of the logical positivist rejection of metaphysics and theology, the nature of religious language continues to be a very live issue in philosophical theology. In the next section we will consider an existentialist interpretation of religious language; for the moment we must pursue a bit further the question of its cognitive status. Legion are the positions and moves that have been recently proposed concerning the logical and empirical placing of religious discourse. Whereas the older issue revolved around the question of verifiability, one of the more recent approaches has centered on the further question of "falsifiability." This received its best-known statement in "Theology and Falsification," a discussion by three British analytic thinkers: Antony Flew, R. M. Hare, and Basil Mitchell. The Flew-Hare-Mitchell debate, along with a response by John Hick, represents, then, at least one very important and contemporary slant on the significance (or non-significance) of religious statements.

A favorite point of departure for what might be called falsification-approaches is John Wisdom's parable of the garden, and it is with this parable that Flew begins:

Two people return to their long neglected garden and find among the weeds a few of the old plants surprisingly vigorous. One says to the other "It must be that a gardener has been coming and doing something about these plants." Upon enquiry they find that no neighbor has ever

[14] Paul Tillich, *Theology of Culture*, ed. Robert C. Kimball (New York: Oxford University Press, 1959), p. 172.

seen anyone at work in their garden. The first man says to the other "He must have worked while people slept." The other says "No, someone would have heard him and besides, anybody who cared about the plants would have kept down these weeds." The first man says "Look at the way these are arranged. There is purpose and a feeling for beauty here. I believe that someone comes, someone invisible to mortal eyes. . . ."[15]

And so the parable goes on, the first man insisting that there is evidence in the garden for the existence of some kind of a gardener, though he continually modifies his idea of the gardener in order to accommodate the second man's evidence to the contrary. Finally, after both men have examined the evidence, pro and con, for a gardener the first man concludes, "I still believe a gardener comes," and the second man, "I don't." According to Flew, the original, fine, brash hypothesis of the gardener has died by inches, the "death by a thousand qualifications." Similarly, we may begin with a meaningful concept but so qualify it step by step that the final result bears little or no relation to what we originally started with—in fact, what we are left with may be nothing at all. For example, the gardener that the first man continues to believe in has, in the last analysis, no more significance than an imaginary gardener or even no gardener.

Now, says Flew, theological utterances appear to have a peculiar weakness for death by a thousand qualifications. Take the statement "God has a plan." On the face of it this seems to be a genuine, meaningful, factual assertion. Consider, however, that the man who asserts, "God has a plan," would be likely to assert it no matter what. That is, there is probably no evidence, no conceivable set of conditions, that could cause him to deny that God has a plan. A tornado destroys part of a community and the qualification-process begins: "Our church and our parishioners remained untouched, witnessing to God's protection of the faithful"; "The tornado destroyed our church and killed several of our parishioners, displaying that God's inscrutable plan requires at times even

[15] Antony Flew (with R. M. Hare and Basil Mitchell), "Theology and Falsification," in *New Essays in Philosophical Theology,* ed. Antony Flew and Alasdair MacIntyre (London: Student Christian Movement Press, 1955), p. 96. Though Flew provides his own version of the parable, the above quotation is actually from Wisdom's version in "Gods," *Proceedings of the Aristotelian Society,* New Series, XLV (1944–45), p. 191.

the suffering of the faithful"; "God has a plan, but . . . ." Thus it turns out that "God has a plan" may be so eroded away with qualification that the result is not a genuine assertion at all. Any statement that is compatible with every conceivable situation does not assert anything about any particular situation and is, therefore, not even in theory falsifiable. And if a statement cannot even in principle be shown to be false, then it cannot be shown to be true either, which means that it has no truth-falsity value, which means that it has no cognitive value, which means that we are back to "Creech creech." Statements like "God has a plan," "God created the world," and "God loves us," may be, according to Flew, as vacuous as the gardener who turned out to be nothing at all. Or at least until someone can say what would have to occur to constitute their disproof.[16]

To this challenge Hare responded simply that Flew is right in judging that religious statements are not assertions of fact. But what are they then? Hare says they are "bliks," a word he coined to suggest the non-verifiable, non-falsifiable, non-factual, though nonetheless very real and deeply rooted feeling we have concerning the truth of some things. Hare asks us to consider his own parable:

A certain lunatic is convinced that all dons want to murder him. His friends introduce him to all the mildest and most respectable dons that they can find, and after each of them has retired, they say, "You see, he doesn't really want to murder you; he spoke to you in a most cordial manner; surely you are convinced now?" But the lunatic replies "Yes, but that was only his diabolical cunning; he's really plotting against me the whole time, like the rest of them; I know it I tell you."[17]

The moral of this story is that the lunatic has a *blik* about dons, though more important, he has a wrong (in fact, an insane) *blik* about dons. The non-assertional character of *bliks* aside, clearly there is a difference between right *bliks* and wrong *bliks* and it is important to have the right *bliks*. From our belief that our cars will not disintegrate as we career down the freeways, to our conviction that tables continue to exist when unperceived, to our confidence in the promise of a friend, our lives are filled with

16 Flew, *ibid.*, pp. 96 ff.
17 R. M. Hare, *ibid.*, pp. 99 f.

bliks, and it obviously matters a great deal whether you think that dons are trying to murder you!

In spite of it all, therefore, *bliks* appear to have some cognitive status, even though Hare himself does not spell this out; they bear upon the truth of things and can be mistaken. But what, then, is the logical status of these peculiar beliefs—unarguable, but so essential to our lives? Where Flew erred, says Hare, is in taking *bliks* as *explanations* of something. *Bliks* (for example, "God has a plan") are not themselves explanations of anything, though taken together they constitute a view of the world, a feeling about the way things are, that in turn makes explanation possible. *Bliks* cannot be verified or falsified because they are themselves the elemental ideas that make possible the verification and falsification of other ideas.[18]

It would appear that Hare is right. On both the practical and intellectual plane, one cannot function without *bliks;* they are constitutive of one's *Weltanschauung* or image of the world. For the religious person to abandon his belief, say, that the world is created and sustained by Almighty God would require that his whole way of seeing the world be remodelled. Since *bliks* are at once determinative of and the products of the sum total of our experiences (sensory, intellectual, emotional, aesthetic), it is often the case that we cannot deny them without, in a way, denying ourselves at the same time. Why one should hold a certain *blik* to begin with, or how one is to decide between competing *bliks,* are questions that remain. Perhaps the notion of *conversion* has some relevance at this point. At any rate, we find ourselves confronting once again a fact of intellectual experience that we have encountered in one form or another throughout our discussions: the presence of the non-rational. Notwithstanding our desire for completely rational justification, our positions are usually shot through and through with non-rational elements which, though non-rational, appear to be inevitable, relevant, and even necessary for our understanding of the world.

Mitchell answered Flew differently, maintaining that religious statements are genuine assertions even though they cannot be conclusively verified or falsified. As we might expect, Mitchell enlists the help of a third parable to make his point. Let us imagine, he

[18] *Ibid.,* pp. 99 ff.

says, that during a war in an occupied country a resistance fighter meets a Stranger who impresses him deeply. The Stranger tells the partisan that he, the Stranger, is also on the side of the resistance. Thus the partisan is won over by the Stranger, who then urges the partisan to trust him no matter what happens. The partisan leaves the meeting confident in the sincerity and truth of the Stranger. But the Stranger is sometimes seen in enemy uniform handing over patriots to the occupation powers. Because the partisan is still convinced of the Stranger's sincerity, he now interprets the Stranger's present actions as part of a secret resistance maneuver. When he asks for help from the Stranger, sometimes he receives it and feels grateful for the confirmation of his belief; at other times, his request is not granted and he thinks to himself, "The Stranger knows best." And so the partisan goes on clinging to his conviction in spite of appearances to the contrary.

The important difference between Hare's parable and Mitchell's is that Hare's lunatic allows nothing to count against his *blik* that dons are trying to murder him, whereas Mitchell's resistance fighter admits that many discrepancies do seem to belie his faith in the Stranger. And if there is evidence that counts against the truth of the statement "The Stranger is on our side," then this statement has (whatever the case with *bliks*) truth-value and it qualifies as a genuine assertion, even though there may be no *conclusive* verification or falsification of it; and (whatever the case with *bliks*) it does explain some things, at least in the eyes of the resistance fighter. Similarly, the theologian does allow certain evidences, like the fact of evil and suffering, to weigh against his belief that "God has a plan" (a genuine assertion that helps explain the way things are) though never *decisively*. And is this not, after all, what is often meant by "having faith?"[9]

Furthermore (though Mitchell does not suggest this), "The Stranger is on our side," would, in fact, be conclusively verified or falsified when the war was over. This is the point of John Hick's concept of "eschatological verification," and still another parable. (That Hick saw his position as an answer to the Flew-Hare-Mitchell discussion is evident from the title of his own article: "Theology and Verification.")

Hick invites us to consider two men walking together down a

---

[9] Basil Mitchell, *ibid.*, pp. 103 ff.

road. One man believes that the road leads, eventually, to a Celestial City; the other man believes that the road leads nowhere. Along the way, both men experience times of refreshment and times of hardship, and both men find it possible to interpret their experiences, the bad as well as the good, as consistent with their different beliefs about their ultimate destination. Thus, as Hick says, during the journey the issue between the two men—like Flew's garden-watchers—is not an experiential one; they have no argument about their experiences along the way, but about their ultimate destination.

And yet when they do turn the last corner it will be apparent that one of them has been right all the time and the other wrong. Thus, although the issue between them has not been experimental, it has nevertheless from the start been a real issue. . . . Their opposed interpretations of the road constituted genuinely rival assertions, though assertions whose status has the peculiar characteristic of being guaranteed retrospectively by a future crux.[20]

Of course it will be noted that if the road leads nowhere, then there is no hope of refuting the one man's claim that it leads to a Celestial City. Similarly, some theological statements, like "The soul is immortal," by their nature can never be falsified: If we die and that is the end of the matter, then we will not be there to observe whether that is the end of the matter. On the other hand, we know what it would be like for the soul to survive death, that is, we know what empirical difference it would make. Such statements are, therefore, potentially verifiable in the future—eschatologically—and that is enough to insure their nature as genuine descriptive assertions. Their meaning is not symbolic, not ceremonial, not emotive, but factual: ". . . the existence or non-existence of the God of the New Testament is a matter of fact, and claims as such eventual experiential verification."[21]

[20] John Hick, *Faith and Knowledge*, second ed. (Ithaca, N.Y.: Cornell University Press, 1966), pp. 177 f. Hick's position was first published as "Theology and Verification," *Theology Today*, XVII (April, 1960).

[21] *Ibid.*, p. 193. One might note also I. M. Crombie's earlier version of the idea of eschatological verification in his contribution to the Flew-Hare-Mitchell discussion, reprinted as Part Two of "Theology and Falsification," in Flew and MacIntyre, *op. cit.*, pp. 109 ff.

Hick, of course, opened a new front on the question and his position was answered in a variety of counterattacks. One thinker responded, for example, that Hick reasons circularly inasmuch as the eschatological verification of Christian theological propositions requires the meaningfulness of those very propositions. To use Hick's examples, the truth of "God exists" may be confirmed in the postmortem state in which we, in our resurrected bodies, discover the fulfillment of God's purpose for us, or in which we experience a communion with God through Christ, God's Son. But clearly the possibility of such experiences, involving God's purposes or involving Christ (the divinely "anointed") or God's Son, presupposes already the meaningfulness of God-talk.[22] To this still another responded that the criticism applies equally to all verification-talk: We cannot ask what evidence is relevant for the verification of any statement unless we know first what the statement means. He concluded that the verificationists are more confused about the meaning of their language than are the theologians, and directed the theologians to proceed with business as usual as if nothing happened:

theologians have no logical reason to be troubled by the current state of the philosophical challenge to the meaningfulness of God-talk. Perhaps at a later time some philosopher will formulate such a challenge in some coherent way. But until then theologians will probably be justified in devoting the major part of their attention to the more substantive problems of their discipline.[23]

No doubt a more charitable estimation of verificationism could be provided. But even so, on what possible grounds could a cogent verificationism commend itself to us in competition with other approaches? Would it not in the end find it necessary like the older Positivism to appeal rather dogmatically to the nature of things and the nature of knowledge, and to take a rather narrow view, at that?

---

[22] Kai Nielsen, "Eschatological Verification," *Canadian Journal of Theology*, IX (October, 1963).

[23] George Mavrodes, "God and Verification," *Canadian Journal of Theology*, X (July, 1964), p. 191. For an argument that Flew's original falsification-challenge was itself ill-conceived, see Alvin Plantinga, *God and Other Minds* (Ithaca, N.Y.: Cornell University Press, 1967), pp. 157 ff.

Symbolic and Poetic Meaning

Most people are naturally inclined to view religious statements (such as "God loves us") as being *cognitive* statements; that is, they take them as being informative, as describing some factual situation or other (such as "Sirius is 8.7 light years away"), and therefore as having truth-falsity status. But we have now seen that whereas the cognitive significance of religious statements has been defended by some (for example, St. Thomas), it has been challenged by others (Flew). Altogether different is the approach of those philosophers who freely grant the *non*-cognitive character of religious statements and proceed to locate their significance and function completely outside the question of their literal truth or falsity.

Some of the attempts to recover the significance of religious language by shifting to a non-cognitive interpretation have been sponsored by the analysts-empiricists themselves. One of the most successful of these is contained in R. B. Braithwaite's *An Empiricist's View of the Nature of Religious Belief*. In place of the Verification Principle Braithwaite substitutes what may be called the Use Principle: The meaning of a statement is disclosed in the way it is used. On inspection it turns out that religious utterances are used by the religious man to express an intention to adopt a certain behavioral policy or to live in a certain way (for example, in a Christian way with its practice of love and so forth) and to support him in his determination to carry through in that policy. These moral intentions are, in this way, related to a story or group of stories (for example, the stories about Jesus) which are "entertained" as the empirical or factual—though not necessarily historical or true—basis of the intention, and which cumulatively suggest that policy or way of life. The essence of religion, he says, lies in its exhortation to a life of love, and the great religions differ only, therefore, in their ritual practices and, more important, the different stories (or sets of stories) entertained as the empirical foundation of their moral teaching.

Braithwaite summarizes his position: "A religious assertion, for me, is the assertion of an intention to carry out a certain behaviour policy, subsumable under a sufficiently general principle to be a moral one, together with the implicit or explicit statement, but not the assertion, of stories."[24] Braithwaite believes that this understanding of religious assertions possesses the advantage of, among other things, doing justice both to the religious man's demand that his beliefs be taken seriously and to the empiricist's demand that religious discourse be factually grounded.

In fact, however, it may be asked whether Braithwaite does justice to either of these. First, the religious man's beliefs usually (depending on the man) extend beyond a mere "entertaining" of hypothetical stories. Rather, he may conceive himself as a participant in a real drama involving the Christ who "for us men and for our salvation, came down from heaven . . . was made man . . . was crucified . . . suffered . . . rose again . . . ." More than a life style or a behavioral policy of love, it may be for the believer a matter of salvation and hope, and hope that is dependent upon real occurrences. It may be Braithwaite himself who does not take religious belief seriously enough.

Second, if Braithwaite's position does justice to the empiricist's demands, it does so at too great a price, for, as was just suggested, the real stuff of religious conviction (depending on the religion) is hardly exhausted in what can be empirically apprehended. That Jesus of Nazareth lived, that he taught certain things, that he was crucified under Pontius Pilate around the year 33 A.D., and even that he was raised from the dead, may be taken as factual, empirical information, even if untrue. But that the Logos was in the beginning, that he was God, that all things were made by him, that he was the light of men, that he himself became a man and atoned for the sins of the world, cannot be empirically apprehended though it is the foundation of Christian belief and hope. Furthermore, in his reduction of the great religions to essentially the same concern for the moral life, Braithwaite underestimates their differences. The story of the Gospels and the story of the *Bhagavad-Gita*, for example, involve very different theologies, very different conceptions of salvation, and have really quite different points. It would appear that the situation of the religious believer may be considerably richer than Braithwaite has allowed.

The interpretation of religious language as symbolic (Braithwaite preferred the more neutral "story" to "myth" or "symbol")

---

[24] R. B. Braithwaite, *An Empiricist's View of the Nature of Religious Belief* (Cambridge, England: Cambridge University Press, 1955), p. 32.

has always been popular and not even the staunchest fundamentalist would deny the presence of symbolism in the Bible. No doubt the most notable attempt to express the symbolic meaning of Christianity is that of the German-American theologian Paul Tillich (1886–1965).

Tillich's concept of the religious symbol is inseparable from his concept of faith. According to Tillich, faith is not merely an intellectual affair, as in an intellectual assent to revealed truths; nor is it merely a volitional matter, an act of the will; nor is it to be identified with emotion or feeling. To identify faith with any one of these (and it has, in fact, been identified with each) is a distortion of its true nature. Faith, rather, involves the total person, the sum of one's faculties; it is "a centered act of the total personality" (in a lecture Tillich once characterized man as "a multidimensional unity") affirming that which is grasped as holding ultimate significance. In two words, faith is "ultimate concern." But faith is idolatrous when it affirms something as ultimate which is not really ultimate, for example, the nation, wealth, and social prestige. We will see in the next chapter that for Tillich what is really ultimate, the Ground of Being, cannot itself be something existing alongside other things but lies infinitely beyond the reach of the finite concepts that designate ordinary realities. In this way, the nature of genuine faith itself requires the transformation of idolatrous concepts into symbols: "That which is the true ultimate transcends the realm of finite reality infinitely. Therefore, no finite reality can express it directly and properly. . . . Whatever we say about that which concerns us ultimately, whether or not we call it God, has a symbolic meaning. . . . The language of faith is the language of symbols."[25]

Tillich is eager to answer the man who is disappointed to learn that religious language turns out to be "only symbolic." There is a difference between a sign and a symbol, a recurring idea in Tillich's works. Whereas signs and symbols both point to something beyond themselves, symbols (whether artistic, political, or religious) participate in that to which they point, they share in the dignity and honor of what they represent. Further, as in art and music, symbols disclose new levels of reality otherwise inaccessible

[25] Paul Tillich, *Dynamics of Faith* (New York: Harper & Row, 1957), pp. 44 f.

to us, and unlock corresponding dimensions of the soul. Finally, because symbols are projections of the collective unconscious and hold significance only insofar as a community (unconsciously) accepts and responds to them, they are born and they die, they are never invented or wilfully discarded. Let us, then, never say, "only a symbol," but rather, "not less than a symbol."[26]

Underlying Tillich's view of the significance of religious symbols is his view of man as an estranged being. This latter idea is, actually, the point of departure for Tillich's whole existential theology. The phrase "existential anxiety" expresses Tillich's appraisal of the human situation. Man is a being who lives continually under the threat of non-being. In the anticipation of death man is confronted with his finitude. His sense of guilt reflects his deviation from his essential nature, what he ought to be. And hope is lost in the experience of meaninglessness. Man finds himself, therefore, estranged from his own being, suffering existential anxiety.

It is precisely these existential dimensions of man and this state of anxiety that religious symbols address. For example, the mythical symbolism of the creation story speaks to man's sense of finitude; it testifies that man is not alone, that he is a creature, that he has been created, and that he thus participates in the inexhaustible depth of reality. Let him then take courage and affirm himself in the infinite Ground of his being. In this way, the symbol of creation gives man the "courage to be"—the title of one of Tillich's works—even in the face of the ever-present threat of nothingness. Or again, central to many religions are the symbols of the fall and salvation, along with a multitude of closely related symbols. The symbol of temptation, as Tillich says, expresses the anxiety of existential decisions. Adam and Eve symbolize the situation of man confronted with the decision between "the dreaming innocence of Paradise and achieving self-realization in knowledge, power, and sex." Their fall symbolizes this transition to existential self-actualization. (Of course, man's essential state "before" the fall is not conceived here as a literal state in time, but rather the potentiality for authentic existence that is present in every stage of man's development; neither is the "transition" a literal or historical transition but a statement about the tragic-universal character of existence.) The symbols of the demonic represent man's "feeling of

---

[26] *Ibid.,* pp. 41 ff.

being possessed by structures of self-destruction." And salvation symbols like redemption, regeneration, and Christ, speak mythologically of man's "passionate quest" in his existential situation.[27]

Such, for Tillich, is the power and significance of religious symbols as they confront us with the reality and the urgency of our existential plight. In reference to the symbol of the Fall he says: "It is a genuine description of man's predicament here and now and should not be vitiated by the absurdities of literalism."[28]

Tillich's analysis of religious symbolism gives rise to several problems, including a rather obvious one. As the ultimate reality to which all religious symbols point, Being Itself may turn out to be (quite opposite to Tillich's intent) both a theologically and religiously empty concept. If nothing non-symbolic can be affirmed about Being Itself, then we may legitimately wonder how any theology can justify itself as more adequate than another. Bare Being Itself, without any elaboration or qualification, can hardly serve as a criterion for theological (symbolic) discussions and appeals. Further, if *all things* by their nature participate in the Ground of Being, then it is devoid of the distinctive character and demand that alone can inspire worship and commitment. We are, in fact, at the opposite extreme from both the distinctive Wholly-Otherness of Otto's numinous and the particularity of Kierkegaard's object of faith. According to Tillich, the First and Great Commandment is a symbolic translation of ultimate concern. But whereas I might feel suitably constrained to love the Lord my God with all my heart, with all my soul, and with all my mind (Matt. 22:37–38), I might have some difficulty experiencing such devotion and excitment towards an impersonal and general Being Itself. Certainly we would be left cold if Billy Graham were to conclude one of his evangelistic broadcasts with the benediction, "And may the Ground of Being bless you real good!"

Another view that sees the meaningfulness of religious language in its essentially non-cognitive function is that of George Santayana (1863–1952). Santayana was a romantic and a poet as well as a philosopher. He believed that the poetic and imaginative impulse, cultivated in accord with intellection or ideation, contributes an

[27] Paul Tillich, "Existential Analyses and Religious Symbols," in *Contemporary Problems in Religion*, ed. Harold A. Basilius (Detroit: Wayne State University Press, 1956), pp. 42 ff.

[28] *Ibid.*, p. 50.

essential element to understanding and life, and that these two together—imaginative impulse and ideation—constitute the essence of human activity. This twofold activity is in turn manifest in every sphere of human endeavor, as is suggested in the five volumes of Santayana's *The Life of Reason* which bear the individual titles *Reason in Common Sense, Reason in Art, Reason in Science, Reason in Society,* and *Reason in Religion.*

That religion belongs essentially to the Life of Reason (the seat of ultimate values) is apparent from its projection of ideals and its shaping of moral aspirations. But although it aims at the ends of the rational life, it does so by means of an imaginative activity, similar to that of the poet: "Religion remains an imaginative achievement, a symbolic representation of moral reality which may have a most important function in vitalising the mind and in transmitting, by way of parables, the lessons of experience."[29] On the relation of religion to poetry he goes so far as to claim that "religion and poetry are identical in essence, and differ merely in the way in which they are attached to practical affairs. Poetry is called religion when it intervenes in life, and religion, when it merely supervenes upon life, is seen to be nothing but poetry."[30]

It is clear, then, that religion functions not on the plane of literal truth (Santayana says that religions may be better or worse but never true or false), and two important observations follow from this. First, the traditional conflict between science and religion is a wholly misguided one. Since religion has nothing at all to say about the factual world, it can hardly oppose the truths of science. It is understandable, however, that the problem arises. Religion has always had a tendency to misunderstand its own true nature, arrogate to itself the role of pronouncing literal truths, and harden into a dogma about the way things are rather than be a "struggling force" for the sake of what ought to be. The sooner we recognize the moral (not factual) and symbolic (not literal) character of religious expression, the better will it be for religion's relation to other disciplines, especially the sciences. On the other hand, and second, we must not allow the positive contribution of the religious-poetic

[29] George Santayana, *The Life of Reason: Reason in Religion* (New York: Scribner, 1905), p. 12.

[30] George Santayana, *Interpretations of Poetry and Religion* (New York: Scribner, 1900), p. v.

imagination to become obscured by the contradictions and confusions of religions:

Nor have we any reason to be intolerant of the partialities and contradictions which religions display. Were we dealing with a science, such contradictions would have to be instantly solved and removed; but when we are concerned with the poetic interpretation of experience, contradiction means only variety, and variety means spontaneity, wealth of resource, and a nearer approach to total adequacy.[31]

For both Tillich and Santayana, religious expression conveys us beyond the world of ordinary experience to the realm of ultimate concern (Tillich) or to the inspiration of moral life (Santayana). Scientific and literal discourse is, of course, appropriate to one kind of situation, but it seems not to be the situation in which we are compelled to ask the questions that matter most.

In this post-positivist time it seems quite incredible to have once thought that meaningful discourse could so simply be sifted through an analytic-*a priori*/synthetic-*a posteriori* linguistic sieve. Even the later Wittgenstein, with his notion of many legitimate "language games" (a total fabric of speech-forms, situation, and behavior) has contributed to a new interest in the richness and diversity of domains and kinds of discourse, each with its own principles and its own purpose. Not the least of these is religious discourse. And we may conclude with Ian T. Ramsey's observations that religious language is necessarily an odd one, commensurate with the oddness of the religious situation itself, and that "the central problem of theology is how to use, how to qualify, observational language so as to be suitable currency for what in part exceeds it—the situations in which theology is founded."[32]

---

[31] Santayana, *The Life of Reason: Reason in Religion, op. cit.*, p. 13.
[32] Ramsey, *op. cit.*, pp. 42 f.

12

Some New Theologies

It should be apparent by now that no survey of philosophical theology (at least in its Western form) can proceed very far without some reference to Biblical theology. Especially in recent years the philosopher and the theologian have been unable to avoid the impact of one another and the lines between the two have become increasingly blurred. There is also the intrinsic interest of the several movements of contemporary theology, an interest suitably evidenced in the phenomenal success of Bishop John A. T. Robinson's *Honest to God* (1963) which brought these positions within reach of a popular reading audience and created a tidal wave of response. It is appropriate, then, that we conclude with a discussion of the new theologies. But who from the continuing procession of theologians shall we choose to represent the most important directions of contemporary theology? Though such a choice may be somewhat prejudicial, no one would deny that four very influential lines of contemporary theological thought are suggested by Rudolf Bultmann, Paul Tillich, Dietrich Bonhoeffer, and the Death of God thinkers.

Kerygma and Mythology

It is not only a problem of whom to include but also where to begin. Most would agree, however, that the Swiss theologian Karl Barth (1886–1968), often regarded as the greatest theologian of

205

modern times, was the fountainhead of the plethora of positions assumed over recent years.

The theological world of the nineteenth and early twentieth centuries was challenged by Barth's 1919 publication *The Epistle to the Romans*. This epochal work was a protest registered primarily against the prevailing liberal theology of his predecessors, a theology with roots in Friedrich Schleiermacher, empowered by Albrecht Ritschl, and popularized by Adolf von Harnack. Von Harnack was one of Barth's own teachers and his *What is Christianity?* (answer: the Fatherhood of God and the Brotherhood of Man) is rightly hailed as the high water mark of theological Liberalism. This movement was scholarly, honest, well-intentioned, and shallow. What came to be the recognized vapidity of Liberalism was characterized by H. Richard Niebuhr (something of an American counterpart to Barth) in his well-known indictment: "A God without wrath brought men without sin into a kingdom without judgment through the ministrations of a Christ without a Cross."[1] In place of this man-centered, optimistic theology ("Every day in every way we're getting better and better"), Barth, writing in the shadow of the First World War and in anticipation of the Second, called for a "corrective" theology that entertains no illusions about man's situation ("God is in heaven, thou art on earth!") and takes seriously God's decisive judgment on sin as well as his gracious offer of salvation in Christ.

Though Barth developed his Biblical theology (he despised the expression "systematic theology") over a period stretching beyond half a century, its essential character is aptly suggested by the labels that have become attached to it. It has been called, for example, a "theology of the Word," reflecting at once Barth's rejection of any and all natural theology—and certainly anything resembling a Thomistic *analogia entis*—and his emphasis on the Word, God's self-disclosure to man, as the central fact of any adequate theology, the only possible point of departure. The *Deus Absconditus* of natural theology must give way to the *Deus Revelatus* of the Word. Closely related is the expression "kerygmatic theology." The word *kerygma* (from a Greek word meaning "proclamation") figures repeatedly in a whole strain of modern theology and is used as a

---

[1] H. Richard Niebuhr, *The Kingdom of God in America* (Chicago: Willett, Clark & Co., 1937), p. 193.

synonym for the essential, fundamental message or good news of the Gospel, the proclamation of God's saving acts in Christ.

Barthianism is also known as "crisis theology," a theology of judgment and decision. It focuses upon man's helpless and hopeless condition before God to whom he must turn in despair and utter dependence for salvation. "Neo-orthodoxy" suggests, correctly, that Barth signals a return to the classical Protestant position of the reformers: *sola scriptura, sola fides, sola gratia*—"scripture alone, faith alone, grace alone." In fact, Barth's estimation of man's spiritual state goes even further than Calvin's: Though man was created in the image of God, that image has been completely obliterated and wiped out through the Fall. On the other hand, it is not an old orthodoxy but a new one; an orthodoxy that is informed by the insights and critical investigations of modern Biblical and theological scholarship. Finally, Barth's has been called a "dialectical theology" inasmuch as it requires that our talk about the transcendent God be paradoxical, a positive statement generating its own qualification or denial. An obvious example of the latter is to be seen in Barth's late essay "The Humanity of God" as a kind of dialectical response to his own earlier emphasis on God's wholly-otherness.

It should not be surprising that the Barthian attempt to recover the substance of the Biblical message has been characterized as a theological positivism. Barth, too, strips away metaphysical, speculative thought as meaningless, but now replacing the logical positivists' Verification Principle with the sole criterion of revelation, limiting the sphere of legitimate theologizing to what can be, as it were, Biblically verified: A theological statement is an irrelevant product of sinful pride if it is not drawn from divine authority.

Though Barth inaugurated the new theological age, Rudolf Bultmann, revolting with Barth against their liberal teachers but moving in a very different direction, marks an even more dramatic and in some ways more far-reaching revolution. First, it might be mentioned that Bultmann, Professor of New Testament at the University of Marburg, was one of the founding fathers of the school known as form-criticism which attempts to uncover the original oral content of the New Testament (which became buried under superimposed layers of tradition) through analysis of the differing linguistic and theological forms present in the text. One of the pioneering works in this field was Bultmann's 1926 *Die Geschichte der synoptischen Tradition* (in the English translation: *Jesus and the Word*), and much of the fruit of the form-critical method is contained in the more recent and acclaimed two-volume *Theology of the New Testament*. It is difficult to overstate Bultmann's contribution to Biblical scholarship. But there is, at least for our purposes, an even more important side to Bultmann. In 1941 he issued a mimeographed pamphlet, eventually published in English under the title *New Testament and Mythology: The Problem of Eliminating the Mythological Elements from the Proclamation of the New Testament*. The result was that the world of theology would never again be the same.

Bultmann begins, rather abruptly, with the judgment that much of the New Testament is, for modern man, irrational and utterly meaningless. To take Bultmann's important example, the New Testament cosmology is obsolete. The New Testament writers believed in a three-storied universe: Heaven is up above, we are here, and hell is down below someplace. Now the fact is that this view of the world is wrong and we can never again believe it. But is it not possible to reject the world-view of the New Testament while continuing to accept its essential teachings? Not quite. As Bultmann explains, the New Testament three-storied universe is even built right into our essential doctrines and creedal statements.

No one who is old enough to think for himself supposes that God lives in a local heaven. There is no longer any heaven in the traditional sense of the word. The same applies to hell in the sense of a mythical underworld beneath our feet. And if this is so, the story of Christ's descent into hell and of his Ascension into heaven is done with. We can no longer look for the return of the Son of Man on the clouds of heaven or hope that the faithful will meet him in the air . . . .[2]

At many other points, as well, the New Testament can no longer speak to contemporary man. A literal interpretation of the whole "eschatological" framework of the New Testament (that is, its teaching concerning last or final, matters) must be abandoned, for the Son of Man did not in fact return on clouds of glory and the new Kingdom did not materialize. The New Testament teachings about

---

[2] Rudolf Bultmann, "New Testament and Mythology," in *Kerygma and Myth*, ed. Hans Werner Bartsch, tr. Reginald H. Fuller (New York: Harper & Row, 1961), p. 4.

the atonement rest upon primitive ideas of guilt and righteousness. The idea of a pre-existent Son of God who enters the world to redeem men is drawn from Gnosticism. In fact, the New Testament reflects at almost every turn the mythologies of Jewish apocalyptic and Greek Gnosticism, with their dualisms, demonic powers, and divine interventions. What can all of this mean to modern technological man, committed as he is to a scientific world-view? A literal interpretation of the New Testament, then, with its three-storied universe and demons, would mean for us today a *sacrificium intellectus*. Bultmann concludes that if modern man "is prepared to take seriously the question of God, he ought not to be burdened with the mythological element in Christianity."[3]

The question then becomes this: Can the *kerygma*, or essential message of the New Testament, survive this elimination of mythology? At this point Bultmann's more positive contribution begins to take shape. He believes that the essential truth and relevance of the New Testament can be preserved through the program of *Entmythologisierung*, "demythologization," the process of liberating the New Testament message from its mythical setting and expression. Actually, the word "demythologization," as Bultmann himself observes, is inadequate because we aim not to eliminate or subtract the mythological elements in the New Testament, but to *interpret* them. The older Liberalism had attempted such a subtraction of the mythological elements with the tragic result that it threw out the *kerygma* itself and left us with only the trite and sentimental ideals of the "Social Gospel"—love thy neighbor and collect used

[3] *Ibid.*, p. 122. In another place, Bultmann concludes that "the Christology of the New Testament exhibits *nothing specifically Christian.* . . . The heathen mysteries knew not only the figure of the dying redeemer-God, but above all the heathen-gnostic mythology knew that figure of the pre-existent being of God that, obedient to the will of the father, clothed himself in the garment of this world and accepted misery and need, hate and persecution, in order to prepare the way for his own into the heavenly world" (*Essays: Philosophical and Theological*, tr. James C. G. Grieg [New York: Macmillan, 1955], p. 247). It must be pointed out, however, that Bultmann's (and others') gnosticizing of the New Testament is highly debatable. The primary source material for the chronological relations of the New Testament to early gnostic mythology is able to bear more than one interpretation. For example, there appears to be no evidence of a gnostic redeemer-myth earlier than the second century, and many conclude, quite contrary to Bultmann, that Gnosticism itself represents a perversion of Christian teaching.

clothing for the Navahos. More accurately, demythologization is "the method of interpretation which tries to recover the deeper meaning behind the mythological conceptions . . . ."[4] What we must do is penetrate to the kernel of eternal truth hidden within the mythological husk. We must free the *existential* meaning, valid for all times, from its local mythological expression in the New Testament. Such a task, says Bultmann, will tax the time and strength of a whole generation, but it will be worth the trouble, for the New Testament does indeed offer even contemporary man "an understanding of himself which will challenge him to a genuine existential decision."[5]

Not that demythologizing began with us. Bultmann believes that the earliest attempts at demythologization are to be found in the New Testament itself, for example, the Fourth Gospel. Written for a generation for whom the apocalyptic Son of Man did not, in fact, return as expected,[6] the Fourth Gospel attempts to translate the futuristic eschatology of the Synoptic Gospels into "realized eschatology"; it spiritualizes the message of a coming kingdom into a message, a truth, a *kerygma* for the present. Judgment and salvation—which Bultmann existentializes into self-understanding and authenticity—may be confronted and enjoyed here and now.

One recognizes in Bultmann's theology the influence of the German philosopher Martin Heidegger and his view of man as "thrown" into the universe, in a state of *Angst*, and in search of responsible or authentic existence. Quite unlike Barth, Bultmann solicits direct aid from philosophy and seeks to demythologize the Bible specifically in light of Heidegger's existentialist approach:

Our question is simply which philosophy today offers the most adequate perspective and conceptions for understanding human existence. Here it seems to me that we should learn from existentialist philosophy, because in this philosophical school human existence is directly the object of attention. . . . Existentialist philosophy, while it gives no answer to the question of my personal existence makes personal existence my own personal responsibility, and by doing so it helps to make me open to the

---

[4] Rudolf Bultmann, *Jesus Christ and Mythology* (New York: Scribner, 1958), p. 18.

[5] Bultmann, "New Testament and Mythology," *op. cit.*, p. 16.

[6] We are overlooking for the moment Bultmann's questionable (late) dating of the Fourth Gospel.

word of the Bible. It is clear, of course, that existentialist philosophy has its origin in the personal-existential question about existence and its possibilities. . . . Thus it follows that existentialist philosophy can offer adequate conceptions for the interpretation of the Bible, since the interpretation of the Bible is concerned with the understanding of existence.[7]

But in contrast to Heidegger's humanistic existentialism, Bultmann believes that the message of the Bible provides for a special and gracious act of God from *outside* in order to make possible the recovery of authentic existence.

How does Bultmann apply all of this to the central datum of Christian faith, that is, the Christ event? The event of Jesus Christ is a unique mixture of history and myth, and if we are to appreciate the existential truth and meaning of that event, we must look beyond its mythological setting; even better, we must try to understand the significance of its mythological setting. After all, says Bultmann, myths are to be interpreted not cosmologically but anthropologically, not as objective pictures of the world but as expressions of man's understanding of himself in his existence. The crucifixion of Jesus was, according to Bultmann, a historical fact, but Jesus was not, literally, the Son of God expiating the sins of the world. Moreover, "an historical fact which involves a resurrection from the dead is utterly inconceivable!" The death and resurrection of Jesus Christ is an "eschatological" event, an event the existential significance of which cannot be located in any historical fact but is apprehensible through the eyes of faith. And what does faith see there? It sees open and authentic existence supremely actualized in Jesus Christ, a more honest view of the world and a better way of living in it. Though we can no longer interpret Jesus' proclamation of the coming Kingdom in terms of space and time, Jesus may yet be for us the bearer of the "last" word—not a temporal but an existential last word, the ultimate and decisive word about God's will.[8]

There is, therefore, an important difference between *Historie* and *Geschichte*, that is, between history conceived as events and history conceived as human situations. It is that latter kind of history that holds existential meaning, and it is the latter that theology is interested in. Theology is not concerned with whether or not some-

---

[7] Bultmann, *Jesus Christ and Mythology, op. cit.*, pp. 55 ff.
[8] Bultmann, "New Testament and Mythology," *op. cit.*, pp. 33 ff.

thing actually happened once upon a time, but with what it could mean for man whether it happened or not. That is why Bultmann, when he was once asked whether he believed that Jesus actually rose from the dead, answered: "I am a theologian, not an archeologist." The historical (*historisch*) status of the cross and resurrection has no bearing at all on its existential significance. There is a difference between the Jesus of history and the Christ of faith.

Of course, Bultmann has been sharply attacked by those who fear, understandably, that he is dissolving the substance of the Gospel right before our eyes into some sort of self-understanding-subjectivism. However, Bultmann has been likened to a man driving his automobile toward a precipice at full speed and swerving to safety at the very last moment. According to Bultmann, though it is necessary to provide modern man with a demythologized and existential interpretation of the New Testament, there is a limit to this procedure. It has just been emphasized that at some point it is also necessary to affirm the objective reality of God's gracious act that provides for men the possibility of self-understanding and salvation. Bultmann does insist on the *kerygma* as the proclamation of God originating from beyond the world of men, and he does believe, as any Christian must, that in some very important sense the *locus* of God's revelation is the Christ event. Critics on the other side do not complain that Bultmann's swerve to safety comes so late but that it comes at all. It has been objected against Bultmann that his program of demythologization, if honestly carried through, would include finally the *kerygma* itself—a dekerygmatization, which of course would be the end of the Gospel.

Another (and very common) objection is that Bultmann is rationalizing the New Testament message, making it intelligible and palatable to modern man when in reality it claims to be an offense. We have encountered some thinkers, such as Kierkegaard and Barth, who are concerned to preserve undiluted the Biblical statement of God's judgment on sinful man as well as his free offer of salvation through the atoning death and real resurrection of Christ —however offensive such talk may seem in a scientific and technological age. Bultmann, on the other hand, seems quite willing, even anxious, to subordinate the expression and interpretation of the Christian *kerygma* to contemporary expectations. How is Bultmann's procedure compatible with the New Testament's announcement that its own message is a "stumblingblock" and "foolishness"

(I Cor. 1:18 ff.)? Bultmann answers that what is indeed incomprehensible about God is not the way he relates to our theoretical thought but the way he deals with our personal existence. For Bultmann, demythologization thus removes only a superficial or false stumblingblock to Christian faith in order to lay bare the real one: the God who in his Word presents himself to us as gracious.[9] Whether the personal and existential aspects of the Gospel can be so neatly separated from the theoretical and historical may be a good question. As we will see a little later, it is probably *the* question.

God above God

Paul Tillich, whom we considered in the earlier discussion of religious symbols, may appropriately be called a systematic theologian. Shifting even more than Bultmann to a decidedly philosophical and metaphysical platform, at home in every period in the history of philosophy and theology, and utilizing the contributions of recent thought such as the insights of depth psychology, Tillich sought to work out his existentialist and "boundary-line" theology for all phases of life and experience.

That Tillich's system has been called a "theology of culture" suggests not only its pervasiveness[10] but also his belief that the political, scientific, and artistic life of every culture reflects an existential situation and an ultimate concern, be it worthy or idolatrous. It follows for Tillich that the expression of the Christian message must be translated for a given cultural situation and the existential questions that it poses. As he expresses it in the opening lines of his *Systematic Theology*, the responsibility of any adequate theology is twofold: "the statement of the truth of the Christian message and the interpretation of this truth for every new generation. Theology moves back and forth between two poles, the eternal

---

[9] Bultmann, *Jesus Christ and Mythology, op. cit.*, pp. 35 ff. Beginning with Chapter 3 of this book Bultmann considers a whole series of important objections to his position.

[10] The breadth of Tillich's interest is reflected very well in a collection of his essays on topics including science, morality, art, education, etc., published under the title *Theology of Culture*, ed. Robert C. Kimball (New York: Oxford University Press, 1959).

truth of its foundation and the temporal situation in which the eternal truth must be received."[11] Persuaded that theology must begin with an existential analysis of man, and that Biblical symbolism must be positively embraced as the only adequate vehicle of theological expression, Tillich develops his contemporary translation of Christianity by means of what he calls the "method of correlation." This method, central to Tillich's whole theology,

tries to correlate the questions implied in the [cultural] situation with the answers implied in the [Christian] message. . . . The method of correlation explains the contents of the Christian faith through existential questions and theological answers in mutual interdependence. . . . The answers implied in the event of revelation are meaningful only in so far as they are in correlation with questions concerning the whole of our existence, with existential questions.[12]

A few short comments on the method of correlation. First, "correlation" may mean correspondence or aligning of items, logical interdependence, and real or factual interdependence. All three meanings have important theological applications. A good example of the last is to be seen in revelation where genuine revelatory disclosure is conditioned both by objective and subjective contributions, the divine revealing and the human receiving. Second, the mutual interdependence and interdetermination of existential questions and theological answers is, for Tillich, symptomatic of man's simultaneous unity with and estrangement from the infinite and, consequently, his ability to ask the questions and his inability to answer them. It is also suggestive of the "theological circle" in which the theologian necessarily finds himself, his theology being the outworking of his own (sometimes hidden) ultimate concern— a fact to be frankly admitted. Third, through the method of correlation Tillich hopes to avoid the error of those theologies that try to deliver answers to questions that men in their particular situations have not asked, and also the error of those theologies that fail to see that the answers must come from beyond the questions themselves. Finally, Tillich sees his method of correlation as having been employed in one form or another throughout the history of Chris-

[11] Paul Tillich, *Systematic Theology* (Chicago: University of Chicago Press, 1951–63), I, 3.
[12] *Ibid.*, pp. 8, 60, 61.

tian theology, and he cites the opening lines of Calvin's *Institutes* as expressing its essence:

The knowledge of ourselves is not only an incitement to seek after God, but likewise a considerable assistance towards finding him. On the other hand, it is plain that no man can arrive at the true knowledge of himself, without having first contemplated the divine character, and then descended to the consideration of his own.[13]

The several parts of Tillich's *Systematic Theology* are each divided into two sections witnessing to Tillich's thoroughgoing attempt to correlate existential questions with theological answers: Reason and Revelation, Being and God, Existence and Christ, Life and Spirit, History and Kingdom.

It is hardly possible even in outline to deal with the many dimensions of Tillich's imposing theology. We will, therefore, focus our attention on one of his doctrines, though the foundational one: God as the symbolic expression of the Ground of all Being and Meaning.

Tillich is sometimes identified as a "Christian atheist." But is it possible to be a Christian theologian, like Tillich, and yet deny that God exists? The answer, of course, depends on what one means by "God" and what one means by "exists." When Tillich says that God does not exist, he refers to the traditional idea of God. Actually, in one sense Tillich and his brand of theology is to our age what ancient Xenophanes was to his. In the same way that Xenophanes attacked the old Homeric, mythological, and anthropomorphic concept of the gods as falling woefully short, so Tillich suggests to us the inadequacy of our own popular concept. Traditional natural theologies possess this significance, that they articulate the existential question of God in a manner appropriate for the situation of a

---

[13] *Ibid.*, I, 3 ff., 8 ff., 60 ff.; II, 13 ff. One might ask, however, whether Tillich's imputation of the method of correlation to Calvin is justified. A careful reading of the lines quoted from Calvin may reveal an unTillichian emphasis, and the following lines from the same context should be noted: "Yet, however the knowledge of God and of ourselves may be mutually connected, the order of right teaching requires that we discuss the former first, then proceed afterward to treat the latter" (*Institutes of the Christian Religion*, I, 1, 3, ed. John T. McNeill, tr. Ford Lewis Battles [Philadelphia: Westminster Press, 1960]).

particular culture.[14] But that culture is rapidly passing on and it behoves us to allow that old theology to give way to a new one, one that can be correlated with the new situation.

Of course, we do not believe naively that God is a nice old man with long white hair sitting on a great white throne. We might, however, yet think of God as a metaphysical principle, transcendent first cause, or necessary being. In short, we conceive God to be a supernatural *thing*. Even this, says Tillich, relegates God to the level of a finite being like ourselves and other things in the universe: It "separates God as a being, the highest being, from all other beings, alongside and above which he has his existence."[15] By thinking of God as an individual thing or substance, by placing him in a supernatural world alongside our own, or by making him a cause alongside other causes, we transform the infinity of God into finitude. Tillich further warns against the Biblical personalism that leads us to think of God as *a* being and *a* person: "The God who is *a* being is transcended by the God who is Being itself, the ground and abyss of every being. And the God who is *a* person is transcended by the God who is the Personal-Itself, the ground and abyss of every person."[16] (Nevertheless, the concept of a personal God is for Tillich an existentially necessary *symbol* because only a person can grasp us and speak to us in our loneliness.)

God is neither "up there" nor "out there" like substances, causes, principles, or people. In this sense it is not appropriate to say either that God *is* or *is not*.

the question of the existence of God can be neither asked nor answered. If asked, it is a question about that which by its very nature is above existence, and therefore the answer—whether negative or affirmative— implicitly denies the nature of God. It is as atheistic to affirm the existence of God as it is to deny it.[17]

[14] For Tillich's existential treatment of the traditional theistic arguments, see *Systematic Theology, op. cit.*, I, 204 ff. For his analysis of the ontological and cosmological approaches (not necessarily arguments) to God, and the superiority of the former, see his important essay "Two Types of Philosophy of Religion," in *Theology and Culture, op. cit.*

[15] Tillich, *Systematic Theology, op. cit.*, II, 6.

[16] Paul Tillich, *Biblical Religion and the Search for Ultimate Reality* (Chicago: University of Chicago Press, 1955), pp. 82 f.

[17] Tillich, *Systematic Theology, op. cit.*, I, 237.

For Tillich, God is surely above and beyond the traditional God of supernaturalism; he is not a super-thing existing out there in the universe someplace. This is the first concept of God that Tillich rejects.

But he also rejects the God of naturalism. The naturalistic interpretation of God identified him in some way with the universe itself, or at least with its essence or special powers. The trouble with this position, according to Tillich, is that it "denies the infinite distance between the whole of finite things and their infinite ground." The naturalistic identification of God and the world makes the word "God" superfluous and simply reveals the naturalist's insensitivity to "a decisive element in the experience of the holy, namely, the distance between finite man, on the one hand, and the holy in its numerous manifestations, on the other. For this, naturalism cannot account."[18] Therefore, the supernaturalist idea of God is inadequate inasmuch as it turns God into another thing out there, and the naturalistic idea is inadequate inasmuch as it fails to distinguish God from the universe and to do justice to our experience of the holy. Both reduce God to an idol.

How, then, shall we speak of God? Tillich answers that there is a third way (grasped in part by classical theologians such as Augustine, Aquinas, Luther, and Calvin) that will liberate us from the two dangerous extremes. God is neither "in" the world nor "above" it; images drawn from the spatial realm can hardly describe God's relation to the world because his relation to the world is hardly spatial. He is, rather, at the very *depth* of being and experience, the infinite ground, the condition, the power of all things. God is *Being Itself*—the only non-symbolic statement that can be made about God. Still, says Tillich, it may be possible for the naturalist to describe his God in much the same way. We must, therefore, add an important qualification. Reality is self-transcending in that finite things point beyond themselves to their infinite depth. In fact, God, the Ground of Being, infinitely transcends that of which he is the ground, a state of reality which has as its counterpart our own self-transcendence in the ecstatic experience of the holy. Tillich's third way thus steers between naturalism and supernaturalism and, as he says, underlies the whole of his theological system.[19]

[18] *Ibid.*, II, 7.
[19] *Ibid.*, pp. 7 ff.

We move now from Tillich's doctrine of God to his doctrine of the Christ. In the discussion of religious symbols we saw that according to Tillich man is guilt-ridden, conscious of his finitude, and threatened with meaninglessness. He is estranged from his essential being and plagued with existential anxiety, a dreadful awareness of his possible non-being. Tillich urges us, nevertheless, to affirm meaning within meaninglessness, to have certitude within doubt, to have "the courage to be." But the source of this courage can never again be the idolotrous God of traditional theism. Our courage lies, instead, in the "God above God," the power of being itself, the God of the third way mentioned above.

Tillich, espousing a partly "adoptionist" Christology, says that this God chose or adopted Jesus who then became the Christ, that is, "the anointed." God has subjected himself to the conditions of spatio-temporal existence, he has shared in man's estrangement, and he has conquered and transformed it through Jesus as the Christ who was "united with the ground of his being and meaning without separation and disruption."[20] (The subjection of the Christ to estranged existence is symbolized in the Cross, and his conquest is symbolized in the Resurrection.) Estrangement thus stands conquered in principle, and the Christ becomes—for those who in faith receive him as such—the bearer and mediator of the "New Being"; he also becomes the center and ultimate criterion of all reconciling revelations, otherwise known as "ecstatic manifestations of the Ground of Being." And for us men, to be grasped (whatever that means) by the healing power of the New Being is salvation or the recovery of our essential being and the fulfillment of our meaning. (Tillich is delighted to point out that the Latin *salvus* means, most fundamentally, "healing.") This involves, first, a participation in God's participation in and victory over the cleavage (or "split," to use one of Tillich's favorite words) between man's essential meaning and his existential state, and therefore victory over man's estrangement from God, the world, and himself. It also means an acceptance of God's acceptance of us through his reconciling and healing work. And it means a transformation in personality and community. The Regeneration, Justification, and Santification of traditional theology is thus restated by Tillich as Participation, Acceptance, and Transformation.[21]

---

[20] *Ibid.*, I, 133.
[21] *Ibid.*, II, 165 ff.

In all of this there is to be seen a new role for the Protestant doctrine of justification by faith alone. Tillich liberates the "Protestant principle" from its merely historical interest and extends it far beyond its traditional Lutheran interpretation, radicalizing and universalizing it for the contemporary situation. When the Bible says in so many places that we are justified not by works but by faith, Tillich understands it to mean (especially in our age of anxiety and doubt) intellectual as well as moral works. The intellectual Pharisee like the sinner stands in need of justification. But God is ready to receive the doubter, for the Ground of Being is present in every act of authentic doubt and faith, accepting and affirming the being of him who quests for Being Itself. It is interesting to note that Bultmann saw his program of demythologization, too, as a means of enriching the doctrine of justification by faith: ". . . demythologizing is the radical application of the doctrine of justification by faith to the sphere of knowledge and thought. Like the doctrine of justification, de-mythologizing destroys every longing for security. There is no difference between security based on good works and security built on objectifying knowledge."[22]

The Protestant principle—at least in Tillich's understanding of it —protests against all idols and deabsolutizes religions and even Protestantism itself, an idea suitably emphasized in Tillich's book *The Protestant Era.* He was, in fact, repulsed by the "absurd and demonic" doctrine, fostered by Christian exclusivism, that only those who heard and received the Christian Gospel would be saved. On the contrary, he believed in a somewhat Platonic way that all men participate more or less in the power of the New Being otherwise they would possess no being at all.

It is probably impossible to summarize succinctly the undergirding movement of Tillich's theology any better than he himself does in the closing lines of one of his most important works: The God above God, the power of being, has appeared in the New Being of Christ, and *"the courage to be is rooted in this God who appears when God has disappeared in the anxiety of doubt."*[23]

At this point we might raise what is for many the most crucial difficulty for both Bultmann and Tillich, at least as viewed from

[22] Bultmann, *Jesus Christ and Mythology, op. cit.,* p. 84.
[23] Paul Tillich, *The Courage To Be* (New Haven, Conn.: Yale University Press, 1952), p. 190.

the standpoint of the mainstream of Christian thought, specifically their view of faith's relation to history. At best, their explanation of this matter leaves something to be desired, but the following seems clear. We have seen that Bultmann claims a certain objectivity for the Christ event, and that Tillich's theology requires a concrete embodiment of the New Being which means that the event of Jesus as the Christ has a "factual element." As it turns out, though, they appear to lay the foundation of faith on a quite different emphasis. Both distinguish the *historischer Jesus* from the *geschichtlicher Christus* (that is, the Jesus who lived once upon a time and the Christ who lives in and for existential situations), and both point faith in the direction of the latter. In fact, Tillich's references to the "factual element" is put into better perspective by the following: "Knowledge of revelation, although mediated primarily through historical events, does not imply factual assertions, and is therefore not exposed to critical analysis by historical research."[24] Historical events (for example, Jesus of Nazareth) may be the occasion of revelation, but revelation is of something not disclosed empirically and the object of faith is thus insulated from any historical or factual investigation. Bultmann has already distinguished the theologian from the archeologist and Tillich speculates that Christianity may be true even if Jesus Christ never lived, much less died and rose again.

It would appear to be very important whether those theologians who have abandoned as a failure the quest of the historical Jesus believe that it is not possible practically and technically to verify the Christ event, or, as Bultmann and Tillich appear to mean, that the Christ event cannot even *in theory* be confirmed as a historical fact. Aside from what the latter may mean for the epistemological question as to the truth-value of Christianity (the reader will recall the problem of gardeners, *bliks*, and strangers in the last chapter), certainly it would be *theologically* vacuous for St. Paul who saw Christian faith as inseparable from its historical substance: ". . . if Christ has not been raised, then our preaching is in vain and your faith is in vain" (I Cor. 15:14). (The present writer cannot bring himself to believe that St. Paul was a proto-Tillichian who regarded the resurrection as a "restitution" of Christ to his Messianic role occurring in the minds of the disciples, or the

---

[24] Tillich, *Systematic Theology, op. cit.*, I, 130.

miracles as an "ecstatically received understanding of constellations of factors which point to the divine Ground of Being."[25]) It would also be vacuous for countless others, including Barth, who have staked their salvation and hope on the objective, historical, and (at least in theory) investigable fact of the miracles, suffering, and resurrection of Jesus Christ:

The truth of Jesus Christ is also in the simplest sense a truth of facts. Its starting-point, the Resurrection of Jesus Christ from the dead, is a fact which occurred in space and time, as the New Testament describes it. The apostles were not satisfied to hold on to an inward fact; they spoke of what they saw and heard and what they touched with their hands.[26]

Obviously there is a big difference between the opinion that a man died and was then raised from the dead, and the further opinion that he was the Christ and that God has acted for our salvation in his death and resurrection. The latter can never be known historically or empirically. But the former can—at least in principle—and the present position maintains that just such historical events or facts are necessarily involved in the network of divine-historical elements that constitute the Christian Gospel. On this view, it is not so much a question of self-understanding but how we are in fact understood by God; it is not a question of what we hope but what we are entitled to hope. Christian faith holds genuine existential-subjective significance only because it rests on a historical-objective foundation, that is, only because God did something "out there," in history, in reality. If a folksy metaphor may be permitted, Christianity issues checks under the name of the Bank of Historical Events. If it turns out that the bank is broke—well, Kierkegaard has already taught us that risk is the measure of faith's intensity.

Religionless Christianity

Another dominant strain in the new theologies was contributed unwittingly, by Dietrich Bonhoeffer, a German pastor and professor who was imprisoned and executed by the Nazis because of his

---

25 *Ibid.*, II, 155 ff., 161.

26 Karl Barth, *Dogmatics in Outline*, tr. G. T. Thomson (London: Student Christian Movement Press, 1949), p. 25.

involvement in the Resistance. It is instructive to note that radical and conservative theologians both have claimed Bonhoeffer as a champion for their causes. It is no wonder that Bonhoeffer has been conscripted by several strands of radical thought and especially by what is called "secular theology." Bonhoeffer's rather startling thesis is that the world has "come of age" and can do without religion: "'God' is being pushed more and more out of life," and "we are moving towards a completely religionless time."[27]

Secular theology received its best-known expression in Harvey Cox's theological best-seller *The Secular City.* Cox's opening statement is: "The rise of urban civilization and the collapse of traditional religion are the two main hallmarks of our era and are closely related movements."[28] Urbanization, or the contemporary cosmopolitan style of life with its freedom of anonymity and mobility, has taken place against the backdrop of scientific and technological advances which were in turn spawned by the "wreckage of religious world-views." A corollary of urbanization, which is a way of living together, is the way in which modern men grasp and understand their life together, or secularization. More specifically, Cox defines secularization as "the loosing of the world from religious and quasi-religious understandings of itself, the dispelling of all closed world-views, the breaking of all supernatural myths and sacred symbols."[29] Secularization (as opposed to secular*ism* which simply substitutes one dogmatic idealogy for another) is interested in this world, not some other world; it is interested in man as the one responsible for the world and history, not some god beyond; and it no longer finds its morality or meanings in religious rules or rituals.

Even though the Church has railed against all that is secular, Cox claims the Bible itself lays the foundation of modern secularization. For example, the Genesis account of Creation portrays nature as "disenchanted," or freed from the supernatural, something to be investigated and mastered by man. The "civil disobedience" of the Hebrews in the story of the Exodus speaks of the desacralization of politics, the rejection of all sacral-political absolutisms. And the Sinai Covenant, with its "Thou shalt have no other gods

27 Dietrich Bonhoeffer, *Letters and Papers from Prison,* ed. Eberhard Bethge, tr. Reginald Fuller, revised ed. (New York: Macmillan, 1967), pp. 168, 139.
28 Harvey Cox, *The Secular City* (New York: Macmillan, 1965), p. 1.
29 *Ibid.*, p. 2.

before me," represents, with its plural "gods," a deconsecration and relativization of cultural creations and human values. In the Creation, the Exodus, and at Sinai, we see God releasing men to their maturity. Calling them to maturity is the task of the Church. In fact, the Church must become God's *avant-garde* in the midst of the city; she, if anyone, must fully embody the Biblical principle of secularization.[30] Something like this, says Cox, is what Bonhoeffer meant by man's coming of age, and by a completely religionless time. But is it?

Some of the more conservative theologians have been distressed over this reading of Bonhoeffer, claiming (more correctly, I think) that the radical interpreters have grasped, at best, only one side of his position and have made him a spokesman for a cause that in fact would have repelled him. The conservatives have suggested, on the other hand, that Bonhoeffer was responding to the preoccupation with the forms of traditional religion rather than with its substance.

When Bonhoeffer claims that the world has come of age and can do without religion, he means that the world can do without *religiosity*. There is, for Bonhoeffer, a difference between superficial religiosity and genuine Christianity. This interpretation of Bonhoeffer agrees with his earlier and emphatic renunciation of the easy religion or "cheap grace" offered by the church, "sold on the market like cheapjack's wares," forgiveness without repentance, faith without involvement.[31] It also agrees with Bonhoeffer's evolving preoccupation with the church's relationship to the world come of age, an interest that can be traced from his *The Cost of Discipleship*, through the *Ethics*, to its final and most dramatic (though fragmentary) expression in *Letters and Papers from Prison*. Of course, the radical interpreters make much out of the "earlier" and "later" Bonhoeffer. But this exaggerated distinction does not, perhaps, do justice to the continuity of Bonhoeffer's works, the changing circumstances of his ministry, and to the numerous friends and students of Bonhoeffer who surely understand better than anyone else what Bonhoeffer was saying.[32]

30 *Ibid.*, pp. 17 ff.

31 Dietrich Bonhoeffer, *The Cost of Discipleship*, tr. R. H. Fuller, second ed. (New York: Macmillan, 1959), pp. 35 ff.

32 For example, Eberhard Bethge, Bonhoeffer's personal friend as well as editor of his works, including *Letters and Papers from Prison* which is the most

Bonhoeffer did believe, to be sure, that God was being pushed out of the world. The God of traditional religion was a "God of the gaps," a God invoked to fill up the gaps in our understanding of the cosmos and ourselves. But the unswerving advance of science has made such a God increasingly unnecessary. With the rise of Darwin, for example, the God of traditional religion took a giant step backward. For the hypothesis of an immediate and special creation of man was now discarded in favor of a better one. That problem was now solved, more naturally, without God. Nor can we allow this God, driven from the public side of life, to take refuge in the personal, inner, and private side of life. For this realm too—the mysterious inner sanctum of the soul—is being exposed and understood, in this case by the light of psychoanalysis. With the rise of Freud, God took another giant step backward. The world is coming of age and can fill up the intellectual and scientific gaps for itself. In the moral as well as the scientific realm, modern man can, as a matter of fact, get along without God, live well, and be happy: "God as a working hypothesis in morals, politics, or science, has been surmounted and abolished; and the same thing has happened in philosophy and religion . . . . For the sake of intellectual honesty, that working hypothesis should be dropped, or as far as possible eliminated."[33]

In this sense, man is not incurably religious, there is no religious *a priori*, no God-shaped blank in the human soul, no numinous consciousness is required, and St. Augustine was simply wrong when he said that the heart is restless until it finds its rest in God. We must, says Bonhoeffer, learn to live in the world *etsi deus non daretur*, "even if God were not given."

Bonhoeffer believes, however, that the demise of such a God is good because this is not the God of Christianity anyway. The sooner we rid ourselves of the felt-necessity of this "religious" God,

---

important source for the radical interpretation. The germs of Bonhoeffer's prison insights were already contained in his first works, *Sanctorum Communio* (published 1930) and *Act and Being* (1931), and the essential continuity of Bonhoeffer's development is unmistakably reflected in Bethge's important biography *Dietrich Bonhoeffer*, ed. Edwin Robertson, tr. Erich Mosbacher, et al. (New York: Harper & Row, 1970). It is encouraging that in the revised edition of the *The Secular City* (New York: Macmillan, 1966), Cox softened his earlier appropriation of Bonhoeffer (see p. xii).

[33] Bonhoeffer, *Letters and Papers from Prison, op. cit.*, p. 187.

the sooner does the God of authentic Christianity become a possibility for us. In this last respect there is a more positive side to Bonhoeffer's theology, apparently not always appreciated by his radical interpreters. The world's coming of age "opens up a way of seeing the God of the Bible," a God who helps us not by a transcendent and otherworldly omnipotence, but by his weakness and suffering with us in the world. We must allow God (as he allowed himself) to be edged out of the world and on to the cross.[34]

This means (as Bonhoeffer says in his unfinished *Ethics*) that the Church must reconsider its understanding of and its relationship to the secular world. Indeed, the Church's ill-conceived distinction between the sphere of the sacred and the sphere of the secular is one of the causes of its ineffectiveness in the modern world. The truth is that God himself entered the world in the Incarnation and "was in Christ, reconciling the world to himself" (II Cor. 5:19). Two-sphere thinking denies the unity of God and the world achieved in the revelation and work of Christ. There is no God apart from the world, no supernatural apart from the natural, no sacred apart from the profane. Christ is the ultimate reality and the world is part of that reality.[35] In fact, the true Church "has essentially nothing whatever to do with the so-called religious functions of man, but with the whole man in his existence in the world with all its implications." The problem now is how to speak in a *secular* way about God and to live a kind of "worldly holiness."[36]

If we are moving, then, toward a completely religionless time, the Christian will have to abandon his *deus ex machina*—his convenient problem-solving God—as well as his other-worldly and ecclesiastical involvements. Quite simply, the Christian must cease to be religious:

He must therefore really live in the godless world, without attempting to gloss over or explain its ungodliness in some religious way or other. He must live a "secular" life, and thereby share in God's sufferings. . . . To be a Christian does not mean to be religious in a particular way, to make

[34] *Ibid.*, pp. 187 f.

[35] Dietrich Bonhoeffer, *Ethics*, ed. Eberhard Bethge, tr. Neville Horton Smith (New York: Macmillan, 1965), pp. 196 ff.

[36] *Ibid.*, pp. 83 f.

something of oneself (a sinner, a penitent, or a saint) on the basis of some method or other, but to be a man—not a type of man, but the man that Christ creates in us. It is not the religious act that makes the Christian, but participation in the sufferings of God in the secular life. . . . The "religious act" is always something partial; "faith" is something whole, involving the whole of one's life. Jesus calls men, not to a new religion, but to life. But what does this life look like, this participation in the powerlessness of God in the world? I will write about that next time, I hope.[37]

By thus breaking in upon the secular world the Christian will be what he is supposed to be: "a man for others." This is the fully human, fully Christian man. And this was the man Bonhoeffer was.

Reacting to Barth's early preoccupation with the divine Wholly-Otherness, bearing the imprint of von Harnack's social consciousness, and, in all, totally Lutheran in his Biblicism and Christology, he felt constrained to cast himself upon the political and moral crisis of his time. From the beginning he opposed the infamous Aryan Clause which banned Jews from positions in the Church, he was instrumental in the formation of the Confessing Church which resisted the German Christians of the Third Reich, and he eventually became implicated in the ill-fated plot to assassinate Hitler. He was shifted around from one prison to another until one day at Flossenburg he concluded a worship service for his fellow prisoners and then, summoned by the guards, he said: "This is the end. For me the beginning of life." He was hanged on April 9, 1945.

Though it is unfortunate that the writings and thoughts of this innovative theological mind must remain forever incomplete, there is, nonetheless, discernible in Bonhoeffer a central and consistent thrust. And although he represents an exciting departure from the usual understanding (or misunderstanding) of what it means to be a Christian in the modern world, it is not necessary to yield to the temptation of interpreting him after the fashion of certain radical secularists or so-called Christian atheists. He was, after all, a man who until the very end continued to speak of the word of God, redemption, and the forgiveness of sins, and he was a man who prayed.

[37] Bonhoeffer, *Letters and Papers from Prison, op. cit.*, pp. 190 f.

The Death of God

Surely the most radical movement within recent theology, and the most deserving of the dubious title "Christian atheism," is the so-called Death of God theology—a macabre locution in more ways than one.

Several thinkers are often associated with this movement, representing different variations on the theme that God himself is dead. Gabriel Vahanian published a book called *The Death of God*, but the title was intended to suggest rather the end of Christian culture: It is no longer possible to objectify God or caricature him through a traditional and antiquated religiosity. Paul M. van Buren has been identified as another Death of God theologian, though he is not happy about it. Prompted both by verificationism and classical Christology, van Buren attempts a reinterpretation of the Gospel for modern empirical man by stressing the factual character of the Christ event. His interest in accommodating especially the insights of recent analytic philosophy is reflected in the full title of his book, *The Secular Meaning of the Gospel: Based on an Analysis of Its Language,* and his rejection of God-talk (including death-of-God-talk) as meaningless. On the Jewish side, Richard L. Rubenstein (*After Auschwitz*) has been aligned with these thinkers. Writing pessimistically for a post-holocaust Judaism, Rubenstein interprets the death of God phenomenologically as a cultural-anthropological fact, preferring the observation that we live in the time of the death of God to the statement "God is dead"; that is, for Rubenstein the Death of God theology, like all theology, is an expression of a way in which the world is experienced. But Thomas J. J. Altizer (*The Gospel of Christian Atheism*) and William Hamilton (*The New Essence of Christianity*) unmistakably and clearly proclaim the actual death of God, and it is to them that one must turn for the most emphatic and authentic expression of this position.

Now it is, at first, difficult to believe that these thinkers actually affirm the real death of God. Upon hearing this phrase we are apt to recall the madman in Friedrich Nietzsche's *The Gay Science* who, after running through the streets in search of God and being unable to find him, cries out:

God is dead. God remains dead. And we have killed him. . . . Is not the greatness of this deed too great for us? Must not we ourselves become gods simply to seem worthy of it? There has never been a greater deed; and whoever will be born after us—for the sake of this deed he will be part of a higher history than all history hitherto.[38]

Nietzsche meant that the idea of God, especially as an absolute lawgiver for men, could no longer be accepted. He himself explains his meaning: "The greatest recent event—that 'God is dead,' that the belief in the Christian God has ceased to be believable—is even now beginning to cast its first shadows over Europe."[39] In this sense, God is dead, and man himself must ascend the throne of God and become the measure of all things. And we rather naturally suppose that the Death of God theologians mean something like that—the traditional idea or concept of God is irrelevant and dead. But this is not the case, at least not with Altizer and Hamilton. Their deicidal tendencies are to be taken quite seriously; they are affirming God's actual death.

In one straightforward statement by Hamilton, appearing (appropriately) in *Playboy*, he lists the possible meanings of the phrase "death of God." The phrase may suggest, for example, that there is no God and there never was one. This is, of course, simply the standard atheistic line. Or the phrase may mean, again, that the idea of God and the word "God" have become vacuous and require radical reformulation. It may mean that classical conceptions of God, such as problem-solver and necessary being, must be abandoned. But after listing these and still other possible interpretations, Hamilton explains that none of these are intended by theologians like himself. By "death of God" they mean, rather, that

there once was a God to whom adoration, praise and trust were appropriate, possible and even necessary, but that there is now no such God. This is the position of the death-of-God or radical theology. It is an atheist position, but with a difference. If there was a God, and if there now isn't, it should be possible to indicate why this change took place, when it took place and who was responsible for it.[40]

[38] Friedrich Nietzsche, *The Gay Science*, no. 125, in *The Portable Nietzsche*, ed. and tr. Walter Kaufmann (New York: Viking Press, 1954).

[39] *Ibid.*, no. 343.

[40] William Hamilton, "The Death of God," *Playboy*, XIII (August, 1966), p. 84.

In another statement, Hamilton says, "We are not talking about the absence of the experience of God, but about the experience of the absence of God." And to those who still think that he must be speaking symbolically, Hamilton says, "We have insisted all along that 'death of God' must not be taken as symbolic rhetoric for something else. There really is a sense of not-having, of not-believing, of having lost, not just the idols or the gods of religion, but God himself."[41]

Yet, to say that God has "died" is somewhat misleading inasmuch as it conjures up an image of a God who once upon a time was living, breathing, and eating, and then suddenly keeled over dead. It would be closer to the truth (though not nearly so spectacular) to say that God has been *transformed*. The supernatural has become immersed in space and time, the spirit has become flesh, the transcendent God has become wholly immanent. Not just our way of talking about God has changed—God himself has changed. This is the real significance of the phrase "death of God."

It is, at best, difficult to say how and when this happened. Both Hamilton and Altizer agree that God died, or at least began to die, at the time of the Incarnation when God transformed himself into the spatio-temporal reality of Jesus Christ, entered human history, and took upon himself not only sin and suffering but mortality as well. Hamilton sees God as still dying in the nineteenth century as reflected in both American and European literary and political movements. He sees Melville's *Moby Dick*, for example, chronicling the death of God: "Perhaps the most unforgettable image of the dying God in our language is that of Ahab finally fixing his harpoon in Moby Dick's side, as the two of them sink together, both of them God, both of them evil."[42] There is, there-

---

[41] William Hamilton (with Thomas J. J. Altizer), *Radical Theology and the Death of God* (New York: Bobbs-Merrill, 1966), pp. 28, 46 f. That Hamilton and Altizer dedicated their book to Paul Tillich should be considered in light of Rubenstein's instructive observation: "Every one of today's radical theologians was either Tillich's student or was profoundly influenced by his writings. In the context of much of today's theological writing, Tillich seems almost conservative. Nevertheless, all radical theologians have elaborated on themes which are at least implicit in Tillich. After all, it was Tillich who asserted in *The Courage To Be* that the God whom Nietzsche said was dead was transcended in a 'God above the God of theism'" (*After Auschwitz* [Indianapolis, Ind.: Bobbs-Merrill, 1966], p. 243).

[42] Hamilton, "The Death of God," *op. cit.*, p. 137.

fore, a three-part answer to the question of when God died: "The coming and death of Jesus makes God's death possible; the 19th century makes it real. And today, it is our turn to understand and to accept."[43]

More important than when and how God died is what it means. Altizer, who is more of an apocalyptic poet than a theologian, makes much of the "kenosis" (Greek: "emptying") passage in Philippians 2:5–8, where it is said that Christ "emptied himself, taking the form of a servant, being born in the likeness of men. And being found in human form he humbled himself and became obedient unto death, even death on a cross." The more orthodox will surely frown on Altizer's use of this Biblical passage as a proof text for his strange theology. Nevertheless, on this particular point Altizer out-orthodoxes the orthodox: He carries the kenotic act of God further than the Bible itself, claiming that the Godhead was *entirely* transformed into Jesus, an idea propagated already in the third century by the heretic Sabellius. At any rate, sifting out Biblical passages to his taste, and greatly influenced by Eastern mysticism, the dialectical thought of Hegel, and the poetic vision of Blake, Altizer is persuaded that God's self-emptying of Spirit in order to become flesh—a descent into the concrete—has achieved, or is achieving, a supreme *coincidentia oppositorum*, a complete union of the sacred and profane.

This in turn means a liberation from the "alien transcendent," the oppressive shadow of the Wholly Other, and a freedom to live in the immediate moment:

The death of God abolishes transcendence, thereby making possible a new and absolute immanence, an immanence freed of every sign of transcendence. Once a new humanity is fully liberated from even the memory of transcendence, it will lose all sense of bondage to the past, and with the loss of that bondage it will be freed from all that No-saying which turns us away from the immediacy of an actual and present "Now."[44]

For Altizer, God gives way to Jesus, otherworldly theology gives way to this-worldly theology, and guilt gives way to a theological-

---

[43] *Ibid.*

[44] Thomas J. J. Altizer, *The Gospel of Christian Atheism* (Philadelphia: Westminster Press, 1966), p. 154.

Dionysiac celebration of life. Hamilton, too, sees the death of God as a joyous and liberating event. God's withdrawal means for man a new openness to the world and an opportunity to bear on his own shoulders the responsibility of suffering and love.[45]

Still, it is not altogether happy that God has withdrawn from our world, and Hamilton speaks of a kind of uneasiness and nostalgia for the absent God and a hope that it may someday be possible to speak of him again. We are reminded of Samuel Beckett's *Waiting for Godot*, an uneventful dialogue, feebly reminiscent of half-forgotten religious images and theological dogmas, in which two characters base their ill-defined hopes on the arrival of some obscure personage named Godot. He never comes, but they continue to wait. This is a summary of the pathetic ambiguity and dim expectation of at least one contemporary state of mind.

Postscript

Many readers are by now certain that theology has indeed managed to find the black cat in a dark room when there is no cat there.

While Karl Barth bent over his desk for more than thirty years and churned out over seven-thousand pages of his *Church Dogmatics* (still unfinished at his death), half a dozen major theological movements and a multitude of minor ones have paraded across the scene, and hundreds of would-be revolutionary theological works have been poured out in a rush for relevance. Rubenstein announced, rather triumphantly, "Radical theology is no fad. It will not be replaced by some other theological novelty in the foreseeable future. Too many tendencies in classical theology, philosophy, and literature have intersected in this movement for it to disappear as rapidly as it has gained attention."[46] It appears that he was wrong. It is now often noted that God-is-dead is dead. And no sooner had the Death of God theology been laid to rest than still another one made its entrance: the Theology of Hope. I mention the Theology of Hope not only to avoid ending

[45] William Hamilton, *The New Essence of Christianity*, revised ed. (New York: Association Press, 1966), pp. 63 f.

[46] Rubenstein, *op. cit.*, p. 246.

with the Death of God, but also because as a substantive theological position it promises neither to appear on the cover of *Time Magazine* nor to fade soon into oblivion as another theological fad.

Though having roots in the hope-oriented philosophy of the Marxist Ernst Bloch, as a Christian movement the Theology of Hope received its initial spark from the German theologian Jürgen Moltmann (*The Theology of Hope*). The most important expressions of this theology from this side of the Atlantic are those of the Catholic Leslie Dewart (*The Future of Belief*) and the Lutheran Carl E. Braaten (*The Future of God*).

Braaten speaks of "the great theologians of the era that has just slipped behind us—Barth, Bultmann, Bonhoeffer, and Tillich" (surely a blow to those who have not yet understood Barth!) and signals a return to the Biblical and more dynamic view of history. The traditional "I AM WHO AM" (Ex. 3:14) now becomes "I WILL BE WHO I WILL BE" (which is in fact a possible translation of the Hebrew); history becomes the stage upon which God works his purposes; the hope of salvation becomes inseparable from Jesus' teaching about the coming Kingdom and the promise of it sealed by his resurrection. God is the Power of the Future. He approaches us not from within, not from above, not from the past, but from ahead. In this there is no sanction of a social *status quo*. Quite to the contrary, this is a theology of revolution pressing for a radical conversion of the present and a making straight of the paths in anticipation of the breaking in of God's Kingdom. On the individual level, the Theology of Hope means that "we can die in a communion of his love, in the assurance of the forgiveness of sins, with undying hope of life and resurrection."[47] In its essential features, of course, this new theology reminds one of something very old.

And this, in a way, brings us back to our thesis stated in the Preface. Although every man necessarily experiences the world from the standpoint of a personal and historical situation and cannot be condemned for not being a god, the man of understanding possesses a wider historical consciousness that liberates him from the imprisonment of his own moment. Ancient Heraclitus said, "It is the mark of a foolish man to get all excited over every new

[47] Carl E. Braaten, *The Future of God* (New York: Harper & Row, 1969), p. 88.

idea." Philosophical and theological understanding comes, rather, through a confrontation with the insights, ideas, experience, and wisdom of the broad sweep of a whole tradition.

In the meantime, Plato summarizes our predicament when, in his dialogue *Phaedo,* he has Cebes say:

I think, Socrates, as perhaps you do yourself, that it is either impossible or very difficult to acquire clear knowledge about these matters in this life. And yet he is a weakling who does not test in every way what is said about them and persevere until he is worn out by studying them on every side. For he must do one of two things; either he must learn or discover the truth about these matters, or if that is impossible, he must take whatever human doctrine is best and hardest to disprove and, embarking upon it as upon a raft, sail upon it through life in the midst of dangers, unless he can sail upon some stronger vessel, some divine revelation, and make his voyage more safely and securely.[48]

---

[48] Plato, *Phaedo,* 85c, tr. Harold North Fowler (London: Heinemann, 1914).

Bibliographical Note

As was stated in the Preface, most of the positions considered in these chapters may be found in my book of readings, *Philosophical and Religious Issues* (Encino, Calif.: Dickenson, 1971). This volume contains a full representation of classical and contemporary approaches to the problems of philosophical theology, as well as extensive bibliographies on each topic. A second collection of readings may be mentioned: George L. Abernethy and Thomas A. Langford (eds.), *Philosophy of Religion*, second ed. (New York: Macmillan, 1968).

Further discussion of the theistic arguments may be found in Donald R. Burrill (ed.), *The Cosmological Arguments* (Garden City, N.Y.: Anchor Books, 1967) and Alvin Plantinga (ed.), *The Ontological Argument* (Garden City, N.Y.: Anchor Books, 1965). In addition, one should note both the April and July, 1970, issues of *The Monist*, LIV, which are devoted entirely to contemporary treatment of the theistic arguments. A useful selection from mystical literature, along with helpful introductions, is provided in Walter T. Stace (ed.), *The Teachings of the Mystics* (New York: New American Library, 1960).

Somewhat more general in their content are the following three anthologies: John Hick (ed.), *The Existence of God* (New York: Macmillan, 1964); Ed. L. Miller (ed.), *Classical Statements on Faith and Reason* (New York: Random House, 1970); and George I. Mavrodes (ed.), *The Rationality of Belief in God* (Englewood Cliffs, N.J.: Prentice-Hall, 1970). Also covering a variety of issues, but wholly contemporary and analytic in its approach is the extremely important collection, *New Essays in Philosophical Theology*, ed. Antony Flew and Alasdair MacIntyre (London: Student Christian Movement Press, 1955).

Individual works of merit that range over the standard problems but from differing standpoints include E. L. Mascall, *He Who Is* (London: Libra Books, 1943) which represents a modern Thomistic approach; James F. Ross, *Philosophical Theology* (Indianapolis, Ind.: Bobbs-Merrill, 1969), an attempt to illuminate the traditional Thomistic approach by the light of contemporary language-philosophy; Alvin Plantinga, *God and Other Minds* (Ithaca, N.Y.: Cornell University Press, 1967), a logical and critical scrutiny of the theistic arguments, the problem of evil, issues in verification and falsification, and so forth; Erich Frank, *Philosophical Understanding and Religious Truth* (Oxford, England: Oxford University Press, 1945), a readable examination of the nature of religious truth as it bears on certain perennial themes; and Frederick Ferré, *Language, Logic and God* (New York: Harper & Row, 1961), which provides a thorough introduction to the language and verification approaches that dominate so much of the contemporary discussion.

In addition, the following recent and worthy treatments of specific themes may be noted: John Baillie, *The Idea of Revelation in Recent Thought* (New York: Columbia University Press, 1956); R. C. Zaehner, *Mysticism: Sacred and Profane* (Oxford, England: Clarendon Press, 1957); John Hick, *Faith and Knowledge*, second ed. (Ithaca, N.Y.: Cornell University Press, 1966); John Hick, *Evil and the God of Love* (New York: Harper & Row, 1966); C. J. Ducasse, *Nature, Mind and Death* (La Salle, Ill.: Open Court, 1951); Ian T. Ramsey, *Religious Language* (New York: Macmillan, 1957).

A popular and very influential statement of recent theological positions is John A. T. Robinson's *Honest to God* (Philadelphia: Westminster Press, 1963). A survey of the whole modern period is provided in James C. Livingston, *Modern Christian Thought: From the Enlightenment to Vatican II* (New York: Macmillan, 1971) and an account of the developments since 1900 (taking account of philosophy also) may be found in John Macquarrie, *Twentieth-Century Religious Thought* (New York: Harper & Row, 1963). Prevailing theological discussion is reflected in the continuing series *New Theology,* ed. Martin E. Marty and Dean G. Peerman (New York: Macmillan, 1964–   ) and theological positions of specifically Continental thinkers are represented in the suggestive journalistic pieces in Werner Harenberg, *Der Spiegel on the New Testament,* tr. James H. Burtness (New York: Macmillan, 1970).

Index